B.C.E. | C.E.

Daniel 8:13-14
page 7

2,300 Evening-Mornings (Passovers)

*The time period from June 8, 632 C.E. to June 7, 1967 C.E.
is exactly 1,335 years to the day.*

?????

Death of Mohammed,
beginning of Muslim Caliphate
June 8, 632 C.E.

Daniel 12:5-7
page 25

Daniel 12:8-12
page 17

3½ Times* (798 Years)

1,335 Days (Day of Atonements)

** "Time" is equal to twelve 19-year Metonic Cycles,
i.e., 12 x 19 years = 228 years.*

1,290 Days

1,290 Years

45 Days

45 Years

*Byzantines recapture Jerusalem
628 C.E., desecrate Temple Mount*

League of Nations
passes Palestine Mandate
July 24, 1922

Roman-Byzantine Period **2nd Persian-Byzantine Period**

*Pompey
captures Jerusalem
63 B.C.E.*

*Julian the Apostate
attempts to rebuild Temple
363 C.E.*

*Chosroes II Parvez
Sassanid Persian Empire
(Nehemiah ben Hushiel)
captures Jerusalem 614 C.E.*

After 638 C.E.
*After Caliph Omar captured Jerusalem in 638 C.E., he visited the Temple
Mount, where he prayed and had a temporary mosque erected. Decades
later, the golden-domed Dome of the Rock (c. 685-691 C.E.) and the silver-
domed al Aqsa Mosque (c. 646-705 C.E.) were built there, probably on the
foundation stones of the Jupiter Temple complex built by Hadrian in 135 C.E.*

Daniel 7:25
page 31

3½ Times* (798 Years)

Roman-Byzantine period ends,
Omar captures Jerusalem and Temple Mount
February, 638 C.E.

Portents and omens of doom
are observed in Jerusalem during
Passover, 66 C.E.

Daniel 7:12
page 31

After Passover in 66 C.E.
*After Passover in 66 C.E., priests reported the departure of the Shekinah from the Temple on the evening of Pentecost
that year; the First Jewish-Roman War started later that year in August, the siege of Jerusalem by Roman legions
under Titus began in the early months of 70 C.E., and ended in August with the city and Temple destroyed; the Second
Jewish-Roman War started in 132 C.E., the victorious Roman emperor Hadrian changed the name of Jerusalem to
Aelia Capitolina and that of Judea to Syria Palestina c. 135 C.E., then built a Temple to Jupiter on the Temple Mount.*

Season and Time*

*Decree of Caesar
(see Daniel 9:24-27 time line below)*

Time = 228 Passovers

228 Years

*Passover of 66 C.E.
(March 27)*

Julius Caesar issues decree
to Hyrcanus II, street and trench
rebuilt in 44/43 B.C.E., count of
weeks begins with first year
in 7-year sabbath cycle

B.C.E. | C.E.

Daniel 9:24-27
page 61

Jesus, the anointed one,
begins 3-year ministry to
confirm New Covenant
(see page 85)

70 Weeks (Pentecosts)

Herod captures
Jerusalem

70th Week
*1) New covenant is introduced.
2) The anointed one is cut off.
3) Vision and prophet is sealed.
4) Most Holy One is anointed.*

7 Weeks
7 Pentecosts

62 Weeks
62 Pentecosts

*43-37 B.C.E.
... coincides with
Sabbath Cycle*

36 B.C.E.-26 C.E.

26/27 C.E.

*Note that time lines are not drawn
to scale, but points are generally shown
in their correct chronological sequence
when read left to right or vice versa.*

43 B.C.E.   37/36 B.C.E.

Pentecost
26 C.E.

Pentecost
27 C.E.

To Rick,

with best wishes,

David

MAY 17, 2009

DANIEL UNSEALED

DANIEL UNSEALED

An explanation of the chrono-specific prophecies in the

Book of Daniel, chapters 7-12, as understood ...

by Daniel

FIRST EDITION

A PROPHECY SOCIETY PUBLICATION

DANIEL UNSEALED

*Scripture quotations are shown in italics throughout this book.
The King James Version is the version quoted, for continuity of style
and to simplify copyright issues, unless noted otherwise.*

Published by The Prophecy Society
www.prophecysociety.org
770-679-0633
Monday-Friday, 10am-5pm Eastern Time

ISBN-13 978-0-9816912-0-6
ISBN 0-9816912-0-X

First Edition, First Printing

Printed in the United States of America

To order additional copies of this book on the internet, go to
http://www.prophecysociety.org/orders

Comments and feedback are invited and can be sent to the author
by e-mail addressed to: daniel@prophecysociety.org

∽

On front cover ...

Public domain photograph of the oil-on-canvas painting
"Daniel in the Lions' Den" by Peter Paul Rubens, *c.* 1614-1616,
original painting on display at The National Gallery of Art
in Washington D.C.

DEDICATION

∽

*To the men and women of faith who have accurately transmitted
the Holy Scriptures of God to this generation.*

ABBREVIATIONS

List of abbreviations and symbols used in this book.

AP	Author's Paraphrase
b.	Born in ... *with year*
B.C.E.	Before the Common Era
	... same as B.C.
BHS	Biblia Hebraica Stuttgartensia
c.	Latin *circa* (about) ... *with year*
cf.	Latin *confer* (compare)
C.E.	In the Common Era*
	... same as A.D.
CJB	Complete Jewish Bible
d.	Died in ... *with year*
JPS	Jewish Publication Society
KJV	King James Version
MT	Masoretic Text
NASB	New American Standard Bible
NET	New English Translation
NIV	New International Version
NJB	New Jerusalem Bible
NJV	New Jewish Version
p.	Page(s) ... *with number(s)*
r.	Reigned ... *with year(s)*
RSV	Revised Standard Version
UBS	United Bible Societies

* Modern-era years occurring in the Common Era are often shown in the text without the "C.E." notation.

TABLE OF CONTENTS

I, DANIEL, UNDERSTOOD

The Book of Daniel[1] is the record of divine revelation given to the people of ancient Israel through the Hebrew prophet[2] and seer Daniel more than twenty-five-hundred years ago. In its pages are found prophecies unlike any others in the Bible, detailed predictive prophecies that set forth a comprehensive chronology encompassing the history of the Jewish people from the time of the exile in Babylon[3] down to the present day. Despite their evident specificity, though, the chrono-specific prophecies in Daniel have been impossible for anyone to interpret conclusively over the years. The reason why they have defied interpretation for so long is explained in the text of Daniel itself. There we are told that the prophecies were sealed up in Babylon by an angel of God. At the same time, we are told why the prophecies were sealed—so as to keep them from being understood until the time of the end.[4]

Indeed, a survey of the many contradictory interpretations of the Danielic prophecies published in the years since they were handed down provides confirmation that their exact meanings have been divinely sequestered from the beginning. Over the centuries, no expositor has interpreted all of the prophecies with any degree of certainty, nor has anyone been able to correlate all of the prophesied events with events documented in history. Acclaimed Torah sages and Talmudists, world-renowned Bible scholars, even one universally recognized scientific genius—Sir Isaac Newton—all have strived to produce the definitive exposition of the prophecies, and all of them have come up short of achieving their goal. Their labors have produced valuable insights and thought-provoking interpretations that have advanced our understanding of biblical prophecy. Still, one undeniable fact remains: Every exposition of the chrono-specific prophecies in Daniel published prior to modern times has now been shown by the events of history to have been inaccurate or incomplete in some substantial way.

Expositions of Daniel published in recent years have proven to be unsatisfactory in various ways as well. All too often, modern expositors have relied on using approximations of history as substitutes for exact fulfillments of prophesied events. This method of close-is-good-enough interpretation is typical of most contemporary expositions of Daniel, chapter 8, for example. Other expositors, in an attempt to achieve the precision necessary for claiming an exact fulfillment of a chrono-specific biblical prophecy, have gone to the opposite extreme, such as resorting to complicated mathematical formulas based on a postulated 360-day "prophetic year" that matches nothing in the Bible, Jewish history, or observable astronomy. This latter method of chronological manipulation is most often associated with expositions

---

[1] See *Appendix One: Background Notes on the Book of Daniel* on *p. 93*.
[2] Daniel never referred to himself as a prophet in the Book of Daniel, even though he did see visions and record prophesies.
[3] 605-536 B.C.E.; Daniel is assumed to have been taken captive to Babylon after the Battle of Carchemish in 605 B.C.E.
[4] Daniel 12:9: *"And he said, Go thy way, Daniel: for the words are closed up and sealed till the time of the end"* (KJV).

of Daniel, chapter 9. Additionally, many modern expositors, unable to find exact matches in history for events mentioned in the prophetic text, have simply consigned all such unmatched events to the time of the end by default, with no justification for doing so other than the fact that the events do not fit anywhere else in their interpretive scheme. These and similar exegetic compromises have produced frequently well-received but nevertheless flawed interpretations of the Danielic prophecies.

Before continuing, let me acknowledge that the above comments may seem to be unflattering criticism at first read. However, they are not meant to disparage in any way the fine work of previous expositors of Daniel, nor are they calling into question the scholarship or spiritual integrity of the many dedicated expositors who have provided commentaries in years past. Their efforts have edified and sustained the faithful through good times and bad, and for that alone they deserve our appreciation and respect. Instead, the comments are simply pointing out the obvious—that God, after giving the chrono-specific prophecies to Daniel, immediately directed that they be sealed up until the time of the end. That act of divine sealing made it impossible for any expositor to expound them fully until the specified time of the end had arrived. No matter how clever the interpreter and diligent the effort, a definitive exposition of the prophecies simply could not be done until then. Even Daniel himself wrote that he did not understand everything that had been revealed to him.[1] The prophecies were sealed, and that was that. Yet, the Bible clearly foretold that they would be unsealed for full understanding at the time of the end.

Recent Jewish history indicates that we are now living in the appointed time of the end. Events central to the Jewish people—the birth of Zionism[2] in 1897, the Palestine Mandate passed by the League of Nations in 1922, the Holocaust in Europe during World War II, the influx of Jews seeking refuge in their ancestral homeland in Palestine after the war, the partition of Palestine by the United Nations in 1947, and the establishment of the modern nation of Israel there in 1948—all of these events taken together are an unmistakable end-time indicator to those who believe the biblical prophecies that require a regathered Jewish people living in *Eretz-Israel*[3] at the end of days. Collectively, those events are an eschatological benchmark that should not have been overlooked by Bible expositors at the time they were happening, although most did so back then. Even the Zionist leaders themselves did not claim eschatological meaning for their movement. Nevertheless, the rebirth of Israel as an independent nation in Palestine was a prophetic turning point. That event, and the accelerated ingathering of Jews from nations all around the world that began immediately afterwards, confirmed for Bible believers that the time of the end was at last underway.[4] This meant that it would henceforth be possible for the chrono-specific prophecies in Daniel to be unsealed by God at any time. The stage was set.

---

[1] Dan. 12:8: *"And I heard, but I understood not: then said I, O my Lord, what shall be the end of these things?"* (KJV).
[2] a worldwide Jewish movement for the establishment in Palestine of a national homeland for Jews.
[3] Hebrew-to-English transliteration meaning "Land of Israel" (*i.e.,* the land promised to the Children of Israel by God).
[4] See *Appendix Five: The Modern Nation of Israel - Is it Biblical?* on *p.* 105.

Meanwhile, as the events of Jewish national rebirth were reaching their climax in Europe and Palestine during the 1940s, I was experiencing my early childhood years in America, far too young to take note of those events or realize their importance for signaling the unsealing of the chrono-specific prophecies in the Book of Daniel. Nor could I foresee that the process of understanding the prophecies would one day involve me. My spiritual awakening came years later, as I was heading into my thirty-second year, when my curiosity about things sacred was quickened by God. Quite literally overnight, I was filled with an overwhelming desire to read the Bible around the clock for days on end, and given clarity of mind to understand what I was reading as I read. During this period of spiritual immersion and illumination, I was especially drawn to the prophecies in Daniel, and my attention was repeatedly focused on the chrono-specific prophecy in the eighth chapter. Unfamiliarity with the historical details that provide context to the events described in Daniel soon required that I supplement my Bible study with a review of ancient Jewish history, and that research resulted in my exposure to the details of modern Jewish history as well. It was the latter that provided the key that unlocked everything.

The breakthrough moment—the instant when I first suspected that the prophecy in the eighth chapter of Daniel might have a modern fulfillment—came in the spring of 1974, while I was reading an account of the Six-Day War that had been fought and won by Israel in 1967. After finishing the portion describing the capture of the Temple Mount in Jerusalem by Israeli army paratroopers on the morning of June 7, the third day of the war, I was struck by how closely the result of the capture—the return of Old Jerusalem and the Temple Mount to Jewish sovereignty—matched the fulfillment event of the prophecy in Daniel, chapter 8, verse 14: "... [then] *the sanctuary will be restored to its rightful state*" (CJB). I asked myself if it was possible that this then-recent event, which had happened literally before my eyes on television seven years earlier, was now to be considered the fulfillment of that ancient Hebrew prophecy? I was aware that, in the interval since it had occurred, no respected Bible scholar had come forward to single out that event as being a prophetic fulfillment, so I was cautious at first. I resisted the inner voice urging me to embrace a new interpretation, especially without further support from the Bible for doing so. Additional years of Bible study and prayer would transpire before I overcame my doubt by finding the Scriptural confirmation needed to support a modern event as a true prophetic fulfillment.

More than three decades have passed since I understood how to correctly interpret the chrono-specific prophecy in Daniel, chapter 8. That breakthrough in understanding, and the gradual strengthening of my faith that resulted as I went through the decade-long process of questioning my interpretation against Scripture until I was certain of its accuracy, opened the door to more understanding. The knowledge gained from the interpretation of Daniel, chapter 8, provided the key for determining the chronological starting point for working out the interpretation of Daniel, chapter 12. Then, the added knowledge gained from understanding the twelfth chapter provided the key for understanding the meanings of the chronological terms "season" and "time" that are required for assembling the continuous time lines that provide the framework for understanding the remaining prophecies in Daniel. And so it went, year after year, as I continued to study and pray and seek understanding. I soon found that the more I understood about one prophecy, the more I was able to understand about another, with the result that over time, one by one, all of the chrono-specific prophecies in Daniel were unsealed to reveal their secrets.

The interpretations of the Danielic prophecies understood thus far, and the steps in the process of understanding that led to those interpretations, are explained in the pages that follow. The prophecies are presented in the order that I understood them, beginning with the all-important chrono-specific prophecy in the eighth chapter of Daniel. As you read the interpretations set forth in this exposition, you will find them to be non-traditional. Giving them a fair hearing may require that you set aside eschatological assumptions and traditional interpretations that you have read in Bible commentaries, or heard expounded at prophecy conferences, on television and radio, and in your local church or synagogue. If you will but follow the presentations set forth herein, however, reserving final judgement and keeping in mind the overall chronological framework into which the individual prophecies fit,[1] I can assure you that it will all come together and make sense in the end. And, as you begin to understand for yourself that the prophecies in Daniel were passed down from antiquity as a divine testimony specifically to those of us living in this end-time generation, my hope and prayer for you is that you will be inspired to join with me in giving praise to the Living God of the Bible.

> *"O Lord, you are my God! I will exalt you in praise, I will extol*
> *your fame. For you have done extraordinary things, and executed plans*
> *made long ago exactly as you decreed."* – ISAIAH 25:1 (NET)

---

[1] The "Prophecy Overview" chart (see PLATE 1 located on inside front cover) provides an easy-to-locate reference that will help you visualize the chronological relationships between the prophecies explained in the expository chapters of this book.

EXPLANATIONS OF PROPHECIES

CHAPTER ONE

THEN SHALL THE SANCTUARY BE RESTORED
Daniel 8:1-27

The accurate interpretation of the chrono-specific prophecy found in Daniel, chapter 8, which I refer to as "The Alexander Prophecy" because it begins with the appearance of Alexander the Great on the stage of biblical history, is the key to deciphering and understanding all of the chrono-specific prophecies in the Book of Daniel. The reason why the interpretation of this prophecy is so important is that it extends the efficacy of Bible prophecy from ancient times into modern times. By so doing, it establishes the chronological framework needed for accurately interpreting the remaining chrono-specific prophecies in Daniel, some of which also have post-biblical fulfillments, as will be shown in subsequent chapters of this book. In this chapter, though, the exposition of the prophecy in Daniel, chapter 8, will receive our full attention, since the correct interpretation of that epoch-spanning prophecy is fundamental to understanding the chronology of everything else.

The eighth chapter of Daniel can be divided into three distinct parts (see text on page 9). The first part is comprised of verses 1-12. These verses set forth a prophetic vision predicting the history of the Jewish people for the immediate future—immediate, that is, from the standpoint of a person living in the Achaemenid (Persian) Empire during the reign of Darius III.[1] The vision describes a ram with two horns pushing westward, northward, and southward. The ram is next seen standing still before a river while a he-goat with a notable horn comes against the ram from the west with fury. The he-goat then proceeds to smite the ram and break his two horns. Thereafter, nothing the ram is able to do can stop the he-goat from waxing great and casting the ram to the ground. However, when the he-goat has achieved greatness, his horn is broken, and four notable ones take his place. Out of one of the four notable horns, a little horn comes forth to wax great toward the pleasant land, and this little horn takes away the daily sacrifice, casts down the sanctuary[2] and hosts to the ground, and prospers. So conclude the events described in the first part. The second part is a parenthesis comprised of verses 13-14, and contains a cryptic chrono-specific prophecy promising that the sanctuary will be restored, or "cleansed" (KJV), in the future. The third part is comprised of verses 15-27. These verses provide a partial interpretation of the prophetic vision recorded in the first part. The ram with two horns is identified in verse 20 as the kings of Media and Persia,[3] and the he-goat with the notable horn is identified in verse 21 as the first king of Greece.[4] The little horn that arises from the four notable horns is not identified by name, but is described as a king of fierce countenance who destroys the holy people. Most Bible expositors agree that

---

[1] Darius III Codomannus (r. 336-330 B.C.E.), last king of the Achaemenid (Persian) Empire.
[2] a reference to Mount Moriah and the Temple in Jerusalem.
[3] a general reference to all Achaemenid kings from Cyrus II the Great (r. 559-529 B.C.E.) to Darius III Codomannus.
[4] Alexander of Macedon (r. 336-323 B.C.E.), who unified the Greek city-states under his rule in 336-334 B.C.E.

the fierce-king imagery is referring to the Seleucid king Antiochus IV Epiphanes,[1] and most agree that the term "holy people" in verse 24 is a reference to the Jews living in Judah (Judea) under his rule. A prediction of harsh oppression and persecution of the holy people by the king of fierce countenance closes part three, but that is not the end of the story. Part three also closes with a reminder that the prophecy in part two—the prophecy in verses 13-14 foretelling that the sanctuary will be restored to its rightful status after 2,300 "evening-mornings"[2]—will most certainly come true. It is the fulfillment of this two-verse prophecy that projects the context of Daniel from ancient times into modern times.

None of the interpretations of verses 13-14 presented in the most widely-used expositions of Daniel allow for a modern-day fulfillment. Instead, most expositors assign the fulfillment event (the restoration of the sanctuary) to the time of Antiochus IV Epiphanes and the Maccabean revolt,[3] or they make it an end-time event that will happen sometime in the distant future. In those expositions that assign fulfillment of verse 14 to the time of Antiochus, the 2,300 "evening-mornings" time period is usually assumed to define a period of persecution of the Jews by Antiochus. The starting point for counting the 2,300 "evening-mornings" (assumed to mean 2,300 literal days) usually begins with an unspecified event in 171 B.C.E., and the count ends with the rededication of the Temple by Judah Maccabee, who captured Jerusalem in the third year of the Jewish revolt against Antiochus, reconsecrated the Temple altar, and began offering daily sacrifices once again. From historical records, we know that the rededication happened on the 25th day of the month of Kislev[4] in the 148th year of the Seleucid Empire,[5] which is equivalent to the Gregorian date of December 14, 164 B.C.E. However, counting backwards 2,300 days from that date, no significant starting event involving Antiochus or the Jews (one that would allow such an interpretation to fit the text of verses 13-14 exactly) is found in the historical record. So, at best, this interpretation gives an approximate fulfillment, and most proponents of this interpretation admit as much. Other expositors have proposed that the 2,300 "evening-mornings" phrase in verse 14 is referring to the continual sacrifices that were offered twice daily in the Temple. Since there were two such sacrifices offered in each calendar day, one in the morning and one in the evening, they reason that there are only 1,150 actual days needed to complete the count. Those who offer this interpretation usually start their count on the date when Antiochus profaned the Jewish Temple in Jerusalem by placing a statue of Zeus in the Holy of Holies and sacrificing a pig on the sacred altar, an act of desecration according to Jewish ceremonial law that made offering further sacrifices on that altar impossible. From historical records, we know that the desecration of the Temple happened on the 25th day of Kislev in the 145th year of the Seleucid Empire, which is equivalent to December 16, 167 B.C.E.

---

[1] Antiochus IV Epiphanes (*r.* 175-164 B.C.E.), king of the Hellenistic Seleucid Empire.

[2] עֶרֶב בֹּקֶר (BHS) translated as *"days"* (KJV) or *"evenings and mornings"* in other translations (NASV, NET, CJB, *etc.*).

[3] The Maccabees were a priestly family that sparked and led a revolt by Jews in 167 B.C.E. against Antiochus IV, who was attempting to replace Biblical Judaism with Hellenism.

[4] The Jewish calendar adopted the Babylonian system for naming months during the exile in Babylon; see *p.* 95.

[5] Josephus, *Antiquities*, 12:7:6; 1 Maccabees 4:52.

Text of Daniel 8:1-27 (KJV)

The Vision

1 In the third year of the reign of king Belshazzar a vision appeared unto me, even unto me Daniel, after that which appeared unto me at the first. *2* And I saw in a vision; and it came to pass, when I saw, that I was at Shushan in the palace, which is in the province of Elam; and I saw in a vision, and I was by the river of Ulai. *3* Then I lifted up mine eyes, and saw, and, behold, there stood before the river a ram which had two horns: and the two horns were high; but one was higher than the other, and the higher came up last. *4* I saw the ram pushing westward, and northward, and southward; so that no beasts might stand before him, neither was there any that could deliver out of his hand; but he did according to his will, and became great. *5* And as I was considering, behold, an he goat came from the west on the face of the whole earth, and touched not the ground: and the goat had a notable horn between his eyes. *6* And he came to the ram that had two horns, which I had there seen standing before the river, and ran unto him in the fury of his power. *7* And I saw him come close unto the ram, and he was moved with choler against him, and smote the ram, and brake his two horns: and there was no power in the ram to stand before him, but he cast him down to the ground, and stamped upon him: and there was none that could deliver the ram out of his hand. *8* Therefore the he goat waxed very great: and when he was strong, the great horn was broken; and for it came up four notable ones toward the four winds of heaven. *9* And out of one of them came forth a little horn, which waxed exceeding great, toward the south, and toward the east, and toward the pleasant land. *10* And it waxed great, even to the host of heaven; and it cast down some of the host and of the stars to the ground, and stamped upon them. *11* Yea, he magnified himself even to the prince of the host, and by him the daily sacrifice was taken away, and the place of his sanctuary was cast down. *12* And an host was given him against the daily sacrifice by reason of transgression, and it cast down the truth to the ground; and it practised, and prospered.

The 2,300 Days (Evening-Mornings)

13 Then I heard one saint speaking, and another saint said unto that certain saint which spake, How long shall be the vision concerning the daily sacrifice, and the transgression of desolation, to give both the sanctuary and the host to be trodden under foot? *14* And he said unto me, Unto two thousand and three hundred days; then shall the sanctuary be cleansed.

The Vision Interpreted

15 And it came to pass, when I, even I Daniel, had seen the vision, and sought for the meaning, then, behold, there stood before me as the appearance of a man. *16* And I heard a man's voice between the banks of Ulai, which called, and said, Gabriel, make this man to understand the vision. *17* So he came near where I stood: and when he came, I was afraid, and fell upon my face: but he said unto me, Understand, O son of man: for at the time of the end shall be the vision. *18* Now as he was speaking with me, I was in a deep sleep on my face toward the ground: but he touched me, and set me upright. *19* And he said, Behold, I will make thee know what shall be in the last end of the indignation: for at the time appointed the end shall be. *20* The ram which thou sawest having two horns are the kings of Media and Persia. *21* And the rough goat is the king of Grecia: and the great horn that is between his eyes is the first king. *22* Now that being broken, whereas four stood up for it, four kingdoms shall stand up out of the nation, but not in his power. *23* And in the latter time of their kingdom, when the transgressors are come to the full, a king of fierce countenance, and understanding dark sentences, shall stand up. *24* And his power shall be mighty, but not by his own power: and he shall destroy wonderfully, and shall prosper, and practise, and shall destroy the mighty and the holy people. *25* And through his policy also he shall cause craft to prosper in his hand; and he shall magnify himself in his heart, and by peace shall destroy many: he shall also stand up against the Prince of princes; but he shall be broken without hand. *26* And the vision of the evening and the morning which was told is true: wherefore shut thou up the vision; for it shall be for many days. *27* And I Daniel fainted, and was sick certain days; afterward I rose up, and did the king's business; and I was astonished at the vision, but none understood it.

Alternate Translation

verses 13-14 ... Then I heard a holy one speaking, and another holy one said to the speaker, "How long will the events of the vision last, this vision concerning the regular offering and the transgression which is so appalling, that allows the sanctuary and the army to be trampled underfoot?" The first said to me, "Two thousand three hundred evenings and mornings, after which the sanctuary will be restored to its rightful state." (CJB) in Gregorian reckoning.[1] The count ends with the date of the Temple rededication by Judah Maccabee mentioned previously, which occurred on December 14, 164 B.C.E. A quick look at these historically verifiable starting dates and ending dates reveals a time interval of 1,093¾ days, but not the 1,150 days required to total the 2,300 twice-a-day sacrifices postulated by this interpretative scheme. Once again, the proposed interpretation is a close approximation, but not an exact fulfillment.

The above approaches for interpreting the chrono-specific prophecy in verses 13-14 are typical of schemes used by most expositors over the years. So far, none of their interpretations fit the chronological and textual constraints of the prophecy exactly, at least, not in both ways at the same time. Either the time interval does not equal 2,300 units, or the starting (or ending) date does not match any event mentioned in the biblical text and independently documented by secular history. Considering that the Bible tells us that the chrono-specific prophecies in Daniel were sealed from our understanding until the time of the end, the inability of past expositors to interpret Daniel, chapter 8, with exactitude was to be expected. The prophecy was sealed away from their understanding. However, a recent event—the capture of the Temple Mount in Jerusalem by Israel on June 7, 1967—unsealed the prophecy for our generation. It did so by allowing the prophesied climactic event, the restoration of the sanctuary that was foretold in verse 14, to be identified.[2] Seven years after this event occurred, during a period of personal spiritual awakening, I recognized the eschatological importance of the modern restoration. My eyes were opened by God to this understanding. Still, I had doubts at the time. I realized that my interpretative scheme postulating a modern-day fulfillment was non-traditional.[3] Right away, I recognized that I had to find biblical confirmation for my new insight before I could believe it beyond doubt. As I searched the Bible, I knew that my interpretation had to fit both Scripture and history exactly to be a true interpretation, and that is what I found. Now, I want to share with you the keys that allowed me to interpret the prophecy.

The Keys to the Interpretation

The first key to interpreting the prophecy in Daniel, chapter 8, is to understand the full scope of the question being asked in verse 13. I realized that past expositors had underestimated the question, *"How long shall be the vision concerning the daily sacrifice, and the transgression of desolation, to give both the sanctuary and the host to be trodden under foot?"* (KJV), assuming it to be asking only how long the interruption of the Temple sacrifices and other transgressions against the Temple and the Jews being perpetrated by Antiochus would last. That was not the question being asked, however. The questioner

---

[1] Josephus, *Antiquities*, 12:5:4, but 1 Maccabees 1:54 gives the date as the 15th day of Kislev.
[2] See photograph of this prophecy being fulfilled on *p. 18.*
[3] I later discovered that Adam Clarke's *Commentary on the Bible (1810-1825)* offered the same exposition, but he did not take into account that there was no year "zero" and thus incorrectly calculated 1966 C.E. as the year of sanctuary restoration. Still, it was a quite remarkable feat of biblical insight and exegesis for that day and time.

was seeking to know the duration of the full vision. A more compelling translation of verse 13 is, *"How long will the events of the vision last, this vision concerning the regular offering and the transgression which is so appalling, that allows the sanctuary and the army to be trampled underfoot?"* (CJB). The first phrase of this translation recognizes correctly that the question of duration pertains to the events of the entire vision, from start to finish, a time period that includes the interruption of the daily sacrifices and transgressions by Antiochus, but also includes the earlier events described in verses 1-12. When the scope of the question is understood, it is easy to see that the first action event of the vision, the beginning of conflict between the king of Persia and the king of Greece that is described in verse 6, is the actual starting point for calculating the duration of the entire vision. Verse 14 then states that the events of the vision will end after 2,300 "evening-mornings" have occurred, at which time the sanctuary will be restored to its rightful state. It is generally agreed by almost all expositors that the word "sanctuary" in verse 14 refers to the Jewish Temple, and after the destruction of the Temple by the Romans in 70 C.E., to the area now known as the Temple Mount in Jerusalem. Putting all of this together, I could deduce that the prophecy was predicting that the Temple Mount would be restored after a period of 2,300 "evening-mornings" had occurred, with the count beginning from the time when Alexander the Great first moved against Darius III of Persia, which history records as the Battle of Granicus in 334 B.C.E.

The second key to interpreting the prophecy is to understand the time period meant by the Hebrew phrase עֶרֶב בֹּקֶר (BHS, Strong's OT: 1242, 6153), literally "evening-mornings," used in verse 14. The King James Version renders it as "days," based on usage in Genesis, chapter 1, verses 5-31, *"the evening and the morning were the* [first, second, third, ...] *day"* (KJV) where a similar Hebrew phrase is used as equivalent to a day. Expositors adopting that translation have traditionally considered the phrase "evening-mornings" to mean literal 24-hour days, but have been unable to make that interpretation fit history. Other translations render the phrase as "evening *and* mornings," adding the conjunction "and" which is not found in the best Hebrew manuscripts of verse 14. Expositors using this translation have often gone on to interpret the phrase as a reference to the daily evening and morning Temple sacrifices interrupted by Antiochus. However, I knew that the verses mentioning the daily sacrifices elsewhere in the Bible always described them as "morning and evening" sacrifices, the reverse of the word order used in verse 14. Interpreting "evening-mornings" as "daily sacrifices" would thus be inconsistent. Plus, the proponents of that interpretation have also been unable to make their exposition fit history. At this point, I realized that another interpretation was needed. Knowing that the ending event of the prophecy had occurred in 1967, and now understanding that the starting event had occurred in the year 334 B.C.E., a quick calculation showed that the interval between the two was essentially 2,300 calendar years. Thus, "evening-mornings" seemed to be equivalent to years in time. Still, I could not see how this could be. As was my custom, I turned to the Bible for clarification. The insight and understanding I sought came while reading the passage about the instructions given by God for instituting and observing the Passover, as recorded in Exodus, chapter 12, verses 6-10, 14: *"And ye shall keep it* [the Pascal lamb] *up until the fourteenth day of the same month: and the whole assembly of the congregation of Israel shall kill it **in the evening**. And they shall take of the blood, and strike it on the two side posts and on the upper door post of the houses, wherein they shall eat it. And they shall eat the flesh in that night, roast with fire, and unleavened bread; and with bitter herbs they shall eat it. Eat not of it raw, nor sodden at all with water, but roast with fire; his head with his legs, and with the purtenance thereof. And ye shall let nothing of it remain until the morning; and that which remaineth of it **until the morning** ye shall burn with fire ... And this day shall be unto you for a memorial; and ye shall keep it a feast to the Lord throughout your generations; ye shall keep it a feast by an ordinance for ever"* (KJV). In those verses was the answer that I was seeking. The oldest memorial observance of the Jews, the Passover, was an annual evening-until-morning event. I now realized that "evening-morning" did not mean a set period of time, as I had first suspected, but instead meant an event, the Passover night, the reminder of God's faithfulness to Israel. Thus, 2,300 "evening-mornings" in verse 14 meant 2,300 Passovers.

The third key to interpreting the prophecy is to understand how to count the 2,300 Passovers that determined the time span stipulated in verse 14, specifically, to know when to begin and when to stop the count. I knew that the initial Passover in the count had to occur after the first action event of the prophecy, which was the Battle of Granicus stipulated in Daniel, chapter 8, verse 6. This battle was the first time that Alexander the Great met and defeated the army of Darius III of Persia. There is no historical reference to a specific date for the Battle of Granicus except a mention in a work by Plutarch of Charonea,[1] which recorded that the battle took place in the Macedonian month of Daesius in the year 334 B.C.E. This meant that Alexander first moved against Persia in late May or early June. Passover was celebrated on March 26th in 334 B.C.E., so it had already occurred before the battle began, and thus the next Passover, the one celebrated in 333 B.C.E., is the one that must be used to start the count that determines the duration of the time span in verse 14. I also knew that the count had to conclude before the Temple Mount was captured by Israeli army paratroopers on June 7, 1967. This meant that the last Passover in the count, the 2,300th Passover, had to be the Passover of 1967, which occurred on April 25th that year. The big question was whether there were 2,300 Passovers between the Battle of Granicus in 334 B.C.E. and the capture of the Temple Mount during the Six-Day War in 1967. There was only one way to find out, and that was to count the Passovers. So, I did, and you can, too. Table 1.1 (on opposite page) demonstrates how the 2,300 Passovers should be counted. Included in the count are all Passovers

---

[1] From *Life of Alexander* (section 16, verses 1-3) by Plutarch of Chaeronea: "In the meantime, Darius' captains, having collected large forces, were encamped on the further bank of the river Granicus, and it was necessary to fight, as it were, in the gate of Asia for an entrance into it. The depth of the river, with the unevenness and difficult ascent of the opposite bank, which was to be gained by main force, was apprehended by most, and some pronounced it an improper time to engage, because it was unusual for the kings of Macedonia to march with their forces in the month called Daesius. But Alexander broke through these scruples, telling them they should call it a second Artemisius. And when Parmenion advised him not to attempt anything that day, because it was late, he told him that he should disgrace the Hellespont, should he fear the Granicus." ... translated by Mr. Evelyn for John Dryden's *Plutarch's Lives by Several Hands*, published in 1683.

occurring ***after*** Alexander the Great led his forces against Persia at the Battle of Granicus in 334 B.C.E., and ***before*** Israeli army paratroopers captured the Temple Mount on June 7, 1967. The count is initiated with the Passover in 333 B.C.E., which is the first Passover that occurred after the Battle of Granicus. The count ends with the Passover that occurred in 1967. Each Passover in the table is denoted as "P#" (where "#" is its number in the count), followed by its corresponding Gregorian year. After the initial ten Passovers (P1 through P10), which are shown on the top line, Passovers are shown in ten-year increments (so that you can verify the count on your fingers). When you have completed verifying the count for yourself, you will see that there are exactly 2,300 Passovers between the starting event of the vision, the Battle of Granicus specified in verse 6, and the ending event of the vision, the restoration of the Temple Mount specified in verse 14, precisely the time span required for this interpretation to be the exact fulfillment of the chrono-specific prophecy set forth inverses 13-14. In addition, the starting and

Table 1.1 - How to Count the 2,300 Evening-Mornings

P1 - 333 B.C.E.	P2 - 332 B.C.E.	P3 - 331 B.C.E.	P4 - 330 B.C.E.	P5 - 329 B.C.E.	P6 - 328 B.C.E.	P7 - 327 B.C.E.	P8 - 326 B.C.E.	P9 - 325 B.C.E.	P10 - 324 B.C.E.
1-10 see above	P20 - 314 B.C.E.	P30 - 304 B.C.E.	P40 - 294 B.C.E.	P50 - 284 B.C.E.	P60 - 274 B.C.E.	P70 - 264 B.C.E.	P80 - 254 B.C.E.	P90 - 244 B.C.E.	P100 - 234 B.C.E.
P110 - 224 B.C.E.	P120 - 214 B.C.E.	P130 - 204 B.C.E.	P140 - 194 B.C.E.	P150 - 184 B.C.E.	P160 - 174 B.C.E.	P170 - 164 B.C.E.	P180 - 154 B.C.E.	P190 - 144 B.C.E.	P200 - 134 B.C.E.
P210 - 124 B.C.E.	P220 - 114 B.C.E.	P230 - 104 B.C.E.	P240 - 94 B.C.E.	P250 - 84 B.C.E.	P260 - 74 B.C.E.	P270 - 64 B.C.E.	P280 - 54 B.C.E.	P290 - 44 B.C.E.	P300 - 34 B.C.E.
P310 - 24 B.C.E.	P320 - 14 B.C.E.	P330 - 4 B.C.E.	P340 - 7 C.E.	P350 - 17 C.E.	P360 - 27 C.E.	P370 - 37 C.E.	P380 - 47 C.E.	P390 - 57 C.E.	P400 - 67 C.E.
P410 - 77 C.E.	P420 - 87 C.E.	P430 - 97 C.E.	P440 - 107 C.E.	P450 - 117 C.E.	P460 - 127 C.E.	P470 - 137 C.E.	P480 - 147 C.E.	P490 - 157 C.E.	P500 - 167 C.E.
P510 - 177 C.E.	P520 - 187 C.E.	P530 - 197 C.E.	P540 - 207 C.E.	P550 - 217 C.E.	P560 - 227 C.E.	P570 - 237 C.E.	P580 - 247 C.E.	P590 - 257 C.E.	P600 - 267 C.E.
P610 - 277 C.E.	P620 - 287 C.E.	P630 - 297 C.E.	P640 - 307 C.E.	P650 - 317 C.E.	P660 - 327 C.E.	P670 - 337 C.E.	P680 - 347 C.E.	P690 - 357 C.E.	P700 - 367 C.E.
P710 - 377 C.E.	P720 - 387 C.E.	P730 - 397 C.E.	P740 - 407 C.E.	P750 - 417 C.E.	P760 - 427 C.E.	P770 - 437 C.E.	P780 - 447 C.E.	P790 - 457 C.E.	P800 - 467 C.E.
P810 - 477 C.E.	P820 - 487 C.E.	P830 - 497 C.E.	P840 - 507 C.E.	P850 - 517 C.E.	P860 - 527 C.E.	P870 - 537 C.E.	P880 - 547 C.E.	P890 - 557 C.E.	P900 - 567 C.E.
P910 - 577 C.E.	P920 - 587 C.E.	P930 - 597 C.E.	P940 - 607 C.E.	P950 - 617 C.E.	P960 - 627 C.E.	P970 - 637 C.E.	P980 - 647 C.E.	P990 - 657 C.E.	P1000 - 667 C.E.
P1010 - 677 C.E.	P1020 - 687 C.E.	P1030 - 697 C.E.	P1040 - 707 C.E.	P1050 - 717 C.E.	P1060 - 727 C.E.	P1070 - 737 C.E.	P1080 - 747 C.E.	P1090 - 757 C.E.	P1100 - 767 C.E.
P1110 - 777 C.E.	P1120 - 787 C.E.	P1130 - 797 C.E.	P1140 - 807 C.E.	P1150 - 817 C.E.	P1160 - 827 C.E.	P1170 - 837 C.E.	P1180 - 847 C.E.	P1190 - 857 C.E.	P1200 - 867 C.E.
P1210 - 877 C.E.	P1220 - 887 C.E.	P1230 - 897 C.E.	P1240 - 907 C.E.	P1250 - 917 C.E.	P1260 - 927 C.E.	P1270 - 937 C.E.	P1280 - 947 C.E.	P1290 - 957 C.E.	P1300 - 967 C.E.
P1310 - 977 C.E.	P1320 - 987 C.E.	P1330 - 997 C.E.	P1340 - 1007 C.E.	P1350 - 1017 C.E.	P1360 - 1027 C.E.	P1370 - 1037 C.E.	P1380 - 1047 C.E.	P1390 - 1057 C.E.	P1400 - 1067 C.E.
P1410 - 1077 C.E.	P1420 - 1087 C.E.	P1430 - 1097 C.E.	P1440 - 1107 C.E.	P1450 - 1117 C.E.	P1460 - 1127 C.E.	P1470 - 1137 C.E.	P1480 - 1147 C.E.	P1490 - 1157 C.E.	P1500 - 1167 C.E.
P1510 - 1177 C.E.	P1520 - 1187 C.E.	P1530 - 1197 C.E.	P1540 - 1207 C.E.	P1550 - 1217 C.E.	P1560 - 1227 C.E.	P1570 - 1237 C.E.	P1580 - 1247 C.E.	P1590 - 1257 C.E.	P1600 - 1267 C.E.
P1610 - 1277 C.E.	P1620 - 1287 C.E.	P1630 - 1297 C.E.	P1640 - 1307 C.E.	P1650 - 1317 C.E.	P1660 - 1327 C.E.	P1670 - 1337 C.E.	P1680 - 1347 C.E.	P1690 - 1357 C.E.	P1700 - 1367 C.E.
P1710 - 1377 C.E.	P1720 - 1387 C.E.	P1730 - 1397 C.E.	P1740 - 1407 C.E.	P1750 - 1417 C.E.	P1760 - 1427 C.E.	P1770 - 1437 C.E.	P1780 - 1447 C.E.	P1790 - 1457 C.E.	P1800 - 1467 C.E.
P1810 - 1477 C.E.	P1820 - 1487 C.E.	P1830 - 1497 C.E.	P1840 - 1507 C.E.	P1850 - 1517 C.E.	P1860 - 1527 C.E.	P1870 - 1537 C.E.	P1880 - 1547 C.E.	P1890 - 1557 C.E.	P1900 - 1567 C.E.
P1910 - 1577 C.E.	P1920 - 1587 C.E.	P1930 - 1597 C.E.	P1940 - 1607 C.E.	P1950 - 1617 C.E.	P1960 - 1627 C.E.	P1970 - 1637 C.E.	P1980 - 1647 C.E.	P1990 - 1657 C.E.	P2000 - 1667 C.E.
P2010 - 1677 C.E.	P2020 - 1687 C.E.	P2030 - 1697 C.E.	P2040 - 1707 C.E.	P2050 - 1717 C.E.	P2060 - 1727 C.E.	P2070 - 1737 C.E.	P2080 - 1747 C.E.	P2090 - 1757 C.E.	P2100 - 1767 C.E.
P2110 - 1777 C.E.	P2120 - 1787 C.E.	P2130 - 1797 C.E.	P2140 - 1807 C.E.	P2150 - 1817 C.E.	P2160 - 1827 C.E.	P2170 - 1837 C.E.	P2180 - 1847 C.E.	P2190 - 1857 C.E.	P2200 - 1867 C.E.
P2210 - 1877 C.E.	P2220 - 1887 C.E.	P2230 - 1897 C.E.	P2240 - 1907 C.E.	P2250 - 1917 C.E.	P2260 - 1927 C.E.	P2270 - 1937 C.E.	P2280 - 1947 C.E.	P2290 - 1957 C.E.	P2300 - 1967 C.E.

Note that there was no year "0" (zero) when going from B.C.E. to C.E., so the count for the Passovers in the transition decade from 4 B.C.E. to 7 C.E. is determined as follows: Passover number 330 in the count (P330 above) occurred in the year 4 B.C.E., P331 in 3 B.C.E., P332 in 2 B.C.E., P333 in 1 B.C.E., P334 in 1 C.E., P335 in 2 C.E., P336 in 3 C.E., P337 in 4 C.E., P338 in 5 C.E., P339 in 6 C.E., P340 in 7 C.E.

ending points used for the count, both of which have times of occurrence that are verifiable in recorded history independent of Scripture, fit the textual constraints of Daniel, chapter 8, exactly.

The Prophecy in History

The events described in Daniel, chapter 8, can be displayed in chronological order as follows:

559 B.C.E.	Achaemenid Persian Empire begins with reign of Cyrus II the Great.
551 B.C.E.	Daniel, chapter 8, is revealed to Daniel in third year of King Belshazzar *(verse 1)*
539 B.C.E.	Cyrus the Great captures Babylon; the Achaemenid Persian Empire expands westward, northward, and southward for the next two-hundred years. *(verses 3, 4)*
336 B.C.E.	Darius III Codomannus becomes king of the Achaemenid Persian Empire. *(verse 20)*
336 B.C.E.	Alexander of Macedon becomes king of Greece. *(verse 21)*
334 B.C.E.	March 26: Passover is observed.
334 B.C.E.	May/June: Battle of Granicus; Alexander the Great defeats the forces of Darius III of Persia for the first time in battle at the Granicus River. *(verses 5, 6)*
333 B.C.E.	April 14: Passover #1 of the 2,300 Passovers is observed. *(verse 14)*
175 B.C.E.	Antiochus IV Epiphanes become king of Seleucid Empire. *(verses 9, 23)*
167 B.C.E.	December 16: Antiochus IV Epiphanes desecrates the Temple altar by sacrificing a pig, sets up statue of Zeus in the Holy of Holies, stops the daily sacrifices, seeks to destroy Judaism. *(verses 10-12, 24, 25a)*
167 B.C.E.	Maccabean revolt begins.
164 B.C.E.	December 14: Judah Maccabee captures Jerusalem, rededicates the Temple and consecrates a new sacred altar, begins offering the daily sacrifices again.
164 B.C.E.	Antiochus IV Epiphanes dies, date uncertain. *(verse 25b)*
1967 C.E.	April 25: Passover #2,300 of the 2,300 Passovers is observed. *(verse 14)*
1967 C.E.	June 7: Israeli army paratroopers restore the Temple Mount to Israel. *(verse 14)*

Daniel, chapter 8, verse 6, successfully predicted[1] that the first king of Greece, Alexander the Great, would defeat the king of Persia, Darius III Codomannus. This prophecy was made more than two-hundred years before the actual event took place in history. Soon after crossing the Hellespont from Greece to Asia in 334 B.C.E., Alexander's disciplined foot soldiers and cavalry clashed with the forces of Darius III near the site of the ruins of Troy, in what history records as the Battle of Granicus because

---

[1] Scholars through the ages have argued that prophecies in the Book of Daniel claiming to foretell events are really nothing more than a record of events written down by scribes *after* those events had already occurred in history. The justification for their attitude of skepticism is that they reject outright the concept of predictive prophecy. The 1967 fulfillment of the predictive prophecy in verses 13-14—verses that even the most skeptical scholar will agree were written down no later than the second century B.C.E.—should settle the argument in favor of the reality of predictive prophecy in Daniel.

it took place on the banks of the Granicus River.[1] Alexander won a great victory over the numerically-superior Persian forces assembled by Darius[2] to oppose him, and he would go on to defeat the army of Darius two more times, in the battle at the Issus River in 333 B.C.E. and then in the climactic battle on the plains of Gaugamela in 331 B.C.E. The latter battle brought the Persian Empire to a close politically. From a biblical standpoint, though, the earlier Battle of Granicus in 334 B.C.E. was the event in history that set into motion the coming conflict between Hellenism and Judaism that would directly shape the history of the Jewish people for many hundreds of years into the future.

The Battle of Granicus was the signal to begin the count prescribed in Daniel, chapter 8, verse 14. As we now know, the count ended twenty-three hundred Passovers later, on April 25, 1967. The Six-Day War began soon after that 2,300th Passover was observed. In the early morning hours of June 7, the third day of the war, soldiers from Israel Defense Forces 55th Paratroopers Brigade were poised to fight their way through the Lion's Gate into the Old City of Jerusalem. Their commander, Colonel Mordechai "Motta" Gur, exhorted his troops with these words: "Soon we will enter the city, the Old City of Jerusalem, about which countless generations of Jews have dreamed, to which all living Jews aspire. To our brigade has been granted the privilege of being the first to enter it ... Now, on, on to the gate!"[3] Within the hour, they had captured the walled Old City and sacred Temple Mount. Five days later, on June 12, the men of Brigade 55 assembled in parade formation atop the Temple Mount to commemorate their victory and remember their fallen comrades. They were again addressed by Colonel Gur, who told them, "You have been privileged to restore to the people of Israel their capital and their sanctuary."[4] As for Alexander the Great, there is no historical evidence that he ever understood the biblical importance of the Battle of Granicus or the role he played in the fulfillment of Hebrew prophecy. Most scholars consider Josephus' story of Alexander being shown the Book of Daniel by the high priest on a visit to Jerusalem to be based on a fable.[5] Likewise, there is no historical evidence that Colonel "Motta" Gur and his men recognized the exegetical significance of their heroic deeds during the Battle for Jerusalem in 1967. They realized that what they had done was significant within the context of Jewish identity and Israeli history, but perhaps not that their actions were the literal fulfillment of a specific biblical prophecy. They were not alone,

---

[1] Kocabaş River in northwestern Turkey on modern maps.

[2] Darius III was not present in person at the Battle of Granicus. The Persian forces were led by three of his satraps, Arsites of Hellespontine Phrygia, Arsamenes of Cilicia, and Spithridates of Lydia and Ionia.

[3] Mordechai Gur, *The Battle for Jerusalem* (New York, New York: Popular Library, 1974), *p.* 354.

[4] Amos Alon, *Jerusalem: City of Mirrors* (London, England: Flamingo, 1996), *p.* 91.

[5] From Josephus, *Antiquities*, 11:8:5 (Whiston translation): "When asked by one of his generals why he welcomed this group [the high priest and his entourage], Alexander replied: 'I did not adore him, but that God who hath honoured him with his high priesthood; for I saw this very person in a dream, in this very habit [garment], when I was at Dios in Macedonia, who, when I was considering with myself how I might obtain the dominion of Asia, exhorted me to make no delay, but boldly to pass over the sea thither, for that he would conduct my army, and would give me the dominion over the Persians; whence it is, that having seen no other in that habit, and now seeing this person in it, and remembering that vision, and the exhortation which I had in my dream, I believe that I bring this army under the divine conduct, and shall therewith conquer Darius [Darius III], and destroy the power of the Persians, and that all things will succeed according to what is in my own mind.'"

though, since no one else at the time recognized the exact prophetic significance of what had transpired. Nevertheless, Gur and his men had carried out the fulfillment of the prophecy set forth in Daniel, chapter 8, verses 13-14, which foretold that the restoration of the Temple Mount to God's people Israel could take place as soon as the Passover of 1967, the 2,300th Passover, had occurred.

The Restoration of the Sanctuary

So, now that the chrono-specific prophecy in Daniel, chapter 8, has been fulfilled by the return of the Temple Mount to Jewish sovereignty in 1967, what are we to make of this restoration? In verse 14, the Hebrew word וְנִצְדַּק (BHS, Strong's OT: 6663), which I have been rendering as *"restored to its rightful state"* (CJB), has been translated in various ways over the years. The King James translators rendered it as *"cleansed,"* whereas the translators of the JPS 1917 edition of the Tanakh[1] rendered it as *"shall be victorious."* Modern translations have been just as diverse in their renderings: *"put right again"* (NET), *"properly restored"* (NASB), *"restored to its rightful state"* (RSV), *"reconsecrated"* (NIV). The UBS Old Testament Handbook says this: "Then the sanctuary shall be restored to its rightful state literally 'and the sanctuary will be justified.' The verb form used here is unique in all the Old Testament, and its precise meaning is uncertain. Some take it to mean 'purified' or *'cleansed'* (NJV). Others have the idea of rededication; NIV reads *'reconsecrated.'* Still others have a more general statement: *'then shall the wrongs of the sanctuary be righted'* (AT) or *' have its rights restored'* (NJB)." Taking all of these approaches into consideration, it seems safe to say that the word reflects a change in status of the Temple Mount that sets things right with respect to God's will. By coming under the control of the Jewish people, the Temple Mount was restored to its rightful legal status as the God-given possession of the people of Israel. Others have ventured the opposite opinion, arguing that the Temple Mount has not been restored to Israel since, within days after it was captured by Brigade 55, administrative control of the platform area and the Islamic structures on it was turned over to the Waqf, an Islamic board similar to a trust in English law, and its administration remains so delegated today. But, make no mistake about it, the Temple Mount is under sole sovereignty of the State of Israel, and has been since June 7, 1967. The government of Israel determines who has access to the Mount, and when, and it is the Jewish people who will eventually determine its final status in the years to come. Judging from the turbulent history surrounding the Temple Mount since its capture, it seems obvious to me that the restoration event that occurred on that June morning forty-plus years ago was but the beginning event in a progressive restoration that is unfolding right before our very eyes.

---

[1] Tanakh (also Tanach) is the English name for the Jewish Bible, a name resulting from the acronym TNK formed by the initial letters of its three main sections, the Torah (Five Books of Moses), Neviim (Prophets), and Ketuvim (Writings).

CHAPTER TWO

WHAT SHALL BE THE END OF THESE THINGS?
Daniel 12:8-12

The capture of the Temple Mount by Israel during the Six-Day War was the fulfillment of the end-time prophecy in Daniel, chapter 8. That event projected the efficacy of Bible prophecy into modern times. It also confirmed that the long-awaited "time of the end" had finally arrived in history. Understanding this development was an important exegetic breakthrough for me, and a spiritual stimulus as well. Armed with my newfound understanding of the commencement of the time of the end, and infused with the knowledge gained by correctly interpreting the chrono-specific prophecy in the eighth chapter, my attention turned to interpreting additional chrono-specific prophecies in the Book of Daniel. I was certain that they were now unsealed and waiting to be fully interpreted. But, where to begin?

Without a clear answer to that question, I began a systematic study of all of the remaining chrono-specific prophecies in Daniel, looking for interpretive clues that would unlock more of them. Although I did not find the clues that I sought during this initial search, I was soon intrigued by and drawn to the chronological specificity and contextual ambiguity of the final prophecy in Daniel, the one at the end of the twelfth chapter, verses 8-12, that says: *"And I heard, but I understood not. Then said I, O my Lord, what shall be the end of these things? And he said, Go thy way, Daniel, for the words are closed up and sealed till the time of the end. Many shall be purified, and made white, and tried, but the wicked shall do wickedly, and none of the wicked shall understand, but the wise shall understand. And from the time that the daily sacrifice shall be taken away, and the abomination that maketh desolate set up, there shall be a thousand two hundred and ninety days. Blessed is he that waiteth, and cometh to the thousand three hundred and five and thirty days"* (KJV). Because this prophecy foretold that it was to be unsealed at the time of the end, and since I knew that the beginning of the time of the end had already commenced, I decided to give it my full attention. I immersed myself in the words of the prophecy, and in the text of the entire twelfth chapter for context (see text on page 23), seeking insight through Bible study and prayer until I found the keys to its interpretation.[1] Now, I am pleased to share those keys with you.

The Keys to the Interpretation

The first key to interpreting the prophecy in Daniel, chapter 12, verses 8-12, is to identify a starting point for counting the time period of 1,290 "days" and 1,335 "days" specified in verses 11-12. For this,

---

[1] Although condensed in the narrative above, this period of seeking through Bible study and prayer actually spanned more than a decade, and final understanding of the prophecy in Daniel, chapter 12, verses 8-12, came more than two decades after the initial breakthrough interpretation of Daniel, chapter 8, discussed in Chapter One of this book.

Israeli halftrack carrying paratroopers kicks up a cloud of dust as it speeds toward the Dome of the Rock atop the Temple Mount on the morning of June 7, 1967, fulfilling ancient prophecies in Daniel.[1]

prophecy, as I quickly discovered, identifying a specific starting point—an event mentioned in the biblical text and also associated with a date verifiable in history from which a count could begin—would not be as simple as it had been with the chrono-specific prophecy in the eighth chapter of Daniel, where the starting point was obvious (Alexander the Great of Greece moving against Darius III of Persia at the Battle of Granicus). From the text of the twelfth chapter, it was apparent that no such obvious starting point or ending point was anywhere mentioned. However, as I read and re-read the text looking for clues, I realized that there were two chronological constraints provided in verses 8-9. The first time constraint was revealed by the question that was asked in verse 8, *"What shall be the end of these things?"* (KJV) or *"My lord, what will be the outcome of these events?"* (NASB). It made clear that the start of the time period specified in the prophecy had to occur after "these things," the events that had just been described in the preceding section, the eleventh chapter of Daniel, had occurred. The latest dated event that I could positively identify in the eleventh chapter was the Maccabean revolt, which began

---

[1] Photo: Copyright © STATE OF ISRAEL, Government Press Office, Israel National Photo Collection. Used by permission.

in 167 B.C.E., so that gave me one end of a chronological bracket containing the specified time period. The other chronological constraint was mentioned in verse 9, *"And he said, Go thy way, Daniel: for the words are closed up and sealed till the time of the end"* (KJV). This verse confirmed that the prophecy would not be understood until the time of the end. This also meant that the conclusion of the time period specified in the prophecy would not happen until sometime during the time of the end. Otherwise, the prophecy would be understood ahead of time in history, and that was not possible. Together, these two chronological constraints meant that the 1,290 "days" and 1,335 "days" had to start sometime after the time of the Maccabees and end some time during the time of the end, which I knew had recently commenced in history. It was at this point that I had insight. Since the time of the end was already underway, and since the time period specified in verses 11-12 had to conclude during the time of the end, the concluding event of the prophecy, if such an end-time event could be identified and dated, could serve as the starting point for a backwards count. In other words, unlike the approach that I had used to interpret the prophecy in the eighth chapter of Daniel, where I found a starting event and then counted forward in time to reveal the meaning of the prophecy, interpreting this prophecy would be accomplished by counting backwards from its end point in time instead. Since the only end-time event in Daniel with which I could associate a specific date was the capture of the Temple Mount by Israel on June 7, 1967—the concluding event that was key to the interpretation of Daniel, chapter 8—I simply assumed that the Temple Mount capture was the concluding event of the time period specified in verses 11-12 of the twelfth chapter as well, an assumption that later proved to be correct. So, ironically, the starting point for doing a count turned out to be the end point of the prophecy in time, and the count of 1,290 "days" and 1,335 "days" would thus need to be done in reverse to reveal the meaning of the prophecy.

The second key to interpreting the prophecy is to understand the time period meant by the word "days" used in verses 11-12. The Hebrew word יָמִים (BHS, Strong's OT: 3117) is translated as "days" in the King James Version, and in most other versions of the Bible as well. It is almost always assumed to mean normal 24-hour days by most expositors of Daniel, but that interpretation did not work for me. Since I had already assumed that the concluding event of the prophecy was the capture of the Temple Mount by Israel on June 7, 1967, I quickly found that counting backwards either 1,290 or 1,335 literal days from that date yielded the identity of no significant event in the modern historical record as far as could be determined, so another interpretation of the word "days" was preferred. Sensing that the term as used in this prophecy probably meant years in real time—an exegetically justifiable assumption since Daniel's contemporary, the prophet Ezekiel, had established the day-for-a-year interpretive principle in Ezekiel, chapter 4, verses 5-6—I looked for a way in which "days" could mean years without such a substitution being specifically prescribed in Scripture, as it was in Ezekiel and was not in this instance. It was then that I recalled the substitution principle that I had discovered during the interpretation of Daniel, chapter 8, in which Passovers, cryptically called "evening-mornings" in that prophecy, were used to mark the passage of years. However, the Hebrew words "evening-mornings" עֶרֶב בֹּקֶר used as a substitute for the word Passover in that chapter were different from the Hebrew word יָמִ֑ים[1] translated as "days" in verses 11-12, so I discounted the possibility that the word "days" was another way of saying Passovers in this prophecy. Still, the idea that the Passover festival had been referred to in such a cryptic manner in the eighth chapter made it reasonable to consider the possibility that this type of substitution, one using the time period associated with a festival of Israel instead of the name of the festival, was a pattern of encryption used by Daniel in other chrono-specific chapters. As I studied the terminology used in the chapters containing references to calendrical time periods—those in the eighth, ninth, and twelfth chapters—I found that a pattern of encryption was possible.[2] The time-period terminology used in each of those chapters could refer to a specific Jewish festival. The eighth chapter used "evening-morning" to mean Passover. The ninth chapter could be using "week" to mean Feast of Weeks (Pentecost), and the twelfth chapter would thus use "day" to refer to the Day of Atonement. In addition, taken together in the order that the chapters were arranged in Scripture, the substitutions would reflect the order of the festivals in the Hebrew calendar.[3] Thus, I felt confident in making the assumption that the 1,290 and 1,335 "days" in verses 11-12 could actually mean 1,290 and 1,335 Day of Atonements.

The third key to interpreting the prophecy is to understand how to count the 1,290 and 1,335 Day of Atonements that determine the time span stipulated in verses 11-12, specifically, to know when to begin and when to stop the count. I had already decided that the starting point for doing the count had to be the concluding event of the prophecy, an end-time event, which I assumed to be the capture of the Temple Mount by Israel that happened on June 7, 1967. I also knew that is was generally agreed by most expositors that the 1,290 "days" time period was to be considered as part of the 1,335 "days." In other words, there were not two separate time periods, one of 1,290 "days" and a second of 1,335 "days," with no overlap, but only one time period extending forward in time for 1,290 "days," and then 45 "days," to make a total time period of 1,335 "days" in duration. So, taking all of these requirements into consideration, the count would need to be done in two stages, a first stage counting backwards for 45 Day of Atonements from the assumed concluding event of the prophecy—the capture of the Temple Mount—to reveal an intermediate date somewhere back in history, and a second stage counting backwards from that revealed intermediate date an additional 1,290 Day of Atonements to reveal a second date even further back in history. Since this backwards count had to begin with the last Day of Atonement observed before the capture of the Temple Mount, the date for the Day of Atonement in the year 1967 had to be determined. By checking a Hebrew calendar, I easily determined that the Day of

---

[1] OT:3117 יוֹם *yowm* (yome); from an unused root meaning to be hot; a day (as the warm hours), whether literal (from sunrise to sunset, or from one sunset to the next) - *New Exhaustive Strong's Numbers and Concordance with Expanded Greek-Hebrew Dictionary* © 1994, 2003, 2006 Biblesoft, Inc. and International Bible Translators, Inc.

[2] I had specialized in cryptography in the military and was predisposed to think in terms of encryption methods.

[3] In the Hebrew calendar: Passover occurs in the first month, Nisan (March/April); Pentecost (Feast of Weeks) occurs in the third month, Sivan (May/June); and the Day of Atonement occurs in the seventh month, Tishri (September/October).

Atonement for that year was observed on October 14, four months after the Temple Mount capture event, so it could not be the one used to initiate the count. Thus, the preceding Day of Atonement, observed on September 24, 1966, would be the initial Day of Atonement from which the backward count for the first stage would have to be initiated. Table 2.1 below demonstrates how to count backwards for 45 Day of Atonements to reveal the intermediate time period that will help to unravel the meaning of the prophecy. The count is initiated with the Day of Atonement in the year 1966, which is the last Day of Atonement observed *before* the capture of the Temple Mount on June 7, 1967. The backwards count of 45 ends with the Day of Atonement that occurred in the year 1922. Each Day of Atonement in the table is denoted as "A#" (where "#" is its number in the count), followed by its corresponding Gregorian year. Day of Atonements are shown in ten-year increments (so that you can verify the count on your fingers). Table 2.2 below demonstrates how to continue the count backwards for another 1,290 Day of Atonements, to reach the total of 1,335 Day of Atonements specified in the prophecy. It picks up the count with the Day of Atonement in the year 1921, and terminates it with the Day of Atonement in the year 632 C.E. Each element in the table is denoted in the same manner as those in Table 2.1. When you have completed verifying the counts for yourself, in both instances counting the specified number of Day of Atonements backwards in time from the capture of the Temple Mount by Israel on June 7, 1967,

Table 2.1 - How to Count the 45 Days

A1 - 1966 C.E.	A2 - 1965 C.E.	A3 - 1964 C.E.	A4 - 1963 C.E.	A5 - 1962 C.E.	A6 - 1961 C.E.	A7 - 1960 C.E.	A8 - 1959 C.E.	A9 - 1958 C.E.	A10 - 1957 C.E.
A11 - 1956 C.E.	A12 - 1955 C.E.	A13 - 1954 C.E.	A14 - 1953 C.E.	A15 - 1952 C.E.	A1306 - 1951 C.E.	A1307 - 1950 C.E.	A1308 - 1949 C.E.	A1309 - 1948 C.E.	A1310 - 1947 C.E.
A21 - 1946 C.E.	A22 - 1945 C.E.	A23 - 1944 C.E.	A24 - 1943 C.E.	A25 - 1942 C.E.	A1316 - 1941 C.E.	A1317 - 1940 C.E.	A1318 - 1939 C.E.	A1319 - 1938 C.E.	A1320 - 1937 C.E.
A31 - 1936 C.E.	A32 - 1935 C.E.	A33 - 1934 C.E.	A34 - 1933 C.E.	A35 - 1932 C.E.	A1326 - 1931 C.E.	A1327 - 1930 C.E.	A1328 - 1929 C.E.	A1329 - 1928 C.E.	A1330 - 1927 C.E.
A41 - 1926 C.E.	A42 - 1925 C.E.	A43 - 1924 C.E.	A44 - 1923 C.E.	A45 - 1922 C.E.	---	---	---	---	---

Table 2.2 - How to Count the 1,290 Days

A1 - 1921 C.E.	A2 - 1920 C.E.	A3 - 1919 C.E.	A4- 1918 C.E.	A5 - 1917 C.E.	A6 - 1916 C.E.	A7 - 1915 C.E.	A8 - 1914 C.E.	A9 - 1913 C.E.	A10 - 1912 C.E.
1-10 see above	A20 - 1902 C.E.	A30 - 1892 C.E.	A40 - 1882 C.E.	A50 - 1872 C.E.	A60 - 1862 C.E.	A70 - 1852 C.E.	A80 - 1842 C.E.	A90 - 1832 C.E.	A100 - 1822 C.E.
A110 - 1812 C.E.	A120 - 1802 C.E.	A130 - 1792 C.E.	A140 - 1782 C.E.	A150 - 1772 C.E.	A160 - 1762 C.E.	A170 - 1752 C.E.	A180 - 1742 C.E.	A190 - 1732 C.E.	A200 - 1722 C.E.
A210 - 1712 C.E.	A220 - 1702 C.E.	A230 - 1692 C.E.	A240 - 1682 C.E.	A250 - 1672 C.E.	A260 - 1662 C.E.	A270 - 1652 C.E.	A280 - 1642 C.E.	A290 - 1632 C.E.	A300 - 1622 C.E.
A310- 1612 C.E.	A320 - 1602 C.E.	A330 - 1592 C.E.	A340 - 1582 C.E.	A350 - 1572 C.E.	A360 - 1562 C.E.	A370 - 1552 C.E.	A380 - 1542 C.E.	A390 - 1532 C.E.	A400 - 1522 C.E.
A410 - 1512 C.E.	A420 - 1502 C.E.	A430 - 1492 C.E.	A440 - 1482 C.E.	A450 - 1472 C.E.	A460 - 1462 C.E.	A470 - 1452 C.E.	A480 - 1442 C.E.	A490 - 1432 C.E.	A500 - 1422 C.E.
A510 - 1412 C.E.	A520 - 1402 C.E.	A530 - 1392 C.E.	A540 - 1382 C.E.	A550 - 1372 C.E.	A560 - 1362 C.E.	A570 - 1352 C.E.	A580 - 1342 C.E.	A590 - 1332 C.E.	A600 - 1322 C.E.
A610 - 1312 C.E.	A620 - 1302 C.E.	A630 - 1292 C.E.	A640 - 1282 C.E.	A650 - 1272 C.E.	A660 - 1262 C.E.	A670 - 1252 C.E.	A680 - 1242 C.E.	A690 - 1232 C.E.	A700 - 1222 C.E.
A710 - 1212 C.E.	A720 - 1202 C.E.	A730 - 1192 C.E.	A740 - 1182 C.E.	A750 - 1172 C.E.	A760 - 1162 C.E.	A770 - 1152 C.E.	A780 - 1142 C.E.	A790 - 1132 C.E.	A800 - 1122 C.E.
A810 - 1112 C.E.	A820 - 1102 C.E.	A830 - 1092 C.E.	A840 - 1082 C.E.	A850 - 1072 C.E.	A860 - 1062 C.E.	A870 - 1052 C.E.	A880 - 1042 C.E.	A890 - 1032 C.E.	A900 - 1022 C.E.
A910 - 1012 C.E.	A920 - 1002 C.E.	A930 - 992 C.E.	A940 - 982 C.E.	A950 - 972 C.E.	A960 - 962 C.E.	A970 - 952 C.E.	A980 - 942 C.E.	A990 - 932 C.E.	A1000 - 922 C.E.
A1010 - 912 C.E.	A1020 - 902 C.E.	A1030 - 892 C.E.	A1040 - 882 C.E.	A1050 - 872 C.E.	A1060 - 862 C.E.	A1070 - 852 C.E.	A1080 - 842 C.E.	A1090 - 832 C.E.	A1100 - 822 C.E.
A1110 - 812 C.E.	A1120 - 802 C.E.	A1130 - 792 C.E.	A1140 - 782 C.E.	A1150 - 772 C.E.	A1160 - 762 C.E.	A1170 - 752 C.E.	A1180 - 742 C.E.	A1190 - 732 C.E.	A1200 - 722 C.E.
A1210 - 712 C.E.	A1220 - 702 C.E.	A1230 - 692 C.E.	A1240 - 682 C.E.	A1250 - 672 C.E.	A1260 - 662 C.E.	A1270 - 652 C.E.	A1280 - 642 C.E.	A1290 - 632 C.E.	---

you will see that the 45th Day of Atonement backwards from that date occurred in the year 1922, and the 1,335th (45 + 1,290) Day of Atonement backwards from that date occurred in the year 632 C.E. This means that three specific years in history are identifiable from the count and can be employed to interpret the chrono-specific prophecy in Daniel, chapter 12, verses 8-12—the starting year of the prophecy, 632; an intermediate year, 1922; and the concluding year, 1967. The significance of the last year in that sequence is already known, of course. 1967 is the year when modern Israel gained possession of the Temple Mount in Jerusalem, significant in Jewish history because it was the first time that a sovereign Jewish people had exercised sovereignty over that piece of real estate since the end of the Bar Kochba revolt in 135 C.E.[1] But what is the significance of the other two years in Jewish history?[2]

The Prophecy in History

To answer that question, I had to identify significant events in Jewish history that had occurred within the constraints of the two time periods, the years 1922 and 632 C.E, defined by counting backwards for 45 and 1,290 Day of Atonements as described above. The 1922 time period could be determined by calculating the time span between the dates for the last Day of Atonement in the backwards count of 45 "days" and the first Day of Atonement in the resumed backwards count of 1,290 "days." In other words, I had to find an event of significance in Jewish history that had occurred between October 12, 1921, and October 2, 1922. When I checked the historical records for that time frame, I found several events that met the requirement of being significant in history, and some of particular significance in Jewish history. All throughout late 1921 and 1922, Adolf Hitler, after having become chairman of the National Socialist German Workers' (Nazi) Party on July 28, 1921, was having his first success at rallying the German people behind his message of virulent anti-Semitism, culminating in a speech before a mass meeting of 50,000 Germans assembled at Konigsplatz in Munich on August 16. In Italy, Hitler's main ally in WWII, Benito Mussolini, became the youngest premier in the history of Italy on October 31. In Russia, Hitler's ally and then nemesis in WWII, Josef Stalin, had been appointed General Secretary of the Communist Party on April 3. Of more pertinence to the prophecy under consideration in this chapter, and to the destiny of the Jewish people, the British White Paper of 1922, also known as the Churchill White Paper because Winston Churchill was the Colonial Secretary at the time, was published on June 3 clarifying how Britain viewed the idea of a Jewish homeland in Palestine, an idea that had been raised in world political circles for the first time by the Balfour Declaration of 1917. The

---

[1] Historians debate whether Bar Kochba actually gained control of Jerusalem during the Second Jewish War. If not, then the last year of Jewish sovereignty over the Temple Mount was 40 B.C.E., when Hyrcanus II was high priest and ethnarch.

[2] Many modern expositors negate the eschatological importance of the Jews as the chosen people of God in post-biblical times, but I do not hold such a view. It was obvious to me from my earlier studies that led to the interpretation of the chrono-specific prophecy in Daniel, chapter 8, that the Book of Daniel is primarily concerned with the destiny of God's people Israel, and that its primary message is about the status of the Jewish people in history with respect to *Eretz-Israel*, Jerusalem, and the Temple Mount. Thus, I focused exclusively on Jewish history to find the prophetic meaning for the years 632 C.E. and 1922.

Text of Daniel 12:1-13 (KJV)

The Time of Trouble

1 And at that time shall Michael stand up, the great prince which standeth for the children of thy people: and there shall be a time of trouble, such as never was since there was a nation even to that same time: and at that time thy people shall be delivered, every one that shall be found written in the book. *2* And many of them that sleep in the dust of the earth shall awake, some to everlasting life, and some to shame and everlasting contempt. *3* And they that be wise shall shine as the brightness of the firmament; and they that turn many to righteousness as the stars for ever and ever. *4* But thou, O Daniel, shut up the words, and seal the book, even to the time of the end: many shall run to and fro, and knowledge shall be increased.

The Time, Times, and a Half

5 Then I Daniel looked, and, behold, there stood other two, the one on this side of the bank of the river, and the other on that side of the bank of the river. *6* And one said to the man clothed in linen, which was upon the waters of the river, How long shall it be to the end of these wonders? *7* And I heard the man clothed in linen, which was upon the waters of the river, when he held up his right hand and his left hand unto heaven, and sware by him that liveth for ever that it shall be for a time, times, and an half; and when he shall have accomplished to scatter the power of the holy people, all these things shall be finished.

The 1,290 Days and 1,335 Days

8 And I heard, but I understood not: then said I, O my Lord, what shall be the end of these things? *9* And he said, Go thy way, Daniel: for the words are closed up and sealed till the time of the end. *10* Many shall be purified, and made white, and tried; but the wicked shall do wickedly: and none of the wicked shall understand; but the wise shall understand. *11* And from the time that the daily sacrifice shall be taken away, and the abomination that maketh desolate set up, there shall be a thousand two hundred and ninety days. *12* Blessed is he that waiteth, and cometh to the thousand three hundred and five and thirty days.

The End of the Days

13 But go thou thy way till the end be: for thou shalt rest, and stand in thy lot at the end of the days

---

White Paper of 1922 separated the lands east of the Jordan River from Palestine and established the territory of Trans-Jordan, which later became the Hashemite Kingdom of Jordan.[1] However, these important events paled in comparison to the momentous event that took place two months after the White Paper. On July 24, 1922, the League of Nations ratified the Palestine Mandate. That act, in which the nations of the world gave official status to "the establishment in Palestine of a national home for the Jewish people,"[2] was the intermediate event identified by the prophecy, and it set in motion the process that eventually resulted in the rebirth of Israel as a nation on May 14, 1948. Still, Jewish sovereignty over Jerusalem and the Temple Mount was not recognized in the Mandate of 1922. It would be another 45 years before both the walled Old City and the Temple Mount would be back under Jewish sovereignty, something that was foreseen by the prophecy in Daniel, chapter 12, verse 12, which says: *"Blessed is he that waiteth, and cometh to the thousand three hundred and five and thirty days"* (KJV).

---

[1] It was from the Arab nation of Jordan that Israel captured the Temple Mount during the Six-Day War in 1967.

[2] This phrase is quoted from the Preamble of the Palestine Mandate approved by the League of Nations on July 24, 1922.

The second time period specified by the prophecy, the one associated with the year 632 C.E., was easy to determine. It could be identified by calculating the time span between the Day of Atonement in the year 632 C.E. and the previous Day of Atonement in the year 631 C.E. In other words, the significant event in Jewish history that marked the beginning of the prophecy would be found somewhere between September 11, 631 C.E., and September 30, 632 C.E. A quick check of the historical records showed that the prior decades had been tumultuous ones in Jewish history. In 614 C.E., the Sassanid Persian Empire under Chosroes II had captured Jerusalem from the Byzantine Empire. The Jews, who were treated harshly under the laws of the Byzantine Empire, had joined forces with the invading Persian king, who they considered a "second Cyrus" after he appointed Nehemiah ben Hushiel, a Jewish mystic and son of the Exilarch de Jure,[1] to lead his army into Palestine. After the conquest of Jerusalem, the Persians allowed the Jews to set up a semi-autonomous government with ben Hushiel as governor, and preparations were even begun for rebuilding the Temple and re-establishing the Levitical priesthood. However, ben Hushiel was killed by a mob of Christian youths before any serious rebuilding could begin. The Persians ended up installing a Christian governor in Jerusalem as a way of placating the Christian majority in the city, and limited Jewish access to the city. In 628 C.E., the Byzantine emperor Heraclius recaptured Jerusalem from the Sassanids and, as punishment for their earlier siding with the Persians, Jews were banished from entering the city on pain of death. Gradually, all of this back-and-forth warfare between the Byzantine Empire and Sassanid Persia exhausted and permanently weakened both sides, setting the stage for an event in the year 632 C.E. that would thereafter be of major significance to the destiny of the Jewish people, and to the future status of Jerusalem and the Temple Mount as well. On June 8, 632 C.E., the self-proclaimed prophet Mohammed died in Arabia to the south. His death was the event that marked the starting point of the prophecy, important from a prophetic standpoint, not because of the man himself but because his death signaled the beginning of the Muslim Caliphate and the start of its military expansion out of Arabia that changed Jewish history forever. Six years after Mohammed's death, in 638 C.E., Muslim forces conquered Palestine and the city of Jerusalem. This event initiated a period of alternating Muslim and European sovereignty over the Temple Mount that would endure for 1,329 years, until 1967 when Israeli troops restored Jewish sovereignty over *Eretz-Israel*, the walled Old City of Jerusalem, and the Temple Mount. Interestingly, the time span from the beginning of the Muslim Caliphate, which began with the death of Mohammed on June 8, 632 C.E., until the capture of the Temple Mount by Israeli paratroopers on June 7, 1967, is precisely 1,335 years to the day, an exact fulfillment of the prophecy in the twelfth chapter of Daniel, verses 8-12.

---

[1] Exilarch ("Head of the Exile") was the title of the leader of the Babylonian Jews in the Sassanid Persian Empire.

CHAPTER THREE

FOR A SEASON AND TIME
Daniel 12:5-7

The knowledge gained from interpreting the chrono-specific prophecy in the eighth chapter of Daniel, namely, understanding the eschatological importance of the capture of the Temple Mount in 1967 and the use of a Jewish festival (Passover) to count the passage of years, was the key that I needed for interpreting the chrono-specific prophecy in the twelfth chapter. In turn, the twelfth chapter, which used Day of Atonements to count the passage of years instead of Passovers, revealed even more knowledge about the divine chronology found embedded throughout the Book of Daniel. Equally important to me as an expositor, I now had confirmation that the process of progressive understanding was underway. This came as no surprise, though. From the start of my quest to interpret the remaining chrono-specific prophecies in Daniel, I had believed that God would reward anyone who was diligently seeking to know his truth through Bible study and prayer. I expected to find answers. So, counting on progressive understanding to help me again, I reasoned that the next step in my quest would involve taking the knowledge gained from correctly interpreting the prophecies in the eighth and twelfth chapters and using it as a key to unlock an additional prophecy, or possibly several prophecies.

It was at this point that I began to use line drawings to display the time spans that were being revealed in each of the prophecies, and this visual representation of chronological information helped me to identify where to next focus my search for new interpretive clues.[1] Once I had drawn parallel time lines for the chronologies given in the eighth and twelfth chapters, I could see that there was a gap in the overall chronology (see diagram on next page). The eighth chapter had produced a time line that stretched from the Battle of Granicus in 334 B.C.E. to the capture of the Temple Mount in 1967. The twelfth chapter had started with the capture of the Temple Mount in 1967 and provided a time line back to the years 1922 and 632 C.E. From previous chronological studies in the Book of Ezekiel, chapter 4, I had found a time line that stretched from 597 B.C.E. to 167 B.C.E., the latter being the year that Antiochus IV Epiphanes desecrated the Temple in Jerusalem.[2] The importance of the Temple desecration event in biblical history is emphasized by Daniel on two occasions, once in the eighth chapter, verse 11, *"Yea, he magnified himself even to the prince of the host, and by him the daily sacrifice was taken away, and the place of his sanctuary was cast down"* (KJV) and again in the eleventh chapter, verse 31, *"And arms shall stand on his part, and they shall pollute the sanctuary of strength, and shall take away the daily sacrifice, and they shall place the abomination that maketh desolate"* (KJV). Since the desecration of

---

[1] The "Prophecy Overview" chart (see PLATE 1 located on inside front cover) grew out of my early efforts to visualize the relationships of the prophecies to one another in real time. I had worked as a draftsman during college, using line drawings to portray spatial relationships, and soon found that method worked well for expressing chronological relationships.

[2] See *Appendix Four: Complementary Chronology in the Book of Ezekiel (Ezekiel 4:5-6)* on *p.* 103.

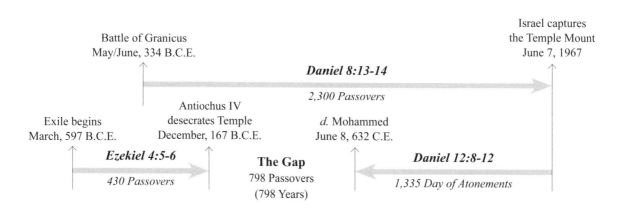

Diagram 3.1 - The Gap in the Chronology

the Temple by Antiochus IV plays such an important role in Daniel, and knowing that Daniel and Ezekiel were contemporaries in Babylon during the exile,[1] I felt comfortable adding the time line from the fourth chapter of Ezekiel to my diagram of time lines from Daniel. Thus, prophecy by prophecy, the chronology of Jewish history as described in Scripture was beginning to take shape. Based on my interpretations of the chrono-specific prophecies in Daniel, chapters 8 and 12, together with the relevant chronological information added from Ezekiel, chapter 4, I could trace a time line from 597 B.C.E. to 167 B.C.E. on my diagram, and then from 1967 in the modern era back to the year 632 C.E. However, there was the gap from 167 B.C.E. to 632 C.E.—a time span of 798 years—and that intrigued me. I knew at once that the gap was where I needed to focus my attention. But where to begin the search for a key to the interpretation? More to the point, what prophecy was to be interpreted?

The Keys to the Interpretation

The first key to the interpreting the prophecy was to understand that I already had the interpretation in hand. The gap itself was the interpretation, at least in chronological terms. What was now required was to identify a chrono-specific prophecy for which the gap was the exact interpretation. Obviously, it would need to be a portion of Scripture that sets forth the 798-year time period defined by the gap, but such a reference in Daniel was not obvious to me at first. As far as I could tell, there was no such mention in that book, so I expanded my search to include the text of the entire Bible, perusing it over and over again, praying for a clue that would point me in the right direction. After searching through every book with not even a hint of success, my attention became focused once again on the place where I had most

---

[1] Ezekiel possibly mentions Daniel by name (see Ezekiel 14:14, 20), but whether they met or corresponded is open to speculation. Both were exiled to Babylon by Nebuchadnezzar, Daniel in 605 B.C.E. and Ezekiel in 597 B.C.E.

recently interpreted a chrono-specific prophecy, the twelfth chapter of Daniel. As I resumed studying and meditating on the words of Daniel, chapter 12 (see text on page 23), I noticed that the gap on my line drawing (see opposite page) was located immediately before the start of the 1,335 Day of Atonements that were described in chapter 12, verses 8-12. It was at this point that I had new insight that eventually led to the identification of the prophecy associated with the gap. I realized that the prophecy about "a time, times, and an half" in verses 5-7 of the text, which came immediately before the prophecy in verses 8-12 describing the 1,335 "days" in the text, might be the prophecy that describes the gap located in the same place on my line drawing. Instead of running concurrently, I realized that the time periods described in verses 5-7 and verses 8-12 could run in sequence, just as the gap and the 1,335 Day of Atonements were depicted on my drawing. This was a breakthrough. For the first time, I felt reasonably confident that the 798 years on my line drawing might be the same as the prophecy about "a time, times, and an half" in verses 5-7 of the twelfth chapter of Daniel. Before exploring further, however, I knew that I needed to verify that there were exactly 798 Passovers between the desecration of the Temple by Antiochus in 167 B.C.E., the starting point of the gap, and the death of Mohammed in 632 C.E., the end point of the gap. I did so by counting the Passovers, and you can, too. Table 3.1 below demonstrates how to count the Passovers that occurred during the gap years. The count is initiated with the Passover of 166 B.C.E, which is the first Passover observed *after* the desecration of the Temple by Antiochus IV on December 16, 167 B.C.E. The count ends with the Passover of 632 C.E., which is the last Passover that was observed *before* the death of Mohammed on June 8, 632 C.E. Each Passover in the table is denoted as "P#" (where "#" is its number in the count), followed by its corresponding Gregorian year. After the initial ten Passovers (P1 through P10), which are shown on the top line, Passovers are shown in ten-year increments (so that you can verify the count on your fingers).

Table 3.1 - How to Count the 798 Passovers

P1 - 166 B.C.E.	P2 - 165 B.C.E.	P3 - 164 B.C.E.	P4 - 163 B.C.E.	P5 - 162 B.C.E.	P6 - 161 B.C.E.	P7 - 160 B.C.E.	P8 - 159 B.C.E.	P9 - 158 B.C.E.	P10 - 157 B.C.E.
1-10 see above	P20 - 147 B.C.E.	P30 - 137 B.C.E.	P40 - 127 B.C.E.	P50 - 117 B.C.E.	P60 - 107 B.C.E.	P70 - 97 B.C.E.	P80 - 87 B.C.E.	P90 - 77 B.C.E.	P100 - 67 B.C.E.
P110 - 57 B.C.E.	P120 - 47 B.C.E.	P130 - 37 B.C.E.	P140 - 27 B.C.E.	P150 - 17 B.C.E.	P160 - 7 B.C.E.	P170 - 4 C.E.	P180 - 14 C.E.	P190 - 24 C.E.	P200 - 34 C.E.
P210 - 44 C.E.	P220 - 54 C.E.	P230 - 64 C.E.	P240 - 74 C.E.	P250 - 84 C.E.	P260 - 94 C.E.	P270 - 104 C.E.	P280 - 114 C.E.	P290 - 124 C.E.	P300 - 134 C.E.
P310 - 144 C.E.	P320 - 154 C.E.	P 330 - 164 C.E.	P340 - 174 C.E.	P350 - 184 C.E.	P360 - 194 C.E.	P370 - 204 C.E.	P380 - 214 C.E.	P390 - 224 C.E.	P400 - 234 C.E.
P410 - 244 C.E.	P420 - 254 C.E.	P430 - 264 C.E.	P440 - 274 C.E.	P450 - 284 C.E.	P460 - 294 C.E.	P470 - 304 C.E.	P480 - 314 C.E.	P490 - 324 C.E.	P500 - 334 C.E.
P510 - 344 C.E.	P520 - 354 C.E.	P530 - 364 C.E.	P540 - 374 C.E.	P550 - 384 C.E.	P560 - 394 C.E.	P570 - 404 C.E.	P580 - 414 C.E.	P590 - 424 C.E.	P600 - 434 C.E.
P610 - 444 C.E.	P620 - 454 C.E.	P630 - 464 C.E.	P640 - 474 C.E.	P650 - 484 C.E.	P660 - 494 C.E.	P670 - 504 C.E.	P680 - 514 C.E.	P690 - 524 C.E.	P700 - 534 C.E.
P710 - 544 C.E.	P720 - 554 C.E.	P730 - 564 C.E.	P740 - 574 C.E.	P750 - 584 C.E.	P760 - 594 C.E.	P770 - 604 C.E.	P780 - 614 C.E.	P790 - 624 C.E.	*P791 see below*
P791 - 625 C.E.	P792 - 626 C.E.	P793 - 627 C.E.	P794 - 628 C.E.	P795 - 629 C.E.	P796 - 630 C.E.	P797 - 631 C.E.	P798 - 632 C.E.	---	---

Note that there was no year "0" (zero) when going from B.C.E. to C.E., so the count for the Passovers in the transition decade from 7 B.C.E. to 4 C.E. is determined as follows: Passover number 160 in the count (P160 above) occurred in the year 7 B.C.E., P161 in 6 B.C.E., P162 in 5 B.C.E., P163 in 4 B.C.E., P164 in 3 B.C.E., P165 in 2 B.C.E., P166 in 1 B.C.E., P167 in 1 C.E., P168 in 2 C.E., P169 in 3 C.E., P170 in 4 C.E.

The second key to interpreting the prophecy, now that the prophecy being interpreted had been identified as the chrono-specific prophecy in Daniel, chapter 12, verses 5-7, was to calculate the duration of the time period called a "time" in that prophecy. Since most Bible expositors agree that the phrase translated as *"a time, times, and an half"* (KJV) means three and a half "times," and since I was assuming that the time span denoted by that phrase was the same as the 798-year gap between the ending point of the chrono-specific prophecy in Ezekiel, chapter 4, verses 5-6, and the starting point of the chrono-specific prophecy in Daniel, Chapter 12, verses 8-12, I did a simple calculation to reveal the result. A "time," in this case, turned out to be 798 years divided by 3½, which equals 228 years (Passovers) in duration.

The third key to the interpreting the prophecy was for me to recognize that the above definition of a "time" was still nothing more than speculation on my part. I needed a more substantial explanation, one that had relevance to the ancient Jewish people and their concept of keeping time, to be able to say with certainty that a "time" meant 228 years (Passovers). I felt confident that my theoretical definition, once applied to understanding additional chrono-specific Danielic prophecies, would prove to be a true definition. At this point in my quest for understanding, however, I could not give a rational explanation for a 228-year time span. Still, I just knew that there had to be some practical meaning associated with the term "time," as used by Daniel, so I set about to find it, and here is what I found.

Defining a Time and a Season

To understand the meaning of the word "time" מוֹעֵד (Strong's OT: 4150) as used by Daniel in his prophecies, it is necessary to consider the historical context in which he wrote. In the Book of Daniel, we are told that he was living in exile in Babylon during the sixth century B.C.E., and for most of that time serving the king as chief of the governors over all of the wise men of Babylon. The wise men were the court astrologers, magicians, and scientists of the day. As chief governor of the wise men, Daniel would have been well-versed in the arts and sciences, especially mathematics and astronomy. Astronomy was the most important scientific discipline of all in ancient times, primarily because it was used to keep track of the reigns of kings and to predict the seasons, accurate knowledge of which was critical to the survival and well-being of the agriculture-based societies of the time. On a spiritual level, the times and seasons, which were directly related to the movement of the heavens, were related by Daniel to the power and influence of God over human affairs. Daniel himself stressed this connection when he said in Daniel, chapter 2, verses 20-21: *"Blessed be the name of God for ever and ever ... he changeth the times and the seasons: he removeth kings, and setteth up kings"* (KJV). So, considering the milieu in which Daniel lived his adult life, it is not surprising to find that elements of Babylonian astronomy, which was quite advanced even by the standards of today, play an important role in the chrono-specific prophecies of Daniel. Prior to the exile, the Jews in *Eretz-Israel* used a calendar that had twelve months of either 29 or 30 days duration, making the Jewish year 354 days in length. The Bible established that the people were to observe the crescent of the new moon as the start of the month. No special instruments were needed. The appearance of the new moon could be determined visually by priests trained to do so. In addition, the Passover was designated to mark the beginning of the months once the Jewish people had entered the promised land, although there is no mention of a "new year" day in the Bible. Neither are there any instructions given about how to reconcile the 354-day lunar year with the 365¼-day solar year, although it can be assumed that some method of intercalation (adjustment to prevent calendar creep) was used since Passover was required in some biblical passages to always be associated with the ripening of the ears of barley, which happens in the spring season. If no intercalation had been done, Passover would have come eleven days earlier each year, eventually being observed in summer, fall, winter, and spring in sequence as the decades progressed. Even with our limited knowledge of the Jewish calendar before the time of the Babylonian exile, we know for certain that Passover was always observed in spring in ancient Israel, proving that intercalation of some sort did take place.

During the exile, the Jews followed the Babylonian lunisolar calendar. Like the Hebrew calendar, it had twelve months of either 29 or 30 days, but it also had a new feature, a leap month which was added to certain years on a fixed schedule to make sure that the seasons always occurred at the proper time, in terms of climate, instead of drifting through the calendar. "Originally, the king decided which month had to be added (intercalated), and when. This was not very satisfying, and the Babylonian astronomers, often called Chaldaeans, gradually developed rules to create the nearly perfect calendar. The key was the discovery, in the mid-eighth century B.C.E. that 235 lunar months are almost identical to 19 solar years [228 solar months]. The difference is only two hours. The Chaldaeans concluded that seven out of nineteen years ought to be leap years with an extra month. From now on, intercalary months were still announced by the king, but he was advised by an astronomer. After Babylon had been captured by the Persian king Cyrus the Great in 539, priestly officials took over. The Chaldaeans now started to look for a standard procedure for the intercalation of months. It was introduced in 503 B.C.E. by Darius I the Great (if not earlier)."[1] The important thing to note in the excerpt just quoted is the reference to the 19-year cycle, in which 235 lunar months equal 19 solar years (228 solar months). This conjunction is called the Metonic Cycle today, mainly because 18th-century classical scholars credited its development to Meton of Greece sometime around 430 B.C.E. Over time, however, this attribution has proven to be incorrect. There is ample evidence that the 19-year cycle was used in the Babylonian calendar at least as early as the time of Daniel's exile, and some evidence that it was being used in Babylon in some form as early as the eighth century B.C.E. It is also important to note that the 19-year cycle is not exact, since 235 lunar months are almost, but not quite, identical in length to 19 solar years (228 solar months), the difference being about two hours and 5 minutes for every 19-year cycle. So, in order to keep a calendar based on this system in near-perfect synchronization, a day (2 hours x 12) has to be

---

[1] Excerpt (in quotes) from "The Babylonian Calendar" © 1996-2008 Jona Lendering (www.livius.org). Used by permission.

subtracted at the conclusion of each twelfth 19-year cycle, or, putting it in its most simple terms, one day must be subtracted at the end of every 228 years to ensure that Passover occurs at the same time of the year over the centuries.[1] It is this 228-year time span, "exotic knowledge" apparently made known to Daniel by the angel of God, or perhaps he learned it from the Babylonian astronomers, that defines the word "time" as used in the chrono-specific prophecy in Daniel, chapter 12, verses 5-7. The 228-year time span derived from astronomical alignments fits exactly when applied to the prophecy about *"a time, times, and an half"* (KJV), the time period specified by verses 5-7, and is sufficient confirmation of the earlier result, which was derived from reasoning alone. Accordingly, for use in interpreting the chrono-specific prophecies in Daniel, a "time" can now be defined with confidence as twelve 19-year cycles, a span of time that equals 228 years, or 228 Passovers in the Danielic way of counting time.

Since the above definition of a "time" will be used in the next chapter to explain more chrono-specific prophecies, it seems appropriate at this point to explain the meaning of the word "season" זְמַן (Strong's OT: 2166, 2165), which is also used by Daniel as a chronological term together with the word "time," as in Daniel, chapter 7, verse 12: *"a season and time"* (KJV). The Aramaic word translated as "season" in Daniel's seventh chapter is the same Hebrew word rendered as "appointed time" in the Book of Esther, where it is referring to the institution of Purim as a Jewish festival. However, the festival of Purim was instituted after the lifetime of Daniel, so another meaning must be found for the word "season" in this instance. The most obvious alternative is to use Passover, the festival that Daniel uses chronologically as a marker in his other chrono-specific prophecies, unless he specifies otherwise as he does in the ninth and twelfth chapters. In addition, Passover is referred to as a "season" numerous times in the Bible, as in Numbers, chapter 9, verses 2-3: *"Let the children of Israel also keep the passover at his appointed season. In the fourteenth day of this month, at even, ye shall keep it in his appointed season: according to all the rites of it, and according to all the ceremonies thereof, shall ye keep it"* (KJV). So, a "season," as used chronologically by Daniel, means simply a single Passover.

Of course, the definitions for "time" and "season" postulated here mean nothing in and of themselves, but have value only insomuch as they can be used to interpret chrono-specific passages in Scripture and correlate them with history, as has been demonstrated above with the interpretation of the prophecy in verses 5-7 of the twelfth chapter. The definitions will be used again in the next chapter of this book to interpret and understand the chronological references in the seventh chapter of Daniel.

---

[1] A slightly more precise adjustment can yield almost exact synchronization (with accuracy of less than half a day of error in 7,500 years), but the rules for this adjustment would have been impossible for ancient astronomers or priests to detect or utilize without the precision of modern time-keeping instrumentation. However, the 228-year adjustment could be employed simply by keeping track of the new moons, something that could be done quite accurately with the naked eye.

CHAPTER FOUR

THAT WHICH SHALL NOT BE DESTROYED
Daniel 7:1-28

The seventh chapter of Daniel is the most diverse chapter in the Book of Daniel, sweeping chronologically across eleven centuries with a three-pronged overview of events relating to God's people Israel as they lived in subjugation to surrounding Gentile empires. It begins in the empire of Cyrus the Great, then progresses through the reigns of his successors in the Achaemenid Persian Empire, then through the empires and kingdoms of Alexander the Great, the Seleucid Greeks, the Hasmoneans, the Romans, the Byzantines, and the Sassanid Persians, ending on the doorstep of the Muslim era. Over the years, many expositors have focused on the empires that populate the narrative of this chapter, and have thus interpreted its main purpose as revealing God's plan for the nations, but such an interpretation is missing the point. The Gentile empires are only incidentally important inasmuch as they provide context for understanding the travails of the Jews under their domination. The real focus is always on the relationship of the Jewish nation and people with Jerusalem and the Temple, and, ultimately, on God and his divine plan for bringing redemption to mankind through Israel. It is this plan for universal redemption that underlies the exposition of Daniel, chapter 7, that is set forth in this chapter.

The seventh chapter of Daniel can be divided into three distinct parts (see text on page 39). The first part is comprised of verses 1-12. These verses record a prophetic vision of future events affecting the Jewish people as seen by Daniel in 553 B.C.E.[1] The vision starts with the four winds of heaven striving upon the great sea, with four beasts, each diverse from the other, rising out of the sea. The first beast appears as a lion with eagle's wings. Daniel watches as the wings are plucked off and the beast is lifted up and made to stand upon feet like a man, and a man's heart is given to it. The second beast is like a bear raised up on one side, with three ribs between its teeth, and it is told to arise and devour much flesh. The third beast is like a leopard with four wings on its back and four heads, and dominion is given to it. The fourth beast is perceived as dreadful and terrible and exceedingly strong, and it has great iron teeth. It is seen to devour and break into pieces and stamp the residue with its feet. It is different from the other beasts, and it has ten horns. After this, a little horn arises and plucks up three horns by the roots, and this horn has the eyes of a man and a mouth speaking great things. Then thrones are cast down and the Ancient of Days sits, with multitudes ministering to him, and the court sits in judgement, and the books are opened. At the same time, the horn is saying great words while the body of the beast is destroyed and burned. The other beasts have their dominion taken away, but their lives are prolonged for a season and time. The second part is a parenthesis comprised of verses 13-14, and involves a son of man coming with the

---

[1] Chronology of Daniel's visions: chapter 7 in the first year of King Belshazzar, *c.* 553 B.C.E. (Daniel 7:1); chapter 8 in the third year of King Belshazzar, *c.* 551 B.C.E. (Daniel 8:1); chapter 9 in the first year of Darius the Mede, son of Ahasuerus, *c.* 538 B.C.E. (Daniel 9:1); chapters 10-12 in the third year of King Cyrus of Persia, *c.* 536 B.C.E. (Daniel 10:1).

clouds of heaven, to be brought before the Ancient of Days, where he is given an everlasting dominion, glory, and a kingdom, so that all nations and peoples should serve him. Daniel is told that this kingdom shall not be destroyed. The third part is comprised of verses 15-28. These verses provide a partial interpretation of the prophetic vision recorded in the first part. In the vision, Daniel sees himself approach one (an angel) standing nearby and, greatly grieved in his spirit and troubled in his thoughts, asks to know the truth of the things that he is seeing. He is told that the four beasts are four kings that will rise out of the earth, but that the kingdom will be taken by the saints of the Most High and they will possess it for ever and ever. Daniel asks for clarification about the fourth beast after recapping what he understands about the vision, and wants to know more about the actions of the fourth beast. He also wants to know more about the ten horns on the head of the beast and the horn that comes up after them before which three fell, and also wants to know about the horn with a mouth speaking great things, which seemed greater than the others and which waged war against and prevailed over the saints of the Most High until the Ancient of Days came and gave the judgement to the saints, and the time came that the saints possessed the kingdom. Daniel is then told that the fourth beast will be an earthly kingdom, different from all the other kingdoms, and that it shall devour the whole earth, and shall tread it down, and break it in pieces. Furthermore, ten kings will arise from this kingdom, and another king will arise after them, and he will be different from the ten kings, and he will subdue three kings, then speak great words against the Most High, wear out the saints, and think to change times and laws. After this, they will be given into his hand for a time, times, and the dividing of time. But, the judgement will sit, and his dominion will be taken away, to be consumed and destroyed to the end. And, the kingdom and dominion, and the greatness of the kingdom under the whole heaven, shall be given to the people of the saints of the Most High, whose kingdom is an everlasting kingdom, and all dominions shall serve and obey him. With this climactic promise, the events of the vision come to an end.

The Keys to the Interpretation

The first key to interpreting the prophecy in Daniel, chapter 7, is to realize that it is composed of three parallel chrono-specific prophecies, each with its own time line that is distinct in intent from the others. In verses 1-12, the first time-defined part tells a story that stretches in time from the rise of the first kingdom to the conclusion of a time period defined by the phrase "season and time" in verse 12. In verses 13-14, the second time-defined part begins with the efficacy on earth of an everlasting kingdom and has no end in time since it is everlasting. In verses 15-26, the third part tells a story that stretches in time from the rise of the fourth kingdom to the conclusion of a time period defined by the phrase "time, times, and the dividing of time" in verse 25.

The second key to interpreting the prophecy in the seventh chapter, which is composed of the three distinct but complementary prophetic time lines described above, is to remember that these prophecies are about Israel as the people and nation of God, and about God's plan of redemption for all mankind through Israel. Maintaining this Israel-centric viewpoint is critical if a proper interpretation is to be derived from the three prophetic time lines.

The third key to interpreting the prophecy is to pick the correct time period in history as the starting point for the events of the chrono-specific prophecy in the first part of the seventh chapter, since these events (the rise of the kings) are the first events to begin in real time. The most obvious place to look for the starting time period is in the historical period immediately following the time the prophecy was given. Daniel experienced and wrote down his vision in the first year of Belshazzar, king of Babylon,[1] which was sometime around the year 553 B.C.E. This was in the closing years of the Neo-Babylonian Empire that had reached its apex under Nebudchadnezzar. As we know from history, Cyrus the Great conquered Babylon in 539 B.C.E., initiating a period of Persian rule over the region that had been predicted in the Bible. Thus, the Achaemenid Persian Empire, beginning with Cyrus, is the logical time period in history for locating the events of Daniel's prophecy.[2]

The Prophecy in History - Part I

The starting events of the prophecy in the seventh chapter of Daniel are described in verses 3-7 and 17, which, taken together. say that four kings will arise from the earth. Then, verses 7b and 24 clarify that the fourth king is really ten kings. The most straightforward interpretation of these statements is to assume that there will be three kings of an empire, then a dynasty of ten kings in that empire. When the Achaemenid Persian Empire is examined—the portion after it became the sovereign empire over the Jews—that is exactly what we find in its history. The first king in the prophecy (the lion with eagle's wings that is made to stand like a man, and given the heart of a man) is Cyrus II the Great, who began his reign as King of Persia in 546 B.C.E. It is Cyrus who is referred to in Scripture as "God's anointed" and who was called to kingship by God for the sake of the Jewish people.[3] He conquered and consolidated what is now most of the Middle East as his empire. His most famous action regarding the Jews was his decree in 538 B.C.E. that allowed them to end their exile in Babylon and return to rebuild Jerusalem and the Temple, both of which had been destroyed by Nebuchadnezzar in 586 B.C.E. After his death in 530 B.C.E., Cyrus was succeeded by his son Cambyses II, who is the second king in the prophecy (the bear with three ribs in its teeth). Cambyses extended the empire into Egypt, and pushed toward Cush (modern Sudan) and across the sand desert toward the Siwa Oasis (on the Libyan border). These

---

[1] Belshazzar was the son of Nabonidus, King of Babylon (r. 556-539 B.C.E.) who, after ruling for three years, moved to Tema in Arabia to worship the moon god, Sin. Belshazzar was made co-regent and ruled in Babylon beginning in 553 B.C.E.

[2] Expositors have often incorrectly applied the fulfillment of the first part of the prophecy in verses 1-12 to the Seleucid Empire or the Roman Empire, or, in recent years, to an end-of-time scenario involving an antichrist personality.

[3] See Isaiah 45:1-4; Cyrus is mentioned by name 23 times in the Hebrew Scriptures, including three times in Daniel.

Kings of the Achaemenid Persian Empire

(showing only rulers exercising dominion over the Jews; all years B.C.E.)

1st Beast - Cyrus II the Great (*r.* 546-530) , sovereignty over the Jews begins with the capture of the
   Neo-Babylonian Empire in 539, allows Jews to return to Jerusalem in 538.

2nd Beast - Cambyses II (*r.* 530-522), adds Egypt to the empire.

3rd Beast - Gautama (*aka* Smerdis, *r.* 522-521), killed by Darius I

4th Beast with Ten Horns - Dynasty of Darius I (10 kings)

1. Darius I Hystaspes (*r.* 521-486), "the Great," Second Temple dedicated in 515, Darius crosses
   the Bosporus to conquer Thrace, expanding the Persian empire into Europe in 512, an act that initiates
   two centuries of Greco-Persian hostilities, invades Greece, defeated at Battle of Marathon.
2. Xerxes I (*r.* 486-465), invades Greece, defeated Greeks at Battle of Thermopylae, burns Athens.
3. Artaxerxes I Longimanus (*r.* 464-424), turmoil in Egypt, empire declines.
4. Xerxes II (*r.* 424), killed by Sogdianus
5. Sogdianus (*r.* 424-423), killed by Darius II
6. Darius II Nothus (*r.* 423-404), troubles in Egypt, Jewish Temple at Elephantine destroyed.
7. Artaxerxes II Memnon (*r.* 404-358), further decline of empire.
8. Artaxerxes III Ochus (*r.* 358-338), minor resurgence of empire, Egypt reconquered
9. Artaxerxes IV Arses (*r.* 338-336), Phillip II of Macedonia attacks empire in 336.
10. Darius III Codomannus (*r.* 336-330), deposes and kills Artaxerxes IV, later defeated by Alexander
   the Great in 334, making him the last king of Achaemenid Persian Empire.

---

ill-conceived desert expeditions seriously depleted his army, with the result that his brother Smerdis[1] led a coup back in the capital and was recognized as king in most of the Asian part of the empire. Cambyses was not able to reestablish his authority as king and either killed himself or was killed in 522 B.C.E. Smerdis, the third king in the prophecy (the leopard with four wings and four heads), reigned as king for only seven months until he was killed by another son of Cyrus, Darius I Hystaspes, the fourth king of the prophecy (the dreadful and terrible beast with ten horns) who began his reign in 521 B.C.E., the first king in a dynasty of ten kings (see list above), exactly the number of kings called for in the prophecy about the fourth beast. As can be seen from the list of kings above, there was much turmoil in the region during the years of Persian dominion, within the ruling families of the empire itself, between the empire and its often rebellious satrapies Egypt and Babylon, and between Persia and Greece. The Bible is silent about how all of this turmoil affected the Jews living in Jerusalem and the land of Israel at the time. The Books of Ezra and Nehemiah both occur during the reign of a king named Artaxerxes, but determining which king is referenced in either book is difficult. Fortunately, the exact dates for the work of Ezra and Nehemiah in Jerusalem, and whether they were contemporaries or served at separate times, are not germane to our understanding of the chrono-specific prophecies in Daniel, chapter 7.

---

[1] Some historians believe that Cambyses II had his younger brother, Smerdis, murdered before leaving to conquer Egypt, and that an impostor named Gautama, a Magian priest, later assumed the name Smerdis and led a coup to depose the unpopular and absent Cambyses. Darius I, who killed and then succeeded Smerdis/Gautama, made this claim in the Behistun Inscription.

Now that the fourth beast has been correctly identified as the Achaemenid dynasty of ten kings that began with the reign of Darius I the Great in 521 B.C.E., the little horn that arises and plucks up three horns by the roots can be identified as Alexander the Great, the first king of Greece. Alexander moved against the Persian Empire in 334 B.C.E., defeated the Darian dynasty in the person of its last king, Darius III Codomannus, and brought the Achaemenid Persian Empire to a close. As to the question of which three kings did Alexander defeat, there are several possible answers. In one sense, Alexander defeated Darius I, Darius II, and Darius III, three kings who bore the name and spanned the duration of the dynasty that had initiated and maintained hostilities with Greece. In another sense, Alexander, in his first battle against Persia on Asian soil at the Granicus River, defeated a Persian army which was being led by three Darian satraps, Arsites of Hellespontine Phrygia, Arsamenes of Cilicia, and Spithridates of Lydia and Ionia. Another possibility, and the one I prefer, is that Alexander defeated one king three times, which was perceived as defeating three kings from Daniel's viewpoint in the vision. This fits the historical record, which shows that Darius' Persian forces were defeated by Alexander at the Battles of Granicus in 334 B.C.E., Issus in 333 B.C.E., and Gaugamela in 331 B.C.E. After the final battle, Darius fled and Alexander reigned supreme over the Persian Empire, including the province of Judea.

There is no credible evidence that Alexander ever visited Judea or Jerusalem. Most scholars consider that Josephus' story of Alexander visiting Jerusalem and bowing before the high priest to be based on a fable. Whether he did or did not visit, Alexander and his empire did bring Hellenism into the lives of the Jewish people, and the influence of Greek civilization was to create tension in the land of Israel for many years. After his death in 323 B.C.E., the empire of Alexander split into several smaller empires. Two of these dominions, one north of Judea ruled by the Seleucids in Syria and one south of Judea ruled by the Ptolemies in Egypt, were destined to wreak havoc on the inhabitants of Israel, which was located geographically between the two contending military powers. The tenth, eleventh, and part of the twelfth chapters of Daniel describe the years of struggle between the Seleucids and Ptolemies in great detail, as will be shown in the next chapter of this book. However, in the seventh chapter, the focus is more limited in verse 8b and verses 20b-21, where the horn represents the Seleucid Empire in its latter days of dominion over the Jewish people. In verse 25a, the horn being given eyes and a mouth to speak great things against the Most High, to make war on and prevail against the saints of the Most High, and to think to change times and laws, is a description of the violently anti-Jewish Seleucid king, Antiochus IV Epiphanes.[1] It was Antiochus who, in an attempt to replace the practice of Judaism with Hellenism in his kingdom, built a fortress called "The Akra" in the City of David,

---

[1] Antiochus IV Epiphanes is identified more clearly in Daniel, chapter 8, verse 23-25: *"And in the latter time of their kingdom, when the transgressors are come to the full, a king of fierce countenance, and understanding dark sentences, shall stand up. And his power shall be mighty, but not by his own power: and he shall destroy wonderfully, and shall prosper, and practise, and shall destroy the mighty and the holy people. And through his policy also he shall cause craft to prosper in his hand; and he shall magnify himself in his heart, and by peace shall destroy many: he shall also stand up against the Prince of princes; but he shall be broken without hand"* (KJV); also, see Daniel 11:31.

stationed a garrison of troops there to enforce his decrees, appointed a Hellenistic high priest, forbade circumcision and sabbath observances on pain of death, confiscated and burned Torah scrolls, and desecrated the Temple by dedicating it to Olympian Zeus. The ultimate desecration was the erection of a secondary altar on top of the altar of burnt offerings, with the subsequent sacrifice of swine on it. The latter sacrilege took place on the 25th day of Kislev in the 145th year of the Seleucid Empire, which is equivalent to December 16, 162 B.C.E. in Gregorian reckoning. Verse 25b adds cryptically, *"and they shall be given into his hand until a time and times and the dividing of time"* (KJV).

The Roman Period

Although I had already learned from the interpretation of Daniel, chapter 12, verses 5-7, that a "time" is defined as 228 Passovers (years) in duration when used in a Danielic prophecy as a chronological marker, I could not figure out how to apply the definition to verse 25b. The logical approach was to assume that the "time, times, and the dividing of time" in this case covered the same time period as the "time, times, and an half" in the twelfth chapter of Daniel (see page 17). After all, verse 25a described Antiochus IV and the desecration of the Temple, which is the starting point for the 3½ "times" in Daniel, chapter 12. However, I could not identify either the "they" or the "his" about whom it said *"and they shall be given into his hand until a time and times and the dividing of time"* (KJV). It was at this point that I had to go back to the history books to refresh my memory about the events surrounding the persecution of the Jews and desecration of the Temple by Antiochus, and about the revolt that followed. The desecration of the Temple by Antiochus in 167 B.C.E. was a major event in the life of the Jewish people. The revolt, led by the Maccabees, started that same year, and the rebels soon gained the upper hand and began to defeat the forces of Antiochus. In late 164 B.C.E., they captured Jerusalem and rededicated the Temple, building a new altar of burnt offerings and reinstituting the daily sacrifices. The rededication took place on the 25th day of the month of Kislev in the 148th year of the Seleucid Empire, which is equivalent to the Gregorian date of December 14, 164 B.C.E. The following year, in early 163 B.C.E., Antiochus IV died and was succeeded by Antiochus V, against whom the Maccabees continued to fight for independence from Seleucid rule. After the Battle of Nicanor in early spring, 161 B.C.E., in which Maccabean irregulars scored a decisive victory over a numerically-superior and better-equipped Seleucid force led by one of their top generals, Nicanor, Judah Maccabee immediately sent emissaries to Rome. He was seeking an alliance to strengthen him in his fight against the Seleucids. He realized that, after such a humiliating defeat, the Seleucid king would redouble his efforts to put down the Judean rebellion, and Judah reasoned that his forces could not long hold out against the Syrian military might without outside help. In Rome, the Senate received the Maccabean delegation, heard their appeal for assistance, and ratified a treaty between Rome and the Jewish rebels. It was the act of reaching out to Rome by the Jewish rebels, an event that happened between the Battle of Nicanor on March 4 and Passover on April 4 in 161 B.C.E. that explains the meaning of verse 25b by identifying the "they" as the Jews and the "his hand" as the protection of Rome. So, the chrono-specific prophecy in Daniel's vision predicted that the Jewish people would be subject to the power of Rome (and its successor empire, Byzantium) for "a time, times, and the dividing of time," which equals 798 Passovers. Table 4.1 below demonstrates how to count the 3½ "times" (798 Passovers). The count is initiated with the Passover of 161 B.C.E, which is the first Passover observed **after** the Battle of Nicanor in that same year. The count ends with the Passover of 637 C.E. which, as it turns out, is the last Passover **before** the capture of the Temple Mount by Caliph Omar in February, 638 C.E., the event which ended Roman-Byzantine dominion over the Mount and began centuries of Muslim sovereignty over the holiest site of the Jews. In the table, each Passover is denoted as "P#" (where "#" is its number in the count), followed by its corresponding Gregorian year. After the initial ten Passovers (P1 through P10), which are shown on the top line, Passovers are shown in ten-year increments (so that you can verify the count on your fingers).

Table 4.1 - How to Count the 3½ Times in Verse 25b									
P1 - 161 B.C.E.	P2 - 160 B.C.E.	P3 - 159 B.C.E.	P4 - 158 B.C.E.	P5 - 152 B.C.E.	P6 - 156 B.C.E.	P7 - 155 B.C.E.	P8 - 154 B.C.E.	P9 - 153 B.C.E.	P10 - 152 B.C.E.
1-10 see above	P20 - 142 B.C.E.	P30 - 132 B.C.E.	P40 - 122 B.C.E.	P50 - 112 B.C.E.	P60 - 102 B.C.E.	P70 - 92 B.C.E.	P80 - 82 B.C.E.	P90 - 72 B.C.E.	P100 - 62 B.C.E.
P110 - 52 B.C.E.	P120 - 42 B.C.E.	P130 - 32 B.C.E.	P140 - 22 B.C.E.	P150 - 12 B.C.E.	P160 - 2 B.C.E.	P170 - 9 C.E.	P180 - 19 C.E.	P190 - 29 C.E.	P200 - 39 C.E.
P210 - 49 C.E.	P220 - 59 C.E.	P230 - 69 C.E.	P240 - 79 C.E.	P250 - 89 C.E.	P260 - 99 C.E.	P270 - 109 C.E.	P280 - 119 C.E.	P290 - 129 C.E.	P300 - 139 C.E.
P310 - 149 C.E.	P320 - 159 C.E.	P 330 - 169 C.E.	P340 - 179 C.E.	P350 - 189 C.E.	P360 - 199 C.E.	P370 - 209 C.E.	P380 - 219 C.E.	P390 - 229 C.E.	P400 - 239 C.E.
P410 - 249 C.E.	P420 - 259 C.E.	P430 - 269 C.E.	P440 - 279 C.E.	P450 - 289 C.E.	P460 - 299 C.E.	P470 - 309 C.E.	P480 - 319 C.E.	P490 - 329 C.E.	P500 - 339 C.E.
P510 - 349 C.E.	P520 - 359 C.E.	P530 - 369 C.E.	P540 - 379 C.E.	P550 - 389 C.E.	P560 - 399 C.E.	P570 - 409 C.E.	P580 - 419 C.E.	P590 - 429 C.E.	P600 - 439 C.E.
P610 - 449 C.E.	P620 - 459 C.E.	P630 - 469 C.E.	P640 - 479 C.E.	P650 - 489 C.E.	P660 - 499 C.E.	P670 - 509 C.E.	P680 - 519 C.E.	P690 - 529 C.E.	P700 - 539 C.E.
P710 - 549 C.E.	P720 - 559 C.E.	P730 - 569 C.E.	P740 - 579 C.E.	P750 - 589 C.E.	P760 - 599 C.E.	P770 - 609 C.E.	P780 - 619 C.E.	P790 - 629 C.E.	*P791 see below*
P791 - 630 C.E.	P792 - 631 C.E.	P793 - 632 C.E.	P794 - 633 C.E.	P795 - 634 C.E.	P796 - 635 C.E.	P797 - 636 C.E.	P798 - 637 C.E.	- - -	- - -

Note that there was no year "0" (zero) when going from B.C.E. to C.E., so the count for the Passovers in the transition decade from 2 B.C.E. to 9 C.E. is determined as follows: Passover number 160 in the count (P160 above) occurred in the year 2 B.C.E., P161 in 1 B.C.E., P162 in 1 C.E., P163 in 2 C.E., P164 in 3 C.E., P165 in 4 C.E., P166 in 5 C.E., P167 in 6 C.E., P168 in 7 C.E., P169 in 8 C.E., P170 in 9 C.E.

The Period of Prolonged Lives

In addition to the prophecy about the period of Roman hegemony, the seventh chapter of Daniel contains another chrono-specific prophecy that incorporates the chronological markers "season" and "time" to describe a period of Jewish history. This prophecy is found in verse 12, *"I beheld then because of the voice of the great words which the horn spake: I beheld even till the beast was slain, and his body destroyed, and given to the burning flame. As concerning the rest of the beasts, they had their dominion taken away: yet their lives were prolonged for a season and time"* (KJV). The key to understanding this prophecy is found in the phrase "their lives were prolonged." It is a reference to the last words spoken by Moses to Israel, recorded in Deuteronomy, chapter 32, verses 46-47, *"And he said unto them, Set your hearts unto all the words which I testify among you this day, which ye shall command your children to observe to do, all the words of this law. For it is not a vain thing for you; because it is your life: and through this thing ye shall prolong your days in the land, whither ye go over Jordan to possess it"* (KJV). This admonition was preceded by the Song of Moses, which foretold that Israel, once it had taken possession of the promised land, would go whoring after strange gods, causing God to render judgement by removing the people from the land. Moses, in his dying words, stressed that the only way Israel could prolong its days in the land was to be faithful to God's law, the observance of which was centered on the Tabernacle, and later, after the time of Solomon, on the Temple permanently located in Jerusalem. As predicted, the people forsook the law of God, so he used the Babylonians to render judgement on Israel by destroying the Temple and removing them from the land, then brought them back after seventy years of exile. The Temple was rebuilt and the people observed the law once again, but soon drifted back to their old practices. When Antiochus desecrated the Temple in 167 B.C.E., he had the participation of many Jews, especially those from the privileged priestly leadership who had adopted the Hellenism of their Seleucid overlords. However, many Jews in the more rural areas resisted Hellenization, and it was a rural priest named Mattathias, together with his five sons, who began the Maccabean revolt against Antiochus that led to the liberation of Jerusalem from Seleucid rule, and to the rededication of the Temple on December 14, 164 B.C.E. With the reinstitution of the daily Temple sacrifices and observance of the law that was centered on the Temple system, the lives of the Jewish people in the land were prolonged for a "season" (a Passover) and a "time" (228 Passovers), as predicted in verse 12. Table 4.2 below demonstrates how to count the "time" in verse 12. The count is initiated with the Passover of 162 B.C.E, which is the first Passover *after* the Passover that was observed on March 27, 163 B.C.E., which was the first Passover to be observed in the rededicated Temple and the "season" referred to in the prophecy. The count ends exactly 228 Passovers later, with the Passover of 66 C.E. which was associated with many portents and omens of doom for Jerusalem and the Temple (see Josephus' record of these associations in the excerpt on page 40). In the table, each Passover is denoted as "P#" (where "#" is its number in the count), followed by its corresponding Gregorian year. Except for the initial ten Passovers (P1 through P10), and final eight (P221 through P228), Passovers are shown in ten-year increments (so that you can verify the count on your fingers).

Table 4.2 - How to Count the Time in Verse 12

P1 - 162 B.C.E.	P2 - 161 B.C.E.	P3 - 160 B.C.E.	P4 - 159 B.C.E.	P5 - 158 B.C.E.	P6 - 157 B.C.E.	P7 - 156 B.C.E.	P8 - 155 B.C.E.	P9 - 153 B.C.E.	P10 - 153 B.C.E.
1-10 see above	P20 - 143 B.C.E.	P30 - 133 B.C.E.	P40 - 123 B.C.E.	P50 - 113 B.C.E.	P60 - 103 B.C.E.	P70 - 93 B.C.E.	P80 - 83 B.C.E.	P90 - 73 B.C.E.	P100 - 63 B.C.E.
P110 - 53 B.C.E.	P120 - 43 B.C.E.	P130 - 33 B.C.E.	P140 - 23 B.C.E.	P150 - 13 B.C.E.	P160 - 3 B.C.E.	P170 - 8 C.E.	P180 - 18 C.E.	P190 - 28 C.E.	P200 - 38 C.E.
P210 - 48 C.E.	P220 - 58 C.E.	P221 - 59 C.E.	P222 - 60 C.E.	P223 - 61 C.E.	P224 - 62 C.E.	P225 - 63 C.E.	P226 - 64 C.E.	P227 - 65 C.E.	P228 - 66 C.E.

Note that there was no year "0" (zero) when going from B.C.E. to C.E., so the count for the Passovers in the transition decade from 3 B.C.E. to 8 C.E. is determined as follows: Passover number 160 in the count (P160 above) occurred in the year 3 B.C.E., P161 in 2 B.C.E., P162 in 1 B.C.E., P163 in 1 C.E., P164 in 2 C.E., P165 in 3 C.E., P166 in 4 C.E., P167 in 5 C.E., P168 in 6 C.E., P169 in 7 C.E., P170 in 8 C.E.

Text of Daniel 7:1-28 (KJV)

The Vision

1 1 In the first year of Belshazzar king of Babylon Daniel had a dream and visions of his head upon his bed: then he wrote the dream, and told the sum of the matters. *2* Daniel spake and said, I saw in my vision by night, and, behold, the four winds of the heaven strove upon the great sea. *3* And four great beasts came up from the sea, diverse one from another. *4* The first was like a lion, and had eagle's wings: I beheld till the wings thereof were plucked, and it was lifted up from the earth, and made stand upon the feet as a man, and a man's heart was given to it. *5* And behold another beast, a second, like to a bear, and it raised up itself on one side, and it had three ribs in the mouth of it between the teeth of it: and they said thus unto it, Arise, devour much flesh. *6* After this I beheld, and lo another, like a leopard, which had upon the back of it four wings of a fowl; the beast had also four heads; and dominion was given to it. *7* After this I saw in the night visions, and behold a fourth beast, dreadful and terrible, and strong exceedingly; and it had great iron teeth: it devoured and brake in pieces, and stamped the residue with the feet of it: and it was diverse from all the beasts that were before it; and it had ten horns. *8* I considered the horns, and, behold, there came up among them another little horn, before whom there were three of the first horns plucked up by the roots: and, behold, in this horn were eyes like the eyes of man, and a mouth speaking great things. *9* I beheld till the thrones were cast down, and the Ancient of days did sit, whose garment was white as snow, and the hair of his head like the pure wool: his throne was like the fiery flame, and his wheels as burning fire. *10* A fiery stream issued and came forth from before him: thousand thousands ministered unto him, and ten thousand times ten thousand stood before him: the judgment was set, and the books were opened. *11* I beheld then because of the voice of the great words which the horn spake: I beheld even till the beast was slain, and his body destroyed, and given to the burning flame. *12* As concerning the rest of the beasts, they had their dominion taken away: yet their lives were prolonged for a season and time.

The Everlasting Kingdom

13 I saw in the night visions, and, behold, one like the Son of man came with the clouds of heaven, and came to the Ancient of days, and they brought him near before him. *14* And there was given him dominion, and glory, and a kingdom, that all people, nations, and languages, should serve him: his dominion is an everlasting dominion, which shall not pass away, and his kingdom that which shall not be destroyed.

The Vision Interpreted

15 I Daniel was grieved in my spirit in the midst of my body, and the visions of my head troubled me. *16* I came near unto one of them that stood by, and asked him the truth of all this. So he told me, and made me know the interpretation of the things *17* These great beasts, which are four, are four kings, which shall arise out of the earth. 18 But the saints of the most High shall take the kingdom, and possess the kingdom for ever, even for ever and ever. *19* Then I would know the truth of the fourth beast, which was diverse from all the others, exceeding dreadful, whose teeth were of iron, and his nails of brass; which devoured, brake in pieces, and stamped the residue with his feet; *20* And of the ten horns that were in his head, and of the other which came up, and before whom three fell; even of that horn that had eyes, and a mouth that spake very great things, whose look was more stout than his fellows. *21* I beheld, and the same horn made war with the saints, and prevailed against them; *22* Until the Ancient of days came, and judgment was given to the saints of the most High; and the time came that the saints possessed the kingdom.*23* Thus he said, The fourth beast shall be the fourth kingdom upon earth, which shall be diverse from all kingdoms, and shall devour the whole earth, and shall tread it down, and break it in pieces. *24* And the ten horns out of this kingdom are ten kings that shall arise: and another shall rise after them; and he shall be diverse from the first, and he shall subdue three kings. *25* And he shall speak great words against the most High, and shall wear out the saints of the most High, and think to change times and laws: and they shall be given into his hand until a time and times and the dividing of time. *26* But the judgment shall sit, and they shall take away his dominion, to consume and to destroy it unto the end. *27* And the kingdom and dominion, and the greatness of the kingdom under the whole heaven, shall be given to the people of the saints of the most High, whose kingdom is an everlasting kingdom, and all dominions shall serve and obey him. *28* Hitherto is the end of the matter. As for me Daniel, my cogitations much troubled me, and my countenance changed in me: but I kept the matter in my heart.

The Prophecy in History - Part II

The Passover of 66 C.E., which was celebrated on March 27, marked the end of the period of prolonged life in the land for Israel that was predicted in Daniel, chapter 7, verse 12. Josephus records the unusual events leading up to and surrounding that Passover in *The Wars of the Jews*, 6.5.2b-4:

2b. "A false prophet was the occasion of these people's destruction, who had made a public proclamation in the city that very day, that God commanded them to get upon the temple, and that there they should receive miraculous signs of their deliverance. Now there was then a great number of false prophets suborned by the tyrants to impose on the people, who denounced this to them, that they should wait for deliverance from God; and this was in order to keep them from deserting, and that they might be buoyed up above fear and care by such hopes. Now a man that is in adversity does easily comply with such promises; for when such a seducer makes him believe that he shall be delivered from those miseries which oppress him, then it is that the patient is full of hopes of such his deliverance."

3. "Thus were the miserable people persuaded by these deceivers, and such as belied God himself; while they did not attend nor give credit to the signs that were so evident, and did so plainly foretell their future desolation, but, like men infatuated, without either eyes to see or minds to consider, did not regard the denunciations that God made to them. Thus there was a star resembling a sword, which stood over the city, and a comet,[1] that continued a whole year. Thus also before the Jews' rebellion, and before those commotions which preceded the war, when the people were come in great crowds to the feast of unleavened bread, on the eighth day of the month Xanthicus [Nisan, March/April], and at the ninth hour of the night, so great a light shone round the altar and the holy house, that it appeared to be bright day time; which lasted for half an hour. This light seemed to be a good sign to the unskillful, but was so interpreted by the sacred scribes, as to portend those events that followed immediately upon it. At the same festival also, a heifer, as she was led by the high priest to be sacrificed, brought forth a lamb in the midst of the temple. Moreover, the eastern gate of the inner court of the temple, which was of brass, and vastly heavy, and had been with difficulty shut by twenty men, and rested upon a basis armed with iron, and had bolts fastened very deep into the firm floor, which was there made of one entire stone, was seen to be opened of its own accord about the sixth hour of the night. Now those that kept watch in the temple came hereupon running to the captain of the temple, and told him of it; who then came up thither, and not without great difficulty was able to shut the gate again. This also appeared to the vulgar to be a very happy prodigy, as if God did thereby open them the gate of happiness. But the men of learning understood it, that the security of their holy house was dissolved of its own accord, and that the gate was opened for the advantage of their enemies. So these publicly declared that the signal foreshowed the desolation that was coming upon them. Besides these, a few days after that feast, on the one and twentieth day of the month Artemisius [Iyar, May/June], a certain prodigious and incredible phenomenon appeared: I suppose the account of it would seem to be a fable, were it not related by those that saw it, and were not the events that followed it of so considerable a nature as to deserve such signals; for, before sun setting, chariots and troops of soldiers in their armor were

---

[1] This was almost certainly a sighting of Halley's Comet, which is recorded as making an appearance on January 23, 66 C.E. in Gregorian reckoning (January 25, 66 C.E. in Julian reckoning; 13 Shevat 3826 on the Jewish calendar).

seen running about among the clouds, and surrounding of cities. Moreover, at that feast which we call Pentecost, as the priests were going by night into the inner court of the temple, as their custom was, to perform their sacred ministrations, they said that, in the first place, they felt a quaking, and heard a great noise, and after that they heard a sound as of a great multitude, saying, 'Let us remove hence.'[1] But, what is still more terrible, there was one Jesus, the son of Ananus, a plebeian and a husbandman, who, four years before the war began, and at a time when the city was in very great peace and prosperity, came to that feast whereon it is our custom for every one to make tabernacles to God in the temple, began on a sudden to cry aloud, 'A voice from the east, a voice from the west, a voice from the four winds,[2] a voice against Jerusalem and the holy house, a voice against the bridegrooms and the brides, and a voice against this whole people!' This was his cry, as he went about by day and by night, in all the lanes of the city. However, certain of the most eminent among the populace had great indignation at this dire cry of his, and took up the man, and gave him a great number of severe stripes; yet did not he either say any thing for himself, or any thing peculiar to those that chastised him, but still went on with the same words which he cried before. Hereupon our rulers, supposing, as the case proved to be, that this was a sort of divine fury in the man, brought him to the Roman procurator, where he was whipped till his bones were laid bare; yet he did not make any supplication for himself, nor shed any tears, but turning his voice to the most lamentable tone possible, at every stroke of the whip his answer was, 'Woe, woe to Jerusalem!' And when Albinus (for he was then procurator) asked him, Who he was? and whence he came? and why he uttered such words? he made no manner of reply to what he said, but still did not leave off his melancholy ditty, till Albinus took him to be a madman, and dismissed him. Now, during all the time that passed before the war began, this man did not go near any of the citizens, nor was seen by them while he said so; but he every day uttered these lamentable words, as if it were his premeditated vow, 'Woe, woe to Jerusalem!' Nor did he give ill words to any of those that beat him every day, nor good words to those that gave him food; but this was his reply to all men, and indeed no other than a melancholy presage of what was to come. This cry of his was the loudest at the festivals; and he continued this ditty for seven years and five months, without growing hoarse, or being tired therewith, until the very time that he saw his presage in earnest fulfilled in our siege, when it ceased; for as he was going round upon the wall, he cried out with his utmost force, 'Woe, woe to the city again, and to the people, and to the holy house!' And just as he added at the last, 'Woe, woe to myself also!' there came a stone out of one of the engines, and smote him, and killed him immediately; and as he was uttering the very same presages he gave up the ghost."

4. "Now if any one consider these things, he will find that God takes care of mankind, and by all ways possible foreshows to our race what is for their preservation; but that men perish by those miseries which they madly and voluntarily bring upon themselves; for the Jews, by demolishing the tower of Antonia, had made their temple four-square, while at the same time they had it written in their sacred oracles, 'That then should their city be taken, as well as their holy house, when once their temple should become four-square.' But now, what did the most elevate them in undertaking this war, was an ambiguous oracle that was also found in their sacred writings, how,' about that time, one from their country should become governor of the habitable earth.' The Jews took this prediction to belong to themselves in particular, and many of the wise men were thereby deceived in their determination. Now this oracle certainly denoted the government of Vespasian, who

---

[1] This was apparently interpreted by priests as evidence of the departure of the Shekinah from the Temple.
[2] *cf.* Daniel 7:2b: *"... the four winds of the heaven strove upon the great sea"* (KJV).

was appointed emperor in Judea. However, it is not possible for men to avoid fate, although they see it beforehand. But these men interpreted some of these signals according to their own pleasure, and some of them they utterly despised, until their madness was demonstrated, both by the taking of their city and their own destruction."

The events that marked the end of the period of prolonged life for the Jewish people in the land occurred in 66 C.E. with the start of the First Jewish-Roman War. Reacting to insults by Roman soldiers in Caesarea, Eleazar, son of Ananias the high priest, stopped the daily Temple sacrifices offered in honor of Caesar, signaling the start of a revolt against Roman rule. Emboldened by this act of defiance, Zealots overran and killed the Roman garrison stationed in the Antonia Fortress in Jerusalem, and the revolt quickly spread throughout the city. The legate of Syria, Cestius Gallus, sent troops to restore order, but his forces were defeated in the Battle of Beth Horon, further encouraging the uprising of Jews in Galilee and Judea. Late in 66 C.E., the Roman emperor Nero commanded one of his best generals, Vespasian, to put down the rebellion. This marked the beginning of the removal of Jews from the land. For the next three years, the Roman legions, first under Vespasian and then under his son Titus, methodically captured cities in the countryside, enslaving and deporting the Jews. Finally, in 69 C.E., Titus began the assault on Jerusalem, which ended in 70 C.E. with the destruction of the city and the Temple.

The Everlasting Kingdom

When God revealed the prophecies in the seventh chapter to Daniel, the things that the prophet saw in his dream-visions caused him much discomfort, or, as he put it in verse 28, *"my cogitations much troubled me, and my countenance changed in me"* (KJV). His reaction was appropriate for a Jewish man looking for Israel's national redemption from exile in Babylon and its restoration to the promised land. Instead, God was telling him that Jerusalem and the Temple, after they had been rebuilt, would be destroyed yet again, and that the Jewish people would be once more exiled from the land. Furthermore, Daniel was shown that other nations would have dominion over both the city and the sanctuary for a very long time. The news made Daniel physically ill. However, in the midst of all of these dire predictions, hope was offered. It was revealed in verses 13-14, in verse 17, and in verse 27, which foretold that there would be an everlasting kingdom given to one like a Son of Man by the Ancient of Days, and to the saints of the Most High for ever and ever. So, spectacular as were the prophecies predicting the Roman period that lasted from 161 B.C.E. until 638 C.E., and the period of prolonged life in the land that ended with the start of the Jewish *Diaspora* in 66 C.E., it seems that the ultimate purpose of the seventh chapter of Daniel was to introduce the promise of the everlasting kingdom, a messianic kingdom to be ruled by one like the Son of Man and possessed forever by the saints of the Most High.

∞

CHAPTER FIVE

WHAT SHALL BEFALL THY PEOPLE

Daniel 10:1-11:45

The tenth and eleventh chapters in the Book of Daniel contain its longest continuous narrative (see text on pages 47-48). Though chronologically sequential, the text can be divided into three distinct parts for interpretive purposes. The first part consists of the entire tenth chapter, plus the first verse of the eleventh chapter, and it serves as the introduction to part two. The second part consists of verses 2-35 of the eleventh chapter, which provide a straightforward foretelling of historical events that happened in the land of Israel from the time of the Achaemenid Persian Empire down to the days of Antiochus IV Epiphanes.[1] The third part consists of verses 36-45, and the interpretation of this part of the eleventh chapter has been the subject of much speculation over the years, with most conservative expositors assigning its fulfillment to a "time of the end" in a still distant future. Since the first part contains no chrono-specific prophecy, it will not be examined except to note that it reveals the purpose of the narrative, which is to foretell what will happen to the Jewish people in the future—that is, future from the standpoint of Jews returning to Israel at the end of the Babylonian exile.[2] The interpretation thus begins with an exposition of the second part, verses 2-35 of the eleventh chapter. The prophetic elements in those verses will be matched with their fulfillment events in history, as recorded by Polybius, Livy, Josephus, 1 Maccabees, and 2 Maccabees, verse by verse as follows:

The Prophecy in History - Part I

546-334 B.C.E.

verse 2: *"And now will I shew thee the truth. Behold, there shall stand up yet three kings in Persia; and the fourth shall be far richer than they all: and by his strength through his riches he shall stir up all against the realm of Grecia."* (KJV) ... This verse was written down in 536 B.C.E., during the reign of Cyrus the Great (r. 546-530), who had brought the Babylonia Empire to an end three years earlier in 539 B.C.E. So, the "yet three kings" are easy to identify. They are the next three Achaemenid Persian kings, Cambyses II (r. 530-522), Gautama (*aka* Smerdis, r. 522-521), and Darius I Hystaspes (r. 521-486) who was eventually known as Darius the Great. The reign of Darius I was a golden age for Persia. He established a new capital, Persepolis, which had walls sixty feet high. Roads were built to all parts of the empire, and a canal was built from the Red Sea to the Nile. Administration was greatly improved and slavery was forbidden. Darius is notable for his military incursions into Europe, the first Persian

---

[1] Some expositors claim that verses 2-35 are not prophecy at all, but are instead later scribal records of the historical events written down as "prophecy" after the events had happened. For comments on this approach, see the first footnote on *p.* 14.

[2] Daniel had this vision around the time the Jews were returning from exile to Jerusalem. The foundation of the Temple had possibly been laid and a new altar of burnt offering built. Daily life in the land had resumed, but the future was uncertain.

king to expand his empire across the Bosporus. In 490 B.C.E., Darius, seeking to punish Athens for encouraging the Ionian revolt among Greek cities along the coast of Asia Minor, invaded Greece, but suffered defeat at the Battle of Marathon. He was succeeded by his son Xerxes I (*r.* 486-465), who immediately set out to remove the threat of Athenian influence and power on his western flank. Xerxes invaded Greece with an army estimated by Herodotus to be more than two million soldiers strong, including 10,000 elite Persian Immortals. After he won the Battle of Thermopylae, he burned Athens in 480 B.C.E., an act that created a lasting hatred for Persia among the Greeks, engendering a hunger for revenge that was to result in Alexander the Great moving with fury against Persia two centuries later.

334-323 B.C.E.

verse 3: "*And a mighty king shall stand up, that shall rule with great dominion, and do according to his will.*" (KJV) ... This verse moves the action forward in time to the empire of Alexander the Great, who avenged the burning of Athens by conquering the Achaemenid Persian Empire under the rule of Darius III Codomannus, defeating him three times, first at the Granicus River in 334 B.C.E., then at the Issus River in 333 B.C.E., and finally on the plains at Gaugamela in 331 B.C.E. Alexander went on to extend his empire as far north as the Hindu Kush (modern Afghanistan) and as far east as India

323-301 B.C.E.

verse 4: "*And when he shall stand up, his kingdom shall be broken, and shall be divided toward the four winds of heaven; and not to his posterity, nor according to his dominion which he ruled: for his kingdom shall be plucked up, even for others beside those.*" (KJV) ... Alexander the Great died a young man in Babylon in 323 B.C.E., at the height of his power. He did not designate an heir and his only legitimate son (the future Alexander IV) was yet unborn. Twenty-plus years of infighting and intrigue among Alexander's generals followed his death, fracturing the empire. In 301 B.C.E., after the Battle of Ipsus, things stabilized. Cassander ruled Greece, Lysimachus ruled Asia Minor, Seleucus I Nicator ruled Persia and Babylon, and Ptolemy I Soter ruled over Egypt and the Jews living in the land of Israel.

301-253 B.C.E., First Syrian War

verse 5: "*And the king of the south shall be strong, and one of his princes; and he shall be strong above him, and have dominion; his dominion shall be a great dominion.*" (KJV) ... By 281 B.C.E., only two major Greek dynasties remained from the remnants of the empire of Alexander, the Ptolomies in Egypt and the Seleucids in Coele-Syria (see list on next page). For the next century, these two dynasties would dominate the lives of the Jews living in the land of Israel, which was located between the two regional powers. The king of the south is a reference to Ptolemy I Soter, and the prince who was strong above him refers to his son Ptolemy II Philadelphus, who expanded the influence of Egypt throughout the eastern Mediterranean basin. The First Syrian War was fought between Ptolemy II Philadelphus and Antiochus I Soter from 274-271 B.C.E., and the result was a victory for the Ptolemies.

Seleucid and Ptolomaic Kings, 311-164 B.C.E.

(shown in order in which reign began; all years B.C.E.)

Seleucus I Nicator, r. 311 . . . . *Seleucus I Nicator*

Ptolemy I Soter . . . . Ptolemy I Soter, r. 305

Ptolemy II Philadelphus . . . . Ptolemy II Philadelphus, r. 284

Antiochus I Soter, r. 281 . . . . *Antiochus I Soter*

Antiochus II Theos, r. 261 . . . . *Antiochus II Theos*

Ptolemy III Euergetes . . . . Ptolemy III Euergetes, r. 246

Seleucus II Callinicus, r. 246 . . . . *Seleucus II Callinicus*

Seleucus III Ceraunus, r. 225 . . . . *Seleucus III Ceraunus*

Antiochus III the Great, r. 223 . . . . *Antiochus III the Great*

Ptolemy IV Philopator . . . . Ptolemy IV Philopator, r. 222

Ptolemy V Epiphanes . . . . Ptolemy V Epiphanes, r. 204

Seleucus IV Philopator, r. 187 . . . . *Seleucus IV Philopator*

Ptolemy VI Philometor . . . . Ptolemy VI Philometor, r. 180

Antiochus IV Epiphanes, r. 175 . . . . *Antiochus IV Epiphanes*

253-246 B.C.E., Second Syrian War

verse 6: *"And in the end of years they shall join themselves together; for the king's daughter of the south shall come to the king of the north to make an agreement: but she shall not retain the power of the arm; neither shall he stand, nor his arm: but she shall be given up, and they that brought her, and he that begat her, and he that strengthened her in these times."* (KJV) ... The Second Syrian War, this time a fight between Ptolemy II and Antiochus II Theos, began in 260 B.C.E. By 253 B.C.E., the armies of the two kings had exhausted one another. Seven years of back-and-forth warfare with no apparent winner showed both sides the futility of more war, so they made peace. As a symbol of reconciliation, Berenice Syra, the daughter of Ptolemy II, the king of the south, was given in marriage to the king of the north, Antiochus II, who was forced to set aside his wife Laodice so that the marriage could take place. In 246 B.C.E., both Ptolemy II and Antiochus II died. Tradition says that Antiochus was poisoned by Laodice, who wanted the throne for her son Seleucus, while Berenice, now an outsider at the Seleucid court, persuaded her brother, the newly crowned Ptolemy III Euergetes of Egypt, to come to Antioch to help her install her infant son as king. By the time Ptolemy arrived, Berenice and her son had been assassinated. Ptolemy then declared war on the new Seleucid king, Seleucus II Callinicus.

246-223 B.C.E., Third Syrian War

verses 7-9: *"But out of a branch of her roots shall one stand up in his estate, which shall come with an army, and shall enter into the fortress of the king of the north, and shall deal against them, and shall prevail: And shall also carry captives into Egypt their gods, with their princes, and with their precious vessels of silver and of gold; and he shall continue more years than the king of the north. So the king of the south shall come into his kingdom, and shall return into his own land." (KJV)* ... Berenice was the daughter of Ptolemy II, so his son and her brother, Ptolemy III Euergetes, is the one being referred to as "a branch from her roots" in the prophecy. After his sister's assassination in 246 B.C.E., Ptolemy III declared war against Seleucus II, thus beginning the Third Syrian War from 246-241 B.C.E. At the beginning, Ptolemy II won impressive victories in Syria and Anatolia, even occupying the port city of Antioch, and his army was successful in battle as far east as Babylon. Later in the war, Seleucus II was betrayed by his younger brother, Antiochus Hierax, who declared his independence from Seleucus after the latter had been persuaded by their mother, Laodice, to grant Antiochus a co-regency and rule over Anatolia and other Seleucid territories. Weakened by the defection and defeats, Seleucus II sued for peace in 241 B.C.E., in exchange giving Ptolemy III extensive territory along the coast of Syria, including Antioch, and large quantities of gold and silver in reparation and tribute. Ptolemy III had a long and successful reign, outliving both Seleucus II and his son, Seleucus III. He died in the second year of the reign of Antiochus III, being succeeded by his son, Ptolemy IV Philopator.

223-218 B.C.E., Fourth Syrian War

verse 10: *"But his sons shall be stirred up, and shall assemble a multitude of great forces: and one shall certainly come, and overflow, and pass through: then shall he return, and be stirred up, even to his fortress." (KJV)* ... The narrative action of the prophecy now switches back to the northern kingdom to focus on the Seleucids. After the death of Seleucus II, the eldest son, Seleucus III Ceraunus, became king and soon attacked Ptolemy III's provinces in Asia, initiating the Fourth Syrian War from 219-217 B.C.E. He was unsuccessful as a military leader and was assassinated by members of the Seleucid army. His ambitious 18-year-old brother, Antiochus III (later known to history as "the Great"), was recognized as king in his place. Once established on the throne, Antiochus III set out to restore glory to the kingdom, his intention being to recover all territorial possessions lost since the days of Seleucus I Nicator. Antiochus first subdued the eastern provinces and Anatolia, then turned his attention toward Syria and Egypt. In 218 B.C.E., he marched his army through Judea to the border of Egypt, where he stayed for a year preparing for a major assault on Egypt. Meanwhile, the new king of Egypt, young Ptolemy IV Philopator, presided over a kingdom in disarray after years of imperial intrigue and maneuvering, and was a pawn of his counselor, Sosibius, who began training an army to oppose the inevitable Seleucid attack. In addition to Greeks, Sosibius conscripted and trained Egyptians as well, the first time that natives had comprised part of an army under the Ptolemies. By the summer of 217 B.C.E., the Battle of Raphia between the king of the north and king of the south was ready to begin.

217-204 B.C.E, Battle of Raphia.

verses 11-12: *"And the king of the south shall be moved with choler, and shall come forth and fight with him, even with the king of the north: and he shall set forth a great multitude; but the multitude shall be*

Text of Daniel 10:1-21 (KJV)

1 In the third year of Cyrus king of Persia a thing was revealed unto Daniel, whose name was called Belteshazzar; and the thing was true, but the time appointed was long: and he understood the thing, and had understanding of the vision. *2* In those days I Daniel was mourning three full weeks. *3* I ate no pleasant bread, neither came flesh nor wine in my mouth, neither did I anoint myself at all, till three whole weeks were fulfilled. *4* And in the four and twentieth day of the first month, as I was by the side of the great river, which is Hiddekel; *5* Then I lifted up mine eyes, and looked, and behold a certain man clothed in linen, whose loins were girded with fine gold of Uphaz: *6* His body also was like the beryl, and his face as the appearance of lightning, and his eyes as lamps of fire, and his arms and his feet like in colour to polished brass, and the voice of his words like the voice of a multitude. *7* And I Daniel alone saw the vision: for the men that were with me saw not the vision; but a great quaking fell upon them, so that they fled to hide themselves. *8* Therefore I was left alone, and saw this great vision, and there remained no strength in me: for my comeliness was turned in me into corruption, and I retained no strength. *9* Yet heard I the voice of his words: and when I heard the voice of his words, then was I in a deep sleep on my face, and my face toward the ground. *10* And, behold, an hand touched me, which set me upon my knees and upon the palms of my hands. *11* And he said unto me, O Daniel, a man greatly beloved, understand the words that I speak unto thee, and stand upright: for unto thee am I now sent. And when he had spoken this word unto me, I stood trembling. *12* Then said he unto me, Fear not, Daniel: for from the first day that thou didst set thine heart to understand, and to chasten thyself before thy God, thy words were heard, and I am come for thy words. *13* But the prince of the kingdom of Persia withstood me one and twenty days: but, lo, Michael, one of the chief princes, came to help me; and I remained there with the kings of Persia. *14* Now I am come to make thee understand what shall befall thy people in the latter days: for yet the vision is for many days. *15* And when he had spoken such words unto me, I set my face toward the ground, and I became dumb. *16* And, behold, one like the similitude of the sons of men touched my lips: then I opened my mouth, and spake, and said unto him that stood before me, O my lord, by the vision my sorrows are turned upon me, and I have retained no strength. *17* For how can the servant of this my lord talk with this my lord? for as for me, straightway there remained no strength in me, neither is there breath left in me *18* Then there came again and touched me one like the appearance of a man, and he strengthened me, *19* And said, O man greatly beloved, fear not: peace be unto thee, be strong, yea, be strong. And when he had spoken unto me, I was strengthened, and said, Let my lord speak; for thou hast strengthened me. *20* Then said he, Knowest thou wherefore I come unto thee? and now will I return to fight with the prince of Persia: and when I am gone forth, lo, the prince of Grecia shall come. *21* But I will shew thee that which is noted in the scripture of truth: and there is none that holdeth with me in these things, but Michael your prince.

Text of Daniel 11:1-45 (KJV)

1 Also I in the first year of Darius the Mede, even I, stood to confirm and to strengthen him *2* And now will I shew thee the truth. Behold, there shall stand up yet three kings in Persia; and the fourth shall be far richer than they all: and by his strength through his riches he shall stir up all against the realm of Grecia. *3* And a mighty king shall stand up, that shall rule with great dominion, and do according to his will. *4* And when he shall stand up, his kingdom shall be broken, and shall be divided toward the four winds of heaven; and not to his posterity, nor according to his dominion which he ruled: for his kingdom shall be plucked up, even for others beside those. *5* And the king of the south shall be strong, and one of his princes; and he shall be strong above him, and have dominion; his dominion shall be a great dominion. *6* And in the end of years they shall join themselves together; for the king's daughter of the south shall come to the king of the north to make an agreement: but she shall not retain the power of the arm; neither shall he stand, nor his arm: but she shall be given up, and they that brought her, and he that begat her, and he that strengthened her in these times. *7* But out of a branch of her roots shall one stand up in his estate, which shall come with an army, and shall enter into the fortress of the king of the north, and shall deal against them, and shall prevail: *8* And shall also carry captives into Egypt their gods, with their princes, and with their precious vessels of silver and of gold; and he shall continue more years than the king of the north. *9* So the king of the south shall come into his kingdom, and shall return into his own land. *10* But his sons shall be stirred up, and shall assemble a multitude of great forces: and one shall certainly come, and overflow, and pass through: then shall he return, and be stirred up, even to his fortress. *11* And the king of the south shall be moved with choler, and shall come forth and fight with him, even with the king of the north: and he shall set forth a great multitude; but the multitude shall be given into his hand. *12* And when he hath taken away the multitude, his heart shall be lifted up; and he shall cast down many ten

Text of Daniel 11:1-45 (KJV) - *continued*

thousands: but he shall not be strengthened by it. *13* For the king of the north shall return, and shall set forth a multitude greater than the former, and shall certainly come after certain years with a great army and with much riches.*14* And in those times there shall many stand up against the king of the south: also the robbers of thy people shall exalt themselves to establish the vision; but they shall fall. *15* So the king of the north shall come, and cast up a mount, and take the most fenced cities: and the arms of the south shall not withstand, neither his chosen people, neither shall there be any strength to withstand. *16* But he that cometh against him shall do according to his own will, and none shall stand before him: and he shall stand in the glorious land, which by his hand shall be consumed. *17* He shall also set his face to enter with the strength of his whole kingdom, and upright ones with him; thus shall he do: and he shall give him the daughter of women, corrupting her: but she shall not stand on his side, neither be for him. *18* After this shall he turn his face unto the isles, and shall take many: but a prince for his own behalf shall cause the reproach offered by him to cease; without his own reproach he shall cause it to turn upon him. *19* Then he shall turn his face toward the fort of his own land: but he shall stumble and fall, and not be found. *20* Then shall stand up in his estate a raiser of taxes in the glory of the kingdom: but within few days he shall be destroyed, neither in anger, nor in battle. *21* And in his estate shall stand up a vile person, to whom they shall not give the honour of the kingdom: but he shall come in peaceably, and obtain the kingdom by flatteries. *22* And with the arms of a flood shall they be overflown from before him, and shall be broken; yea, also the prince of the covenant. *23* And after the league made with him he shall work deceitfully: for he shall come up, and shall become strong with a small people. *24* He shall enter peaceably even upon the fattest places of the province; and he shall do that which his fathers have not done, nor his fathers' fathers; he shall scatter among them the prey, and spoil, and riches: yea, and he shall forecast his devices against the strong holds, even for a time. *25* And he shall stir up his power and his courage against the king of the south with a great army; and the king of the south shall be stirred up to battle with a very great and mighty army; but he shall not stand: for they shall forecast devices against him. *26* Yea, they that feed of the portion of his meat shall destroy him, and his army shall overflow: and many shall fall down slain. *27* And both these kings' hearts shall be to do mischief, and they shall speak lies at one table; but it shall not prosper: for yet the end shall be at the time appointed. *28* Then shall he return into his land with great riches; and his heart shall be against the holy covenant; and he shall do exploits, and return to his own land. *29* At the time appointed he shall return, and come toward the south; but it shall not be as the former, or as the latter. *30* For the ships of Chittim shall come against him: therefore he shall be grieved, and return, and have indignation against the holy covenant: so shall he do; he shall even return, and have intelligence with them that forsake the holy covenant. *31* And arms shall stand on his part, and they shall pollute the sanctuary of strength, and shall take away the daily sacrifice, and they shall place the abomination that maketh desolate. *32* And such as do wickedly against the covenant shall he corrupt by flatteries: but the people that do know their God shall be strong, and do exploits. *33* And they that understand among the people shall instruct many: yet they shall fall by the sword, and by flame, by captivity, and by spoil, many days. *34* Now when they shall fall, they shall be holpen with a little help: but many shall cleave to them with flatteries. *35* And some of them of understanding shall fall, to try them, and to purge, and to make them white, even to the time of the end: because it is yet for a time appointed. *36* And the king shall do according to his will; and he shall exalt himself, and magnify himself above every god, and shall speak marvellous things against the God of gods, and shall prosper till the indignation be accomplished: for that that is determined shall be done. *37* Neither shall he regard the God of his fathers, nor the desire of women, nor regard any god: for he shall magnify himself above all. *38* But in his estate shall he honour the God of forces: and a god whom his fathers knew not shall he honour with gold, and silver, and with precious stones, and pleasant things. *39* Thus shall he do in the most strong holds with a strange god, whom he shall acknowledge and increase with glory: and he shall cause them to rule over many, and shall divide the land for gain. *40* And at the time of the end shall the king of the south push at him: and the king of the north shall come against him like a whirlwind, with chariots, and with horsemen, and with many ships; and he shall enter into the countries, and shall overflow and pass over. *41* He shall enter also into the glorious land, and many countries shall be overthrown: but these shall escape out of his hand, even Edom, and Moab, and the chief of the children of Ammon. *42* He shall stretch forth his hand also upon the countries: and the land of Egypt shall not escape. *43* But he shall have power over the treasures of gold and of silver, and over all the precious things of Egypt: and the Libyans and the Ethiopians shall be at his steps. *44* But tidings out of the east and out of the north shall trouble him: therefore he shall go forth with great fury to destroy, and utterly to make away many. *45* And he shall plant the tabernacles of his palace between the seas in the glorious holy mountain; yet he shall come to his end, and none shall help him.

given into his hand. And when he hath taken away the multitude, his heart shall be lifted up; and he shall cast down many ten thousands: but he shall not be strengthened by it." (KJV) ... The Battle of Raphia was fought on June 22, 217 B.C.E., between the massive armies of Antiochus III and Ptolemy IV. The battle took place on the sands of what is today called Gaza, near the modern town of Rafah. According to the historian Polybius, Antiochus III had the superior force, perhaps as many as 70,000 foot soldiers and 5,000 cavalry, with 73 war elephants of Indian stock. Ptolemy had fewer soldiers and calvary, and his war elephants from Africa were easily spooked by the Indian elephants of Antiochus. At first the battle went heavily in favor of Antiochus, but, thinking he had victory in hand, he made a strategic blunder that allowed Ptolemy's better-disciplined army to counter-attack and route his forces. Antiochus was forced to withdraw to Lebanon while Ptolemy re-consolidated his dominion over Coele-Syria. The native Egyptians recruited and trained by Sosibius performed well and much of the victory was attributable to their effectiveness, but they would rebel against the rule of Ptolemy in his last years and form a separate government in Upper Egypt that lasted from 207-186 B.C.E. So, Ptolemy IV gained the victory but lost about half of his kingdom in the process.

204-194 B.C.E., Fifth Syrian War

verses 13-17: *"For the king of the north shall return, and shall set forth a multitude greater than the former, and shall certainly come after certain years with a great army and with much riches. And in those times there shall many stand up against the king of the south: also the robbers of thy people shall exalt themselves to establish the vision; but they shall fall. So the king of the north shall come, and cast up a mount, and take the most fenced cities: and the arms of the south shall not withstand, neither his chosen people, neither shall there be any strength to withstand. But he that cometh against him shall do according to his own will, and none shall stand before him: and he shall stand in the glorious land, which by his hand shall be consumed. He shall also set his face to enter with the strength of his whole kingdom, and upright ones with him; thus shall he do: and he shall give him the daughter of women, corrupting her: but she shall not stand on his side, neither be for him."* (KJV) ... Ptolemy IV died in 204 B.C.E., leaving the throne of Egypt to the child king, Ptolemy V. The power stuggle that resulted among the Egyptian leaders soon led to anarchy. Antiochus III took advantage of the situation and invaded Coele-Syria in 202 B.C.E., after making a military alliance with Philip V of Macedon. The Seleucid forces overran the coastal areas of Judea and achieved a decisive victory over the army of Ptolemy in the Battle of Panium in 198 B.C.E. At this point, Rome, fearing disruption of vital grain supplies from Egypt, warned Antiochus and Philip not to invade Egypt, and they complied. Antiochus was content to consolidate his rule over Coele-Syria and the coastal areas. Since Ptolemy was facing a revolt at home, he sued for peace in 195 B.C.E., signing away Coele-Syria and agreeing to marry Antiochus' daughter, Cleopatra I. The marriage took place in 194 B.C.E., with Antiochus hoping to gain power in the Egyptian court through his daughter, but she proved to be loyal to her husband. Notable during this period is the permanent transfer of Judea and Jerusalem to Seleucid rule by the treaty of 195 B.C.E.

195-187 B.C.E.

verses 18-19: *"After this shall he turn his face unto the isles, and shall take many: but a prince for his own behalf shall cause the reproach offered by him to cease; without his own reproach he shall cause it to turn upon him. Then he shall turn his face toward the fort of his own land: but he shall stumble and fall, and not be found."* (KJV) ... With peace secured on his southern flank, Antiochus III attacked into Europe, invading Greece with 10,000 soldiers to aid the revolt of the Aetolians, who elected him commander in chief. This westward thrust soon brought Antiochus into conflict with the emerging Mediterranean power, Rome. He even entertained Rome's nemesis, Hannibal, at his court. The Romans responded by defeating Antiochus at Thermopylae, and he was forced to withdraw back into Asia. The Roman army then proceeded to wrest Anatolia away from Seleucid control by winning the Battle of Magnesia. This defeat, combined with the defeat of Hannibal at sea, gave Rome control of Asia Minor for good, a fact that was made official on the ground by the Treaty of Apamea that was signed in 188 B.C.E. The treaty saddled Antiochus with heavy debt to Rome, and he had to send his son, Mithridates (later to be called Antiochus IV Epiphanes), to Rome as a hostage. With the Seleucid authority thus weakened, the eastern provinces rebelled and gained independence. Antiochus III died in 187 B.C.E. in Persia, trying to reassert his authority over his rapidly diminishing empire.

187-175 B.C.E.

verse 20: *"Then shall stand up in his estate a raiser of taxes in the glory of the kingdom: but within few days he shall be destroyed, neither in anger, nor in battle. And in his estate shall stand up a vile person, to whom they shall not give the honour of the kingdom: but he shall come in peaceably, and obtain the kingdom by flatteries."* (KJV) ... Antiochus III was succeeded by his eldest son, Seleucus IV Philopater. Because of the heavy tribute now being demanded by Rome and the greatly reduced territory from which to generate revenue, Seleucus resorted to heavy taxation of his remaining subjects. Judea suffered terribly under this burden. At one point, Seleucus ordered his treasurer, Heliodorus, to plunder the Temple treasury in Jerusalem. The priests and people wailed and lamented and entreated God to prevent the sacrilege, but Heliodorus persisted. A vivid account of what happened next is given in the apocryphal book of 2 Maccabees 3:23-40 (KJV):

"Nevertheless Heliodorus executed that which was decreed. Now as he was there present himself with his guard about the treasury, the Lord of spirits, and the Prince of all power, caused a great apparition, so that all that presumed to come in with him were astonished at the power of God, and fainted, and were sore afraid. For there appeared unto them an horse with a terrible rider upon him, and adorned with a very fair covering, and he ran fiercely, and smote at Heliodorus with his forefeet, and it seemed that he that sat upon the horse had complete harness of gold. Moreover two other young men appeared before him, notable in strength, excellent in beauty, and comely in apparel, who stood by him on either side; and scourged him continually, and gave him many sore stripes. And Heliodorus fell suddenly unto the ground, and was compassed with great darkness: but they that were with him took him up, and put him into a litter. Thus him, that lately came with a great train and with all his guard into the said treasury, they carried out, being unable to help himself with his weapons: and manifestly they acknowledged the power of God. For he by the hand of God was cast down, and lay speechless without all hope of life. But they praised the Lord, that had miraculously honoured his own place: for the temple; which a little afore was full of fear and trouble, when the Almighty Lord appeared, was filled with joy and gladness. Then straightways certain of Heliodorus' friends prayed Onias, that he would call upon the most High to grant him his life, who lay ready to give up the ghost. So the high priest, suspecting lest the king should misconceive that some treachery had been done to Heliodorus by the Jews, offered a sacrifice for the health of the man. Now as the high priest was making an atonement, the same young men in the same clothing appeared and stood beside Heliodorus, saying, Give Onias the high priest great thanks, insomuch as for his sake the Lord hath granted thee life: And seeing that thou hast been scourged from heaven, declare unto all men the mighty power of God. And when they had spoken these words, they appeared no more. So Heliodorus, after he had offered sacrifice unto the Lord, and made great vows unto him that had saved his life, and saluted Onias, returned with his host to the king. Then testified he to all men the works of the great God, which he had seen with his eyes. And when the king Heliodorus, who might be a fit man to be sent yet once again to Jerusalem, he said, If thou hast any enemy or traitor, send him thither, and thou shalt receive him well scourged, if he escape with his life: for in that place, no doubt; there is an especial power of God. For he that dwelleth in heaven hath his eye on that place, and defendeth it; and he beateth and destroyeth them that come to hurt it. And the things concerning Heliodorus, and the keeping of the treasury, fell out on this sort."

In the waning years of Seleucus IV's rule, the Roman Senate, wanting a better guarantee of the king's fealty, demanded that he send his son and heir, Demetrius, as a hostage, releasing Seleucus' brother Mithridates at the same time as a token of good will. Seleucus IV died in 175 B.C.E., possibly poisoned by Heliodorus, but many historians attribute his demise to the machinations of his brother. Whatever the case, this left the door open for Mithridates, who was now living in Athens, to work his mischief, since the legitimate heir to the throne, Demetrius, was still held hostage in Rome. He moved quickly to secure the throne for himself when he heard of his brother's death, making his way to Pergamum, where he sought the help of King Eumenes II to establish his claim. Heliodorus had already placed another son of Seleucus named Antiochus, a five-year-old, on the throne, but Mithridates quickly maneuvered himself into a co-regency. The child-king Antiochus did not fair well under this arrangement, being murdered not long after it began. This left the throne in the sole possession of Mithridates.

175-168 B.C.E., Sixth Syrian War

verses 22-28: *"And with the arms of a flood shall they be overflown from before him, and shall be broken; yea, also the prince of the covenant. And after the league made with him he shall work deceitfully: for he shall come up, and shall become strong with a small people. He shall enter peaceably even upon the fattest places of the province; and he shall do that which his fathers have not done, nor his fathers fathers; he shall scatter among them the prey, and spoil, and riches: yea, and he shall forecast his devices against the strong holds, even for a time. And he shall stir up his power and his courage against the king of the south with a great army; and the king of the south shall be stirred up to battle with a very great and mighty army; but he shall not stand: for they shall forecast devices against him. Yea, they that feed of the portion of his meat shall destroy him, and his army shall overflow: and many shall fall down slain. And both these kings' hearts shall be to do mischief, and they shall speak lies at one table; but it shall not prosper: for yet the end shall be at the time appointed. Then shall he return into his land with great riches; and his heart shall be against the holy covenant; and he shall do exploits, and return to his own land."* (KJV) ... After the death of the infant-king Antiochus, Mithridates overpowered all opposition, usurped the throne, and changed his name to Antiochus IV Epiphanes to bolster his authority. Immediately, Antiochus set about to Hellenize and unify his realm, including Judea, initiating a struggle for the hearts and minds of the Jewish people that would dominate the history of the Jews for centuries. Onias III was the high priest in Jerusalem when Antiochus IV became king and was known for his faithfulness to the traditions of Judaism and resistance to Hellenization. He had a brother, Joshua, who had adopted the Hellenistic ways of the Seleucids, and had even changed his name to its Greek equivalent, Jason. Aware that Antiochus was in severe need of money, Jason offered him a bribe to set aside Onias and appoint him as high priest in his place. Antiochus was only too happy to do so, installing Jason as high priest in 174 B.C.E. Jason thus became the first high priest over the Jewish people to be appointed by a secular government, much to the chagrin of the many faithful Jews still residing in the land. Two years later, Jason sent a Temple official named Menelaus to Antiochus bearing his tribute in gold and silver for that year. Instead of delivering the money, Menelaus added more talents of gold to Jason's tribute and, representing the total as his own, bribed Antiochus to supplant Jason and install him as high priest in his place. While these priestly machinations were taking place in the Temple hierarchy, Antiochus, eager to add the riches of the Nile to his imperial revenue, decided to tour Egypt, entering with a relatively small army as a bodyguard and ostensibly as the benevolent protector of his nephew, the newly crowned 14-year-old king, Ptolemy VI Philometor, son of Antiochus' sister Cleopatra I. Once in Egypt as a friend of Ptolemy, Antiochus distributed money to gain the favor of the Egyptian people. At the same time, his generals reconnoitered the kingdom's defenses. In these ways, Antiochus laid the groundwork for a later attempt to conquer Egypt by force. By 170 B.C.E., Antiochus deemed everything in readiness, so he set out to invade Egypt. He moved his army to the border, where he was met by a large Egyptian force, but the army of Ptolemy VI was unable to stop him. He quickly captured Pelusium and Memphis, including his nephew Ptolemy VI, and set out to attack Alexandria. To curry favor with the Egyptians, Antiochus publicly supported Ptolemy VI as a puppet king, having many friendly meetings and war conferences with him in Memphis, and, to appease Rome, retained him on the throne when he left Egypt to return to Syria. As he passed through Judea in 169 B.C.E., Antiochus' soldiers killed anyone who opposed them and plundered the city of Jerusalem, a portent of even worse things to come on his next visit to the city. Back in Egypt, the Alexandrians, once Antiochus and his army had gone home, renounced Ptolemy VI and declared their independence, crowning his younger brother, Ptolemy VII Euergetes, as their king. Still a puppet king in Memphis, Ptolemy VI initially praised his uncle Antiochus, but later formed a strategically wise but uneasy alliance with his brother, Ptolemy VII, agreeing to rule Egypt jointly and oppose Antiochus as one.

<u>168 B.C.E.-66 C.E.</u>

verses 29-35: *"At the time appointed he shall return, and come toward the south; but it shall not be as the former, or as the latter. For the ships of Chittim shall come against him: therefore he shall be grieved, and return, and have indignation against the holy covenant: so shall he do; he shall even return, and have intelligence with them that forsake the holy covenant. And arms shall stand on his part, and they shall pollute the sanctuary of strength, and shall take away the daily sacrifice, and they shall place the abomination that maketh desolate. And such as do wickedly against the covenant shall he corrupt by flatteries: but the people that do know their God shall be strong, and do exploits. And they that understand among the people shall instruct many: yet they shall fall by the sword, and by flame, by captivity, and by spoil, many days. Now when they shall fall, they shall be holpen with a little help: but many shall cleave to them with flatteries. And some of them of understanding shall fall, to try them, and to purge, and to make them white, even to the time of the end: because it is yet for a time appointed."* (KJV) ... Angered by the alliance between the two Ptolemy brothers, Antiochus IV invaded Egypt a second time in 168 B.C.E. The Ptolemies called upon Rome to help them, and the Senate complied, sending several legions by ship. As Antiochus approached Alexandria, he was met by three Roman senators on the outskirts of the city. Popillius, speaking for the Senate, demanded that Antiochus withdraw from Egypt. The historian Livy described the meeting in his history of Rome, *Ab Urbe Condita*, xlv.12, as follows:

"After receiving the submission of the inhabitants of Memphis and of the rest of the Egyptian people, some submitting voluntarily, others under threats, [Antiochus] marched by easy stages towards Alexandria. After crossing the river at Eleusis, about four miles from Alexandria, he was met by the Roman commissioners, to whom he gave a friendly greeting and held out his hand to Popilius. Popilius, however, placed in his hand the tablets on which was written the decree of the senate and told him first of all to read that. After reading it through he said he would call his friends into council and consider what he ought to do. Popilius, stern and imperious as ever, drew a circle round the king with the stick he was carrying and said, 'Before you step out of that circle give me a reply to lay before the senate.' For a few moments he hesitated, astounded at such a peremptory order, and at last replied, 'I will do what the senate thinks right.' Not till then did Popilius extend his hand to the king as to a friend and ally. Antiochus evacuated Egypt at the appointed date, and the commissioners exerted their authority to establish a lasting concord between the brothers [Ptolemy VI and Ptolemy VII], as they had as yet hardly made peace with each other."

While Antiochus was preparing his army to return to Syria after his humiliation by the Romans, news that he had been killed in Egypt arrived in Jerusalem. This erroneous report stimulated the former high priest Jason, the one who had been replaced by the appointment of Menelaus to that post by Antiochus, to gather a force of a thousand men and launch an attack on the city of Jerusalem and the Temple, hoping to regain his seat of authority. Menelaus was forced to take refuge inside the Akra fortress, where a garrison of Seleucid soldiers held out against the rebels. When Antiochus heard about the revolt, he hurried to Jerusalem to put down the insurrection, which he did with brutality, killing 40,000 Jewish men, women, and children, and enslaving even more.[1] He also reinstated Menelaus to his post as high priest. This was the beginning of a time of trouble for the Jewish people and Jerusalem that surpassed anything they had yet seen. During the next year or so, the practice of Judaism was forbidden by royal decree, as was the rite of circumcision and the observance of the sabbath. Torah scrolls were confiscated and burned. Anyone caught trying to observe Jewish rituals was summarily executed, usually by being burned alive. The Temple was looted with the help of Menelaus, its vessels removed and the treasury emptied, and the daily sacrifices were stopped for the first time since the return from Babylon. To make a place for his soldiers to worship, Antiochus ordered that the inner Temple area be profaned. An altar to Zeus Olympius, complete with a statue of the Greek god, was built over the altar of burnt offering. Then, on the 25th day of Kislev in the 145th year of the Seleucid Empire, which is equivalent to December 16, 167 B.C.E. in Gregorian reckoning, a swine was offered to Zeus on that pagan altar, the ultimate desecration of the place considered most holy by the Jewish people. Scholars debate whether the desecration of the Temple was the spark that caused the Maccabean[2] revolt that began that year, but one thing is certain, the Jews had more than enough reason to rebel. The insurrection itself started in the rural town of Modin when a local priest named Mattathias refused to sacrifice to a Greek god on the town altar, publicly disobeying the decree by Antiochus that all of his subjects must worship the gods of the Hellenistic pantheon. Mattathias then proceeded to kill a Hellenized Jew who tried to comply in his place. He and his five sons immediately fled to the Judean wilderness to escape death and begin the fight for religious freedom, but Mattathias died within the year. His eldest son, Judah, gathered an army of irregulars and began the effort to gain independence from the rule of the Seleucids. The guerrilla tactics employed by the Maccabees were successful against the more-regimented Syrian troops, especially since the rebels knew the lay of the difficult Judean landscape infinitely better than their foreign adversaries. After three years, the Maccabean forces had captured Jerusalem. The Maccabean priests immediately

---

[1] Scholars disagree about the number of times Antiochus IV visited and plundered Jerusalem. Only one visit is indicated in the apocryphal books of 1 Maccabees 1:20-30 and 2 Maccabees 5:1-16, with plundering mentioned in both instances. A case can be made that two separate instances are recorded, one in each book, thus providing evidence that there were two visits. Two distinct visits are indicated in Josephus, *Antiquities*, 12.246-251, in the Dead Sea Scrolls (4Q248), and in Daniel, chapter 11, verses 28-32. Josephus mentions plundering on the second visit, as do the other two-visit sources. Since Antiochus invaded Egypt twice, it makes sense that he visited Jerusalem two times, once in 169 B.C.E. and again in 168 B.C.E. It also makes sense that his army would have plundered and killed opponents on both occasions. However, it seems much more likely that the wholesale plundering of the Temple itself, and the widespread massacring described in several sources, both of which would have caused a severe reaction among the Jews in both Jerusalem and the countryside, is more logically associated with the period of unrest leading into the Maccabean revolt that began in 168/167 B.C.E.

[2] The term Maccabean is derived from the nickname of Judah, "The Maccabee," which means "the Hammer." (Aramaic *maqqaba*). An alternative explanation is that it is an acronym for the Torah verse "**Mi CH**amocha **BA**'elim YHWH", *"Who is like unto thee among the mighty, O Lord!"* from Exodus 15:11 (KJV).

set about to rededicate the Temple. Daily sacrifices were resumed on the 25th day of the month of Kislev in the 148th year of the Seleucid Empire, which is equivalent December 14, 164 B.C.E. in Gregorian reckoning, exactly 1,093¾ days after they had been taken away by Antiochus.

The prophecy in verses 2-32 of the eleventh chapter goes into great detail about the struggle between the Seleucids and the Ptolemies, and, more important theologically since it relates to the relationship of the Jewish people with God, between Hellenism and Judaism. After Antiochus profanes the Temple and stops the daily sacrifices, the prophecy comes to a turning point, which is the date on which the Temple was reconsecrated and the daily sacrifices resumed, as described in verse 32b, *"but the people that do know their God shall be strong, and do exploits"* (KJV). The prophecy then jumps ahead to the future in verses 33-35, *"And they that understand among the people shall instruct many: yet they shall fall by the sword, and by flame, by captivity, and by spoil, many days. Now when they shall fall, they shall be holpen with a little help: but many shall cleave to them with flatteries. And some of them of understanding shall fall, to try them, and to purge, and to make them white, even to the time of the end: because it is yet for a time appointed"* (KJV). The meaning of the last phrase in verse 35b, *"even to the time of the end: because it is yet for a time appointed"* (KJV), can be understood chronologically by recalling that the interpretation of Daniel, chapter 7, verse 12, in which the phrase *"their lives were prolonged for a season and time"* (KJV) is also referenced from that turning-point date, December 14, 164 B.C.E. Apparently this "time of the end" reference in verse 35 is looking ahead to and foretelling the beginning of the *Diaspora*, which happened in 66 C.E. (see page 37).

At this point, it is good to remember the stated purpose of the eleventh chapter, which is revealed in its introductory tenth chapter, verse 14, *"Now I am come to make thee understand what shall befall thy people in the latter days"* (KJV). In pursuit of this goal of revealing what shall befall the Jewish people after the time of the prophet Daniel, the prophecy has so far described events that have taken the Jewish people from the Achaemenid Persian period that followed the exile in Babylon through the challenge of Hellenism, the trauma of the profanation of the Temple by Antiochus, and the subsequent temporary loss of the sacrificial system so central to observance of the Mosaic Law, then through the restoration of the Temple and sacrificial system by the Maccabees, then down to the start of the First Jewish War in 66 C.E., which marked the beginning of the dispersal of the Jewish people among the nations and the destruction of the Temple building itself in 70 C.E. Not surprisingly, all of the events described in the prophecy so far have involved the Temple, the city of Jerusalem, and the covenant governing Jewish people living in the land to some degree. Most will agree that it is logical to assume that the rest of the prophecy will involve the fate of the city of Jerusalem, the Temple site, and the people in the land as well, and so it does. After jumping forward in time in verse 35 to "the time of the end," which, in this case, means looking forward in time to the beginning of the *Diaspora* in 66 C.E., the prophecy resumes its forward movement in time, picking up the narrative with verses 36-45.

The Prophecy in History - Part II

The placement in history of the events described in verses 36-45 has been the subject of much speculation by expositors over the years. Some expositors claim that the prophecy in those verses was fulfilled completely during the time of Antiochus IV. Others say that history has yet to see any fulfillment of those verses. A few expositors have proposed fulfillments that fall in between the two extremes chronologically. However, none have proposed fulfillments that are post-biblical, yet found in recorded history looking backwards from our viewpoint today. Nevertheless, that is where the fulfillments are to be found. Using clues in the verses themselves, the time frame for the events in these verses can be determined, and, once that time frame has been established, the various events mentioned in the verses can be identified as they correlate with history, and as they relate to the fate of the Jewish people.

The first key to understanding the prophecy is found in verses 42-43: *"He shall enter also into the glorious land, and many countries shall be overthrown: but these shall escape out of his hand, even Edom, and Moab, and the chief of the children of Ammon. He shall stretch forth his hand also upon the countries: and the land of Egypt shall not escape. But he shall have power over the treasures of gold and of silver, and over all the precious things of Egypt: and the Libyans and the Ethiopians shall be at his steps"* (KJV). These verses describe a king that will conquer Egypt after coming through the land of Israel, and will approach near or go into both Libya and Ethiopia (ancient Cush). Fortunately, there have been only a handful of conquerors of Egypt since 66 C.E., the year at which the prophecy in verse 35 left off. The second key to understanding the prophecy is to realize that the eleventh chapter of Daniel has a parallel chronology with respect to the seventh chapter of Daniel.[1] In the same way that the time period described in verse 35 of the eleventh chapter was related to the "season and time" in the seventh chapter, as explained on the previous page, verses 36-45 have a parallel structure in the seventh chapter as well, in verse 25b: *"and they shall be given into his hand until a time and times and the dividing of time"* (KJV). This parallel time period is the 798-years of Roman-Byzantine hegemony over the Jewish people and the city of Jerusalem that began in 161 B.C.E., when Judah Maccabee appealed to Rome for help against the Seleucid army, and ended when Caliph Omar captured Jerusalem and the Temple Mount for Islam in the year 638 C.E. This gives the time frame in which the conqueror of Egypt described in the prophecy in verses 42-43 will be found in history. Since Antiochus IV never captured all of Egypt, and there is no record in history that he ever threatened Libya or Ethiopia militarily, he cannot be the conqueror of Egypt described in the last section of the eleventh chapter. Looking at the history of Egypt during the specified time frame—after the time of the Maccabean revolt and before the time of Caliph Omar in Jerusalem—there is only one king who came down through the land of Israel and conquered all of

---

[1] See the "Prophecy Overview" chart (see PLATE 1 on inside front cover) to compare the time lines for the seventh and the eleventh chapters. Note that the seventh chapter divides into three time lines, one for a "season and time" ending in 66 C.E., another for "time and times and the dividing of time" (3½ "times") ending in 638 C.E., and a third that is without end.

Egypt, then made military excursions into both Libya and Ethiopia that are documented in the historical record. That king is Chosroes II Parvez, the twenty-second king of the Sassanid Persian Empire, who reigned from 590-628 C.E. Skipping over verses 36-39 for the moment,[1] the narrative in verses 40-44 describes the struggle between the Byzantine and Sassanids Persian empires from 602-628 C.E., and it specifically describes the conquests of Chosroes II during that period. Verse 45 goes on to reveal why this period was so important in Jewish history, important enough to be included in the prophecy.

624-638 C.E.

verse 40a: *"And at the time of the end shall the king of the south push at him: and the king of the north shall come against him like a whirlwind, with chariots, and with horsemen, and with many ships ..."* (KJV) ... In this case, "time of the end" refers to the conclusion of the time period defined in Daniel, chapter 7, verse 25b, the 3½ "times." A description of the events that will happen at the very end of this time period is being given in verse 40a, and three political entities are described: 1) the king of the south, who shall push at *him*, 2) the king of the north who will come against *him*, 3) and then the entity described as *him*. Since the "him" can be identified as the king of the Sassanid Empire (Chosroes II and his successors), the identities of the other two personalities can be easily determined from history. The king of the south is Mohammed and the army of Islam, which was pushing northward against the Persians after consolidating their rule of Arabia, even making a few tentative excursions into the Persian lands east of the Jordan River just before Mohammed's death in 632 C.E. The king of the north is the emperor of the Byzantine Empire, Heraclius, who reigned as emperor from 610-641 C.E. Using his large navy, he sailed his army across the Black Sea in 624 C.E., landed in Armenia, then marched overland and attacked the Sassanid Empire through its northern back door while Chosroes was still preoccupied with solidifying his gains in Anatolia and Egypt, and was thus unprepared to defend his heartland. The events described in verse 40a come ***after*** the events described in verses 40b-44, which detail the rapid expansion of the Sassanid Persian Empire. Verse 40a foretells the decline and final defeat of the Sassanid Persians by Byzantium in 628 C.E., and gives the first hint at the rise of Islam, which would go on to supplant both powers in the region, conquering Judea and Jerusalem in 638 C.E.

602-616 C.E.

verses 40b-43a: *"... and he shall enter into the countries, and shall overflow and pass over. He shall enter also into the glorious land, and many countries shall be overthrown: but these shall escape out of his hand, even Edom, and Moab, and the chief of the children of Ammon. He shall stretch forth his hand also upon the countries: and the land of Egypt shall not escape. But he shall have power over the treasures of gold and of silver, and over all the precious things of Egypt: ..."* (KJV) ... Verses 40b-44 are a description of the rapid expansion of the Sassanid Persian Empire from 605-628 C.E. As pointed out in the preceding

---

[1] Verses 36-39 describe another king, not Chosroes II, as will be shown later in this section.

section, this period of expansion of the empire comes immediately before the events describing the decline of the empire found in verse 40a in real time.[1] The expansion began in earnest in 602 C.E. That year, the Byzantine emperor Maurice, who had helped establish Chosroes II on the Sassanid throne, was killed in a palace coup in Constantinople. The young Sassanid king, using the murder of Maurice as a pretext to break the peace treaty that had been signed with Maurice, attacked the Byzantine provinces in Asia Minor, the area known today as central and western Turkey. Between 605-613 C.E., the Sassanid armies of Chosroes captured the important cities of Dara, Amida, Edesa, Hierapolis, Aleppo, Apamea, Caesarea, and Damascus, plus all of the surrounding provincial territories. Emboldened by his relatively easy victories, Chosroes declared a holy war against the Christian Byzantines, with plans to extend the empire and its Zoroastrian religion beyond the far-flung boundaries that had existed under Darius III a thousand years before. Pausing in Damascus, Chosroes made a strategic political decision that was designed to weaken the Byzantine defenses in Judea, through which he had to pass to invade Egypt. He appointed the son of the Jewish Exilarch in Babylon, a mystic named Nehemiah be Hushiel, as nominal head of his armies (although his general, Shahrbaraz, "the king's boar," actually led the invasion). The Jews in the land of Israel rallied behind the invading army of Chosroes, who was considered by many Jews to be a "second Cyrus" who would return them back to self-governance and restore their Temple in Jerusalem. They had been treated harshly by the Byzantine Christians for more than three-hundred years and were eager for a change of regimes. With the help of thousands of Jewish citizens inside its walls, Jerusalem was captured by the Persians in 614 C.E., and a massacre began. Centuries of hatred and resentment were unleashed against the Christian populace, holy sites, and clerics.[2] The bishop of Jerusalem, Zechariah, and the "true cross" were carried captive back to the Sassanid capital. As for the lands of Moab, Edom, and the chief of Ammon mentioned in verse 41, that is referring to the Arabs living in the lands formerly occupied by those kingdoms, since all three kingdoms had long since ceased to exist as recognizable political entities by the time of Chosroes II. The former territories of the Moabites, Edomites, and Ammonites were occupied by the Bani Ghassanids, a tribe of Monophysite Christians who had been allied with Byzantium for many years as buffers against Sassanid Persia. When Chosroes captured Syria and Judea in 614 C.E., he partially overran some of the territory of the Ghassanids. Ten years later, when Heraclius began his final push against Persia in 624 C.E., the Ghassanids came against Chosroes and reclaimed their lands east of the Jordan River. This guerilla warfare against the Sassanids in what is today eastern Syria and western Jordan greatly aided the Byzantine cause. In appreciation, Heraclius later appointed the chief of the Ghassanids, Jabala ibn al-Ayham, as King of the Arabs. The part of the prophecy about Egypt was fulfilled in 616 C.E., two years after the capture of Jerusalem, when Egypt was captured by the army of Chosroes II under the command of Shahrbaraz.

---

[1] Apparently this part of the vision was not recalled by Daniel in strict chronological sequence.

[2] The sack of Jerusalem by the Sassanids and their Jewish allies was undoubtedly a bloody affair, but the best-preserved account, that of the monk Antiochus Strategos, is probably an exaggeration skewed toward a Byzantine perspective.

616-624 C.E.

verses 43b-44: *"... and the Libyans and the Ethiopians shall be at his steps. But tidings out of the east and out of the north shall trouble him: therefore he shall go forth with great fury to destroy, and utterly to make away many."* (KJV) ... After capturing Egypt, the army of Chosroes apparently made incursions into Libya as far as Tripoli, and pushed up the Nile toward Ethiopia. There is no evidence that the Sassanids captured these territories during this period, but historical documents, and some archeological evidence, indicate that the Sassanians plundered in Cyrenaica (on the coast of Libya) in the west and in Nubia (Sudan) in the south.[1] Whether or not the Sassanids actually entered Libya and Ethiopia in force is not the point of the prophecy, however. It merely says that these regions "shall be at his steps," and this was certainly the case. Chosroes II had expanded his empire to its greatest extent by 624 C.E., being almost unstoppable for more than two decades, but his fortunes began to turn that year when Heraclius felt strong enough to begin a counteroffensive. With Chosroes' resources devoted to consolidating his gains in Egypt and Anatolia, the eastern provinces began to revolt, Heraclius then sailed his Byzantine army across the Black Sea and attacked through Armenia. This required Chosroes to leave Egypt and rush his army to met the challenges in the north and east, as the prophecy had foretold.

614-617 C.E., Second attempt to rebuild the Temple

verse 45: *"And he shall plant the tabernacles of his palace between the seas in the glorious holy mountain; yet he shall come to his end, and none shall help him."* (KJV) ... Verse 45 now drops back in time to the capture of Jerusalem in 614 C.E. After taking the city, Chosroes II established Nehemiah ben Hushiel, the Jewish figurehead commander of the Persian army, as governor in Jerusalem, thus planting the tabernacles of his palace[2] on the holy mountain. Nehemiah governed the city with a twelve-man "council of the righteous," exercising political and religious authority. Soon after being installed as governor, Nehemiah began making preparations for rebuilding the Temple, and also began sorting out genealogies in anticipation of resuming the Temple priesthood. However, Nehemiah was killed by a mob of rioting Christians a few months after being appointed governor. Chosroes, needing to placate the city's anti-Jewish Christian majority, appointed a Christian governor to replace Nehemiah and banned Jews from approaching within three miles of the city gates, dashing all hopes for a rebuilt Temple or even a Jew-friendly Jerusalem. In 628 C.E., Jerusalem was recaptured by Heraclius and the city reverted to Byzantine rule. A decade later, the Muslim caliphate replaced Byzantium when Caliph Omar captured Jerusalem, built a small mosque on the Temple Mount, and offered prayers to Allah.

That leaves the identity of the king described in verses 36-39 still to be determined, since those verses were skipped over several paragraphs ago to examine verses 40-45. The explanation of verses 40-45

---

[1] Comparetti, Matteo "The Sassanians in Africa," *Transoxiana*, vol. 4 (July, 2002).

[2] King James translation of the Old Persian word אַפַּדְנוֹ (MT) denoting a military commander's headquarters tent (UBS).

established that the last time period specified by the prophecy in the eleventh chapter of Daniel is the one from 602-638 C.E, so now the interpretation of verses 36-39 can be done. Remember, the king must be a monarch who ruled after 66 C.E. and before 602 C.E., who was important with respect to the fate of the Jewish people, and whose life fits the description given in the prophecy. Looking at the historical record, we find an emperor of Rome, Julian the Apostate, who meets the requirements.

363 C.E., First attempt to rebuild the Temple

verse 36-39: *"And the king shall do according to his will; and he shall exalt himself, and magnify himself above every god, and shall speak marvellous things against the God of gods, and shall prosper till the indignation be accomplished: for that that is determined shall be done. Neither shall he regard the God of his fathers, nor the desire of women, nor regard any god: for he shall magnify himself above all. But in his estate shall he honour the God of forces: and a god whom his fathers knew not shall he honour with gold, and silver, and with precious stones, and pleasant things. Thus shall he do in the most strong holds with a strange god, whom he shall acknowledge and increase with glory: and he shall cause them to rule over many, and shall divide the land for gain."* (KJV) ... Twenty-three years after the death of Constantine I, who opened the Roman Empire to Christianity, his nephew Julian, known to history as "the Apostate," was installed and sustained as emperor by the power of the western Roman army. During his reign from 360-363 C.E., Julian encouraged paganism, and forcefully rejected the teachings of both Judaism and Christianity. He wrote a number of blasphemous treatises whose sole purpose was to convince his subjects that both religions were nothing more than hoaxes. He was a Neo-Platonist, but, judging from his writings, he seems to have had no real religious convictions. However, Julian is especially important in Jewish history because of his attempt to rebuild the Temple in 363 C.E., the first serious attempt to rebuild the Temple after its destruction in 70 C.E. The historian Ammianus Marcellinus, in his *Roman History* (Book 23), recorded this about Julian's attempt to rebuild:

> "But though Alypius [of Antioch, who was the superintendent of construction] applied himself vigorously to the work, and though the governor of the province co-operated with him, fearful balls of fire burst forth with continual eruptions close to the foundations [of the Temple Mount], burning several of the workmen and making the spot altogether inaccessible. And thus the very elements, as if by some fate, repelling the attempt, it was laid aside."

A month after the first attempt to rebuild the Temple was halted, Julian died from wounds suffered in battle against the Sassanid Persians. After Julian, only one more serious attempt to rebuild the Temple would be made, that being the attempt made by Nehemiah ben Hushiel in 614 C.E. That second and final attempt was foretold in verse 45 (see previous page), the verse that brings the vision of Jewish destiny recorded by Daniel in the tenth and eleventh chapters of his book to a close.

∽

CHAPTER SIX

SEVENTY WEEKS ARE DETERMINED
Daniel 9:1-27

The ninth chapter of Daniel says that it was revealed in *"the first year of Darius the son of Ahasuerus, of the seed of the Medes, which was made king over the realm of the Chaldeans"* (KJV). This description is probably a reference to Cyrus the Great or, more likely, to his general Gubaru, who led the assault on the city and was appointed governor of Babylon after its capture on October 29, 539 B.C.E. It thus dates the prophecy to the first year following the conclusion of the seventy years of subjugation to Babylon that had been prophesied by Jeremiah. The ninth chapter features the well-known and much-debated prophecy of the seventy "weeks" in verses 24-27, which are perhaps the four most misinterpreted verses in the entire Bible. Christian scholars and expositors have long disagreed with Jewish rabbis and sages about their interpretation and meaning. Much of the disagreement comes from the theological biases inherent in each faith. In modern times, neither has been able to approach the ninth chapter without preconceived ideas and notions, in the case of Christian expositors notions that it must end with the crucifixion of Jesus or, in the case of Jewish expositors, that it cannot say anything about him at all.

The ninth chapter of Daniel can be divided into three distinct parts (see text on page 65). The first part is comprised of verses 1-2. These verses confirm that Daniel was familiar with the chrono-specific prophecies that had been made before he was born by his contemporary, Jeremiah, foretelling the seventy-year duration of Babylon's hegemony over the people of Judea. The Jewish subjugation to Babylon ended in 539 B.C.E. when the Achaemenid Persians under their king, Cyrus the Great, captured Babylon. Daniel may also be referring to the prophecies of Isaiah that foretold the appearance of Cyrus on the stage of Jewish history, even though the prophet Isaiah is not mentioned by name in Daniel. The second part is comprised of verses 3-23. These verses contain Daniel's prayer of confession and repentance as proscribed by Moses in Leviticus, chapter 26, verses 39-45. The prophet acknowledges the reason for the calamities that have befallen the Jewish people in verses 11-14 of his prayer, *"Yea, all Israel have transgressed thy law, even by departing, that they might not obey thy voice; therefore the curse is poured upon us, and the oath that is written in the law of Moses the servant of God, because we have sinned against him. And he hath confirmed his words, which he spake against us, and against our judges that judged us, by bringing upon us a great evil: for under the whole heaven hath not been done as hath been done upon Jerusalem. As it is written in the law of Moses, all this evil is come upon us: yet made we not our prayer before the Lord our God, that we might turn from our iniquities, and understand thy truth. Therefore hath the Lord watched upon the evil, and brought it upon us: for the Lord our God is righteous in all his works which he doeth: for we obeyed not his voice"* (KJV). The third part, which is comprised of verses 24-27, sets forth the aforementioned chrono-specific prophecy of the seventy "weeks," which will be the focus of the remainder of this chapter.

The Keys to the Interpretation

The first key to interpreting the prophecy of the seventy "weeks" is to understand which commandment is being referred to in verse 25, *"Know therefore and understand, from the going forth of the commandment to restore and to build Jerusalem unto the Messiah the Prince: ... the street shall be built again, and the wall, even in troublous times"* (KJV). The Hebrew word used for commandment is דָּבָר (BHS, Strong's OT: 1697), which can also be interpreted as "decree," That is the better translation, because it is a decree of Julius Caesar that is the "commandment" referred to in the prophecy of the seventy "weeks." Between 47 B.C.E. and 44 B.C.E., Julius Caesar issued a number of decrees pertaining specifically to the Jews. One decree in particular has all of the elements mentioned in verse 25. It was issued by Caesar just before his assassination on the Ides of March (or March 15), 44 B.C.E., and is recorded in Josephus as follows:

> "Gaius Caesar, consul the fifth time, hath decreed, That the Jews shall possess Jerusalem, and may encompass that city with walls; and that Hyrcanus, the son of Alexander, the high priest and ethnarch of the Jews, retain it in the manner he himself pleases; and that the Jews be allowed to deduct out of their tribute, every second year the land is let [in the Sabbatic period], a corus of that tribute; and that the tribute they pay be not let to farm, nor that they pay always the same tribute"... *Antiquities of the Jews* 14.10.5 (Whiston translation).

This decree fits the prophetic description in the Bible text exactly. In it, Julius Caesar decreed that Hyrcanus II, who served as high priest and ethnarch of the Jews from 63-40 B.C.E., was to receive the city and people of Jerusalem to rule as he wished, and the decree gave him permission to rebuild the walls of Jerusalem that had been destroyed by Pompey twenty years earlier in 63 B.C.E. The lack of walls had left the city vulnerable to its enemies, especially the hated Parthians to the east. Caesar wanted Judea as a buffer between the Parthians and Egypt, Rome's breadbasket. so he was eager that his figurehead ruler in Judea, Hyrcanus, and Rome's appointed power behind the throne, the procurator Antipater, fortify the city as quickly as possible. The walls were rebuilt by Antipater sometime in the year 44/43 B.C.E., soon after the decree was issued, and obviously before Antipater died in 43 B.C.E. As for the phrase rendered "unto the Messiah the Prince" in the King James Version, it is usually interpreted as a reference to Jesus by Christian expositors. Instead, it is a reference to Hyrcanus II. The King James translators capitalized the Hebrew word מָשִׁיחַ (BHS, Strong's OT: 4899), from which we get the English word "messiah," but it should not be capitalized in this instance. It means simply an "anointed one," which was the appellation given to the Jewish high priest. The same is true for the Hebrew word נָגִיד (BHS, Strong's OT: 5057), which means "governor, leader, prince, chief ruler," or in this case the office Hyrcanus held, ethnarch, but certainly not "The Prince" as the King James capitalization suggests. Taking all of these clarifications into account, a modern paraphrase of verse 25, inserting the appropriate historical elements in place of the prophetic language, would read: "Observe with your eyes and calculate with your mind, that after the issuing of the decree by Julius Caesar to Hyrcanus II, high priest and ethnarch of the Jews, granting him by the authority of Rome the right to receive Jerusalem as his political and religious dominion and giving him permission to rebuild (fortify) the city ... the street and trench (in front of the wall) will be rebuilt" (AP). Note that the Hebrew word מִן (BHS, Strong's OT: 4480), translated as "from" in verse 25 in the King James Version, is rendered as the word "after" in the paraphrase. This is a chronological distinction that will help determine the historical placement of the seven "weeks" and sixty-two "weeks" mentioned in the verse.

The second key to interpreting the prophecy is to understand the time period meant by the Hebrew word "weeks" שָׁבֻעִים (BHS, Strong's OT: 7620) in verse 25, *"Know therefore and understand, from the going forth of the commandment ... shall be seven weeks, and threescore and two weeks: the street shall be built again, and the wall, even in troublous times"* (KJV). Most expositors have interpreted "weeks" in that verse to mean a "week of years," or, in other words, a "week" is interpreted as meaning a period of seven years. In this scenario, the seven "weeks" then become forty-nine years, and the sixty-two "weeks" become 434 years. However, "week of years" is not the meaning of the word "weeks," at least not with respect to the seven "weeks" and sixty-two "weeks" in verse 25. In that verse, "weeks" refers to the Feast of Weeks. Such usage of a calendar unit as a cryptic reference to a festival is typical of the Book of Daniel. In the eighth chapter, as you may recall, the phrase "evening-morning" was used to indicate the Passover. In the twelfth chapter, the word "day" was used to indicate Day of Atonement. Thus, here in the ninth chapter of Daniel, the word "weeks" means the Feast of Weeks, or, more specifically, it refers to the fiftieth day of the Festival of Weeks, the Day of Pentecost. The time periods being designated in verse 25 are thus seven Pentecosts and sixty-two Pentecosts, for a total of sixty-nine Pentecosts. Chronologically, this represents a time period of about sixty-nine years, divided into two segments, one of seven years, and a second of sixty-two years.

The third key to interpreting the prophecy is to understand that the starting point for counting the seven "weeks" (Pentecosts) is given at the end of verse 25: *"... the street shall be built again, and the wall, even in troublous times"* (KJV). The word "street" רְחוֹב (BHS, Strong's OT: 7339) is a reference to the wide space inside the wall of the city, directly behind a tower gate where troops were assembled to defend the city, as revealed by its usage in 2 Chronicles, chapter 32, verse 6: *"And he [Hezekiah] set captains of war over the people, and gathered them together to him in the street of the gate of the city ..."* (KJV). In addition, the word translated as "wall" וְחָרוּץ (BHS, Strong's OT: 2742) in the King James Version is better translated "trench" according to the UBS Old Testament Handbook, which says, "The second word, rendered 'moat' by RSV, is literally the word for 'cut' and refers to a trench cut into the rock on the exterior walls of a city in order to make the wall a more difficult obstacle for those who would attempt to attack from the outside." According to Josephus (*Wars*, 1.7.3), Pompey had destroyed the wall of Jerusalem and its tower gates, and his troops had filled in the trench in front of the wall to make a platform for his siege engines. The decree of Caesar to Hyrcanus II gave permission to rebuild the defenses which Pompey had destroyed twenty years earlier. The street and trench were part of the fortifications. Their being rebuilt was a time marker that had to occur before the count of the seventy "weeks" could begin. Antipater finished the rebuilding just before his death in 43 B.C.E.

The fourth key to interpreting the prophecy is to understand that the seven "weeks" (meaning seven Pentecosts) specified in verse 25 were contiguous with a seven-year sabbath cycle. In other words, the prophecy was predicting that there would be a seven-year sabbath cycle containing seven Pentecosts, followed by sixty-two years, each containing a Pentecost. So, all that is needed to interpret the prophecy is to match the seven years specified in the prophecy with the sabbath cycle that occurred after the street and trench had been completed in 44/43 B.C.E., then begin counting Pentecosts. However, this presents a challenge since there are no universally accepted records of the sabbath and jubilee cycles as they were observed by Jews in ancient times. Instead, several competing sabbath-jubilee systems have been suggested by Jewish scholars over the years. The system put forth in the 19th century by Benedict Zuckermann, professor of mathematics and calendric science at the Jewish Theological Seminary of Breslau, is perhaps the system most widely accepted in Jewish circles today, and the one recognized as authoritative by most Orthodox Jews. In more recent decades, a competing system has been proposed by Dr. Ben Zion Wacholder, professor of Talmud and Rabbinics at Hebrew Union College-Jewish Institute of Religion, and his cycle of sabbath years has generally found favor in academic circles. Both systems rely heavily on Josephus and various rabbinical writings for determining their sabbath cycles. However, a verification of the sabbath-jubilee cycles that is derived from the biblical record alone is preferred. That will be accomplished in the next section, after which the seven-year sabbath cycle in the prophecy of the seventy "weeks" will be related to the decree that Julius Caesar issued to Hyrcanus II.

Calculating the Sabbath and Jubilee Years

The Jewish people were commanded to observe sabbath and jubilee years, as recorded in Leviticus, chapter 25, verses 1-10a: *"And the Lord spake unto Moses in mount Sinai, saying, Speak unto the children of Israel, and say unto them, When ye come into the land which I give you, then shall the land keep a sabbath unto the Lord. Six years thou shalt sow thy field, and six years thou shalt prune thy vineyard, and gather in the fruit thereof; But in the seventh year shall be a sabbath of rest unto the land, a sabbath for the Lord: thou shalt neither sow thy field, nor prune thy vineyard ... And thou shalt number seven sabbaths of years unto thee, seven times seven years; and the space of the seven sabbaths of years shall be unto thee forty and nine years. Then shalt thou cause the trumpet of the jubilee to sound on the tenth day of the seventh month, in the day of atonement shall ye make the trumpet sound throughout all your land. And ye shall hallow the fiftieth year, and proclaim liberty throughout all the land unto all the inhabitants thereof: it shall be a jubilee unto you"* (KJV).

Text of Daniel 9:1-27 (KJV)

The Understanding

1 In the first year of Darius the son of Ahasuerus, of the seed of the Medes, which was made king over the realm of the Chaldeans; *2* In the first year of his reign I Daniel understood by books the number of the years, whereof the word of the Lord came to Jeremiah the prophet, that he would accomplish seventy years in the desolations of Jerusalem.

The Prayer

3 And I set my face unto the Lord God, to seek by prayer and supplication, with fasting, and sackcloth, and ashes: *4* And I prayed unto the Lord my God, and made my confession, and said, O Lord, the great and dreadful God, keeping the covenant and mercy to them that love him, and to them that keep his commandments; *5* We have sinned, and have committed iniquity, and have done wickedly, and have rebelled, even by departing from thy precepts and from thy judgments: *6* Neither have we hearkened unto thy servants the prophets, which spake in thy name to our kings, our princes, and our fathers, and to all the people of the land. *7* O Lord, righteousness belongeth unto thee, but unto us confusion of faces, as at this day; to the men of Judah, and to the inhabitants of Jerusalem, and unto all Israel, that are near, and that are far off, through all the countries whither thou hast driven them, because of their trespass that they have trespassed against thee. *8* O Lord, to us belongeth confusion of face, to our kings, to our princes, and to our fathers, because we have sinned against thee. *9* To the Lord our God belong mercies and forgivenesses, though we have rebelled against him; *10* Neither have we obeyed the voice of the Lord our God, to walk in his laws, which he set before us by his servants the prophets. *11* Yea, all Israel have transgressed thy law, even by departing, that they might not obey thy voice; therefore the curse is poured upon us, and the oath that is written in the law of Moses the servant of God, because we have sinned against him. *12* And he hath confirmed his words, which he spake against us, and against our judges that judged us, by bringing upon us a great evil: for under the whole heaven hath not been done as hath been done upon Jerusalem. *13* As it is written in the law of Moses, all this evil is come upon us: yet made we not our prayer before the Lord our God, that we might turn from our iniquities, and understand thy truth. *14* Therefore hath the Lord watched upon the evil, and brought it upon us: for the Lord our God is righteous in all his works which he doeth: for we obeyed not his voice. *15* And now, O Lord our God, that hast brought thy people forth out of the land of Egypt with a mighty hand, and hast gotten thee renown, as at this day; we have sinned, we have done wickedly. *16* O Lord, according to all thy righteousness, I beseech thee, let thine anger and thy fury be turned away from thy city Jerusalem, thy holy mountain: because for our sins, and for the iniquities of our fathers, Jerusalem and thy people are become a reproach to all that are about us. *17* Now therefore, O our God, hear the prayer of thy servant, and his supplications, and cause thy face to shine upon thy sanctuary that is desolate, for the Lord's sake. *18* O my God, incline thine ear, and hear; open thine eyes, and behold our desolations, and the city which is called by thy name: for we do not present our supplications before thee for our righteousnesses, but for thy great mercies. *19* O Lord, hear; O Lord, forgive; O Lord, hearken and do; defer not, for thine own sake, O my God: for thy city and thy people are called by thy name. *20* And whiles I was speaking, and praying, and confessing my sin and the sin of my people Israel, and presenting my supplication before the Lord my God for the holy mountain of my God; *21* Yea, whiles I was speaking in prayer, even the man Gabriel, whom I had seen in the vision at the beginning, being caused to fly swiftly, touched me about the time of the evening oblation. *22* And he informed me, and talked with me, and said, O Daniel, I am now come forth to give thee skill and understanding. *23* At the beginning of thy supplications the commandment came forth, and I am come to shew thee; for thou art greatly beloved: therefore understand the matter, and consider the vision.

The Seventy Weeks

24 Seventy weeks are determined upon thy people and upon thy holy city, to finish the transgression, and to make an end of sins, and to make reconciliation for iniquity, and to bring in everlasting righteousness, and to seal up the vision and prophecy, and to anoint the most Holy. *25* Know therefore and understand, that from the going forth of the commandment to restore and to build Jerusalem unto the Messiah the Prince shall be seven weeks, and threescore and two weeks: the street shall be built again, and the wall, even in troublous times. *26* And after threescore and two weeks shall Messiah be cut off, but not for himself: and the people of the prince that shall come shall destroy the city and the sanctuary; and the end thereof shall be with a flood, and unto the end of the war desolations are determined. *27* And he shall confirm the covenant with many for one week: and in the midst of the week he shall cause the sacrifice and the oblation to cease, and for the overspreading of abominations he shall make it desolate, even until the consummation, and that determined shall be poured upon the desolate.

The observance of sabbath and jubilee years by the Israelites is rarely mentioned in the Bible, but one jubilee year can be identified with relative certainty. The year that Solomon dedicated the First Temple is generally accepted to have been a jubilee year. That year can be located in time with respect to the years of Solomon's reign by using the following information available from Scripture:

(1) Construction on the Temple began in the second month (called Ziv before the exile), in the fourth year of the reign of Solomon, see 1 Kings 6:37;

(2) Construction was completed in the eighth month (called Bul before the exile), in the eleventh year of the reign of Solomon, see 1 Kings 6:38;

(3) Solomon dedicated the Temple on the Day of Atonement in the seventh month (called Ethanim before the exile) of the year following its completion, see 1 Kings 8:2.

Assuming that Solomon had an accession year, and numbering the years of his reign in order after that accession year (with Passovers marking the years), the years of his reign and the known Temple events mentioned in items 1-3 above can be shown in their proper chronological relationship, as shown on Diagram 6.1 on page 66. However, the calendar year for the start of his reign must still be calculated.

To determine the calendar year that corresponds to the start of Solomon's reign, more chronological data is needed. Using the definition of the term "time" as 228 years (see page 28), or more accurately using 228 Passovers, the necessary information can be derived from Daniel, chapter 4, verses 31-32: *"The kingdom is departed from thee. And they shall drive thee from men, and thy dwelling shall be with the beasts of the field: they shall make thee to eat grass as oxen, and **seven times** shall pass over thee, until thou know that the most High ruleth in the kingdom of men, and giveth it to whomsoever he will"* (KJV). Ostensibly, this passage is addressed to Nebuchadnezzar, king of Babylon, but there is no indication in the historical record that any of the things described in verses 31-32 ever happened to him in real life. Absent such corroborating evidence, Daniel, chapter 4, is better understood as an allegory about the fate of Israel,[1] with Nebuchadnezzar representing the kings of Israel. Focusing only on the chronological aspects, verse 32 predicts that, after "twelve full months," seven "times" of insanity will pass over Nebuchadnezzar (Israel), followed by a period of "days" (verse 34) at the end of which Nebuchadnezzar's sanity will be restored. This sequence of events seems to coincide with the events and time periods in the time line which was developed from the interpretation of Daniel, chapter 12, which has been shown to describe a "time, times, and an half" (3½ "times") followed by a period of

---

[1] The terminology, narrative structure, and meaning of Daniel, chapter 4, is based on the words of Moses recorded in Leviticus, chapter 26; compare Daniel 4:10, 15, 23, 25, 32, 34 to Leviticus 26:4, 18, 19, 21, 22, 24, 28, 32, 33, 40, and notice the theme of unfaithfulness to the covenant and eventual restoration of Israel; also, see Deuteronomy, chapter 32. Note that Daniel, chapter 4, clarifies the chronology of Israel's punishment for unfaithfulness. The key that relates the chronology of chapter 4 to the time of Solomon is given in verse 16, which says: *"Let his heart be changed from man's, and let a beast's heart be given unto him; and let seven times pass over him"* (KJV). This is a reference to what David told Solomon in 1 Kings, chapter 2, verses 1-4, about having the heart a man (*i.e.,* about remaining faithful to the covenant). Right away, Solomon ignores this charge by marrying Pharaoh's daughter. This is the beginning of Solomon's heart being changed according to 1 Kings, chapter 11, verses 1-10. Having a heart of a beast means having a heart that worships the gods/idols of the nations.

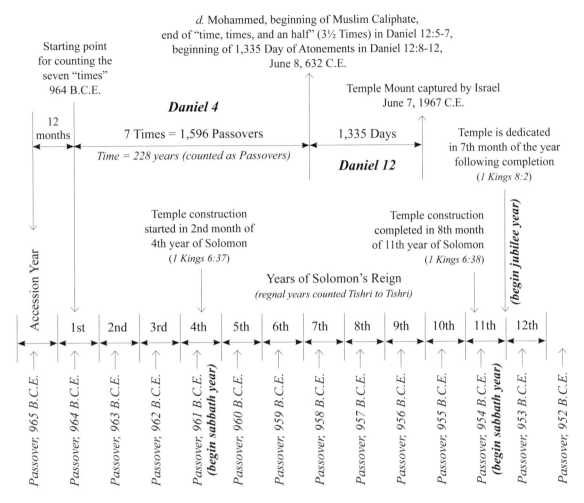

Diagram 6.1 - Calculating Solomon's Jubilee
(to reveal the year 954/953 B.C.E.)

1,335 "days," after which Israel is restored to dominion over Jerusalem and the Temple Mount. The logical assumption is to equate the 3½ "times" in the twelfth chapter is the last half of the seven "times" described in the fourth chapter of Daniel. When counting back seven "times (7 x 228 = 1596 Passovers) from the terminus of the "time, times, and an half" in the twelfth chapter, which is the date June 8, 632 C.E., the Passover that occurred in the year 964 B.C.E. is identified as the starting point for the seven "times." This starting point can then be correlated with the first year of Solomon's reign as shown on the diagram. By moving forward in time to the eleventh year of Solomon's reign, the year that the Temple was completed can be identified as 955/954 B.C.E. Solomon dedicated the Temple in the seventh month of the following year, on 10 Tishri, waiting eleven months after the completion of the Temple to dedicate it. He chose to do the dedication at the time of blowing of the trumpets, indicating that the dedication year, 954/953 B.C.E., was a jubilee year. Once this Gregorian date has been identified as a jubilee year, it is possible to compute all sabbath and jubilee years in history in terms of Gregorian years. *Appendix Three: Calendar of Sabbath and Jubilee Years* is the result of such computation. It should be noted that the sabbath and jubilee years listed in that section agree with the cycles offered by Zuckermann and Wacholder if both are changed from Tishri-to-Tishri into Nisan-to-Nisan reckoning for the Jewish year, as Scripture demands, and if the last year of a Zuckermann year (*e.g.,* 68/69 C.E.) and first year of a Wacholder year (*e.g.,* 69/70 C.E.) are used as the starting year for the sabbath and jubilee years. This would yield a sabbath year running from Nisan 69 C.E. to Nisan 70 C.E.

Now that the calendar of sabbath and jubilee years has been established in history, the date of the decree issued by Julius Caesar to Hyrcanus II in 44 B.C.E. can be examined in relationship to the seven-year sabbath cycles. By referring to the *Appendix Three*, it can be seen that the year 44/43 B.C.E. was a sabbath year. That means that the next sabbath cycle began in the following year, 43/42 B.C.E., so the first Pentecost ("week") in the count of the seven Pentecosts ("weeks") in verse 25 was the one that occurred in 43 B.C.E., and the count ended with the Pentecost in 37 B.C.E. The sixty-two Pentecosts followed the seven Pentecosts, which means that the first Pentecost in the count of sixty-two was the one that occurred in the year 36 B.C.E., and the sixty-second Pentecost in the count of the sixty-two occurred in the year 26 C.E. Table 6.1 on the opposite page shows the seven Pentecosts and the sixty-two Pentecosts and how they are to be counted according to the prophecy of the seventy "weeks."

The Prophecy in History

The prophecy of the seventy "weeks" began with the decree of Julius Caesar establishing Hyrcanus II as ruler in Jerusalem. Based on the authority given him by Caesar, Hyrcanus returned to Jerusalem as the high priest and ethnarch (anointed one and prince), along with the procurator Antipater, father of Herod the Great. By 44/43 B.C.E., they had rebuilt the trench and street of Jerusalem that had been destroyed by Pompey when he brought Judea under Roman control in 63 B.C.E. When Antipater was poisoned in 43 B.C.E., his son Herod began his rise to power. In the year 40 B.C.E., Antigonus, brother of Hyrcanus II, lead a rebellion against Rome, capturing Jerusalem with the aid of the Parthians and setting himself up as high priest. Herod fled to Rome, appealed for help, was declared King of the Jews by the Roman Senate, then sent back to Judea with several legions to put down the rebellion. In January of 36 B.C.E., Herod recaptured Jerusalem, doing so between the seventh Pentecost in the seven-year sabbath cycle and the first Pentecost in the count of sixty-two Pentecosts that would begin in 36 C.E.

verse 25: *"Know therefore and understand, that from the going forth of the commandment to restore and to build Jerusalem unto the Messiah the Prince shall be seven weeks, and threescore and two weeks: the street shall be built again, and the wall, even in troublous times"* (KJV). The capitalized King James

Table 6.1 - How to Count the 70 Weeks (Pentecosts)

Each Pentecost in the count is shown under its equivalent Gregorian year. Sabbath and jubilee years begin in the Gregorian year shown and end in the next year. Jubilee years begin on the 10th day of Tishri (usually corresponding to September-October) in the 49th sabbath year in the cycle. For a listing of all sabbath and jubilee years, see page 97.						**44** B.C.E. *Sabbath Year* Caesar's Decree to Hyrcanus II
1st Year	*2nd Year*	*3rd Year*	*4th Year*	*5th Year*	*6th Year*	*7th Year*
43 B.C.E. Pentecost - May 11 *1 of 7 Pentecosts*	**42** B.C.E. Pentecost - May 29 *2 of 7 Pentecosts*	**41** B.C.E. Pentecost - May 18 *3 of 7 Pentecosts*	**40** B.C.E. Pentecost - May 8 *4 of 7 Pentecosts*	**39** B.C.E. Pentecost - May 28 *5 of 7 Pentecosts*	**38** B.C.E. Pentecost - May 15 *6 of 7 Pentecosts*	**37** B.C.E. *Sabbath Year* Pentecost - Jun 3 *7 of 7 Pentecosts*
36 B.C.E. Pentecost - May 23 *1 of 62 Pentecosts*	**35** B.C.E. Pentecost - May 13 *2 of 62 Pentecosts*	**34** B.C.E. Pentecost - Jun 1 *3 of 62 Pentecosts*	**33** B.C.E. Pentecost - May 19 *4 of 62 Pentecosts*	**32** B.C.E. Pentecost - May 9 *5 of 62 Pentecosts*	**31** B.C.E. Pentecost - May 28 *6 of 62 Pentecosts*	**30** B.C.E. *Sabbath Year* Pentecost - May 17 *7 of 62 Pentecosts*
29 B.C.E. Pentecost - Jun 4 *8 of 62 Pentecosts*	**28** B.C.E. Pentecost - May 25 *9 of 62 Pentecosts*	**27** B.C.E. Pentecost - May 13 *10 of 62 Pentecosts*	**26** B.C.E. Pentecost - Jun 1 *11 of 62 Pentecosts*	**25** B.C.E. Pentecost - May 21 *12 of 62 Pentecosts*	**24** B.C.E. Pentecost - May 11 *13 of 62 Pentecosts*	**23** B.C.E. *Sabbath-Jubilee Year* Pentecost - May 29 *14 of 62 Pentecosts*
22 B.C.E. Pentecost - May 18 *15 of 62 Pentecosts*	**21** B.C.E. Pentecost - May 8 *16 of 62 Pentecosts*	**20** B.C.E. Pentecost - May 28 *17 of 62 Pentecosts*	**19** B.C.E. Pentecost - May 16 *18 of 62 Pentecosts*	**18** B.C.E. Pentecost - June 3 *19 of 62 Pentecosts*	**17** B.C.E. Pentecost - May 23 *20 of 62 Pentecosts*	**16** B.C.E. *Sabbath Year* Pentecost - May 12 *21 of 62 Pentecosts*
15 B.C.E. Pentecost - May 30 *22 of 62 Pentecosts*	**14** B.C.E. Pentecost - May 20 *23 of 62 Pentecosts*	**13** B.C.E. Pentecost - May 8 *24 of 62 Pentecosts*	**12** B.C.E. Pentecost - May 28 *25 of 62 Pentecosts*	**11** B.C.E. Pentecost - May 16 *26 of 62 Pentecosts*	**10** B.C.E. Pentecost - Jun 6 *27 of 62 Pentecosts*	**9** B.C.E. *Sabbath Year* Pentecost - May 24 *28 of 62 Pentecosts*
8 B.C.E. Pentecost - May 14 *29 of 62 Pentecosts*	**7** B.C.E. Pentecost - Jun 1 *30 of 62 Pentecosts*	**6** B.C.E. Pentecost - May 21 *31 of 62 Pentecosts*	**5** B.C.E. Pentecost - May 10 *32 of 62 Pentecosts*	**4** B.C.E. Pentecost - May 30 *33 of 62 Pentecosts*	**3** B.C.E. Pentecost - May 18 *34 of 62 Pentecosts*	**2** B.C.E. *Sabbath Year* Pentecost - May 8 *35 of 62 Pentecosts*
1 B.C.E. Pentecost - May 26 *36 of 62 Pentecosts*	**1** C.E. Pentecost - Jun 4 *37 of 62 Pentecosts*	**2** C.E. Pentecost - May 16 *38 of 62 Pentecosts*	**3** C.E. Pentecost - May 23 *39 of 62 Pentecosts*	**4** C.E. Pentecost - May 12 *40 of 62 Pentecosts*	**5** C.E. Pentecost - Jun 1 *41 of 62 Pentecosts*	**6** C.E. *Sabbath Year* Pentecost - May 21 *42 of 62 Pentecosts*
7 C.E. Pentecost - May 10 *43 of 62 Pentecosts*	**8** C.E. Pentecost - May 28 *44 of 62 Pentecosts*	**9** C.E. Pentecost - May 17 *45 of 62 Pentecosts*	**10** C.E. Pentecost - Jun 4 *46 of 62 Pentecosts*	**11** C.E. Pentecost - May 25 *47 of 62 Pentecosts*	**12** C.E. Pentecost - May 13 *48 of 62 Pentecosts*	**13** C.E. *Sabbath Year* Pentecost - Jun 2 *49 of 62 Pentecosts*
14 C.E. Pentecost - May 21 *50 of 62 Pentecosts*	**15** C.E. Pentecost - May 10 *51 of 62 Pentecosts*	**16** C.E. Pentecost - May 29 *52 of 62 Pentecosts*	**17** C.E. Pentecost - May 19 *53 of 62 Pentecosts*	**18** C.E. Pentecost - May 8 *54 of 62 Pentecosts*	**19** C.E. Pentecost - May 26 *55 of 62 Pentecosts*	**20** C.E. *Sabbath Year* Pentecost - May 16 *56 of 62 Pentecosts*
21 C.E. Pentecost - Jun 2 *57 of 62 Pentecosts*	**22** C.E. Pentecost - May 23 *58 of 62 Pentecosts*	**23** C.E. Pentecost - May 12 *59 of 62 Pentecosts*	**24** C.E. Pentecost - May 31 *60 of 62 Pentecosts*	**25** C.E. Pentecost - May 21 *61 of 62 Pentecosts*	**26** C.E. Pentecost - May 10 *62 of 62 Pentecosts*	**27** C.E. *Sabbath-Jubilee Year* Pentecost - May 28 *70th Pentecost*

translation "Messiah the Prince" has been discredited in recent years by a better understanding of the Masoretic Text. One modern translation adds this footnote, "The accents in the MT indicate disjunction at this point, which would make it difficult, if not impossible, to identify the 'anointed one/prince' of this verse as messianic" (NET). The anointed one and the prince were one person, and that one person was Hyrcanus II. The meaning of verse 25 is captured by the following paraphrase from pages 62-63: "Observe with your eyes and calculate with your mind, that after the issuing of the decree by Julius Caesar to Hyrcanus II, high priest and ethnarch of the Jews, granting him by the authority of Rome the right to rule Jerusalem as his dominion and giving him permission to rebuild the city ... the street and trench (in front of the wall) will be rebuilt" (AP). Comparing this paraphrase with the events of history, it is easy to see a perfect match. Caesar's decree in 44 B.C.E. restored Jerusalem to the rule of Hyrcanus II, the anointed one/prince, and the street and trench were rebuilt sometime in the year 44/43 B.C.E. After seven Pentecosts that coincided with a sabbath cycle, Herod the Great captured Jerusalem from Antigonus in January of 36 B.C.E. (see verse 24 below) and ruled as King of the Jews. During his tumultuous reign, Herod was renowned throughout the known world for his building projects, especially those in the city of Jerusalem. He is best known for the magnificence of the renovated Jewish Temple, known today as Herod's Temple, but there were hundreds of impressive structures built by Herod during his lifetime, including the Antonia Fortress, Masada, Herodium, and the port city of Caesarea. Herod died in the year 4 B.C.E., but the building of Jerusalem and the Temple was still underway when the sixty-ninth Pentecost in the seventy "weeks" was observed in 26 C.E.

The chronology of the first sixty-nine Pentecosts of the seventy "weeks" has now been established as having already occurred during Roman times, between 43 B.C.E. and 26 C.E., but what about the seventieth "week" (or Pentecost)? Since rebuilding the street and trench of Jerusalem had not been completed before the Pentecost in 44 B.C.E., that rules against adding that "week" before the start of the sixty-nine "weeks" to make seventy "weeks." Thus, the Pentecost of 27 C.E., the "week" after the sixty-nine "weeks," is the "week" that must be added to complete the seventy "weeks" (see Diagram 6.2 on the next page). That seventieth "week" added after the sixty-nine "weeks" to complete the seventy "weeks" will be examined in detail in the next chapter. Before moving on to do so, however, some additional items in verse 24 and verses 26-27 need to be correlated with Jewish history, as follows:

verse 24: *"Seventy weeks are determined upon thy people and upon thy holy city, to finish the transgression, and to make an end of sins, and to make reconciliation for iniquity, and to bring in everlasting righteousness, and to seal up the vision and prophecy, and to anoint the most Holy"* (KJV). This verse sets forth six things that must be accomplished during the seventy "weeks." The first item, "to finish the transgression," can be translated as "to shut up the (national, moral or religious) revolt" by using alternate definitions from Strong's for the words rendered in the King James Version as "to finish" לְכַלֵּא (BHS, Strong's OT: 3607) and "the transgression" הַפֶּשַׁע (BHS, Strong's OT: 6588).

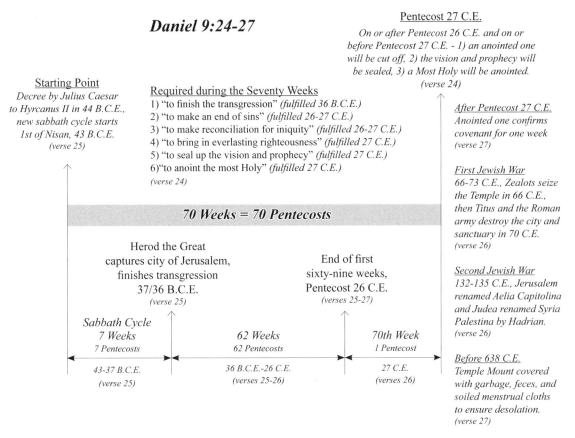

Diagram 6.2 - Time Line for the Seventy Weeks

The alternate translation more accurately fits the history of that period. After the decree made by Caesar in 44 B.C.E., Jewish history records a major revolt by Antigonus, brother of the Hasmonean high priest and ethnarch, Hyrcanus II, in 40 B.C.E. Antigonus, in alliance with Rome's archenemy Parthia, overran Judea and captured Jerusalem and its Temple from Hyrcanus. Antigonus installed himself as high priest after biting off the ear of Hyrcanus to make him ritually ineligible to serve as high priest in the future, then sent him to Parthia in chains. Herod fled to Rome to escape Antigonus. There he was proclaimed King of the Jews by the Roman Senate and sent back to Judea with several Roman legions to put down the insurrection of Antigonus. Herod "finished the transgression" by besieging Jerusalem until the city fell to him in January, 36 B.C.E. It is this sequence of events that fulfills the first item in the list of six things in verse 24 that had to be accomplished during the seventy "weeks." The remaining five items from verse 24 will be discussed at length in the next chapter of this book.

verses 26-27: *"And after threescore and two weeks shall Messiah be cut off, but not for himself: and the people of the prince that shall come shall destroy the city and the sanctuary; and the end thereof shall be with a flood, and unto the end of the war desolations are determined. And he shall confirm the covenant with many for one week: and in the midst of the week he shall cause the sacrifice and oblation to cease. And the people of the prince that shall come shall destroy the city and the sanctuary, and the end thereof shall be with a flood, and unto the end of the war desolations are determined, and for the overspreading of abominations he shall make it desolate, even until the consummation, and that determined shall be poured upon the desolate"* (KJV). In history, the sixty-two "weeks" ended on the Day of Pentecost in the year 26 C.E., after which date it was predicted that an anointed one[1] would be cut off. The Hebrew word "cut off" יִכָּרֵת (BHS, Strong's OT: 3772) is better translated as "will be made a covenant," which is the sense in which it is most frequently used in the Hebrew Scriptures.[2] Chronologically, verse 24 requires the seventieth "week" to be brought to a close with an event that will happen after Pentecost in 26 C.E. and on or before Pentecost in 27 C.E., an event that is described simply as *"to anoint the most Holy"* (KJV). The first part of verse 27 continues the covenant narrative, revealing that the anointed one of verse 26 will confirm the covenant for one week, causing the sacrifice and oblation in the Temple to cease in the midst of the week (these events will be covered in the next chapter). Verse 26 goes on to state that after the above sequence of events *"the people of the prince that shall come shall destroy the city and the sanctuary; and the end thereof shall be with a flood, and unto the end of the war desolations are determined"* (KJV), foretelling the destruction of the Temple by the Romans under Titus during the First Jewish War (66-73 C.E.).[3] The final words of the ninth chapter look even further forward in time to the total destruction of Jerusalem and Judea by Hadrian in the Second Jewish War (132-135 C.E.), which ended with the Temple Mount being plowed under, a new city named Aelia Capitolina replacing Jerusalem, and the name of Judea being changed to Syria Palestina. The phrase translated "overspreading of abominations" in the final part of verse 27 is an interpretation of Hebrew words meaning literally "wing of abominable filth." By using this imagery of being covered over with a wing (as a mother hen covers her chicks with her protective wing), but this time with filth, the prophecy comes to its end by again looking forward in time to the final days of Byzantine rule over Jerusalem, just before the fall of the city to Caliph Omar as predicted in the seventh chapter of Daniel. During this period, the Byzantine Christians had intentionally covered the Temple Mount with their garbage, feces, and soiled menstrual cloths in a misguided effort to ensure that it remained ritually impure for use by Jews, and thus desolate. Even greater insult was to come, though. In the year 638 C.E., Omar, leading the armies of Islam, captured the walled city of Jerusalem, and a few decades afterwards his successors erected the (now golden) Dome of the Rock and the al Aqsa Mosque on the Temple Mount, where they intrude on the sacred site to this day.

---

[1] This anointed one in verse 26 cannot be Hyrcanus II again, since Herod had executed him decades earlier in 30 B.C.E.

[2] The same word translated "cut off "in this verse in Daniel is translated "made a covenant" in Genesis, chapter 15, verse 18.

[3] Roman soldiers offered sacrifices to their standards (containing the image of their deified emperor) on the Temple ruins (Josephus, *Wars of the Jews*, 6:6:1), the "abomination of desolation" foretold in the Gospel of Matthew, chapter 24, verse 15.

CHAPTER SEVEN

HE SHALL CONFIRM THE COVENANT
Daniel 9:24-27

The prophecy of the seventy "weeks" in Daniel, chapter 9, verses 24-27, sets forth three distinct time periods that make up the seventy "weeks"—an initial period of seven "weeks," followed by another period of sixty-two "weeks," followed by a third period of one "week," together totaling seventy "weeks"—all of which have already happened in history as explained in the last chapter. The first time period was a "week" of seven Pentecosts that coincided with the seven-year sabbath cycle that began in 43 B.C.E. and ended in 37 B.C.E. The second time period of sixty-two "weeks" followed the first time period, beginning with the Pentecost observed in 36 B.C.E. and continuing for sixty-two Pentecosts, ending with the Pentecost that was observed in 26 C.E. Both of these time periods together accounted for sixty-nine of the seventy "weeks." The third time period followed immediately after the sixty-nine "weeks," beginning with events in Jewish history that happened after the Pentecost of 26 C.E., and ending before or during the seventieth "week," which was brought to a conclusion by the Pentecost of 27 C.E. Then, according to verse 27, a covenant was confirmed for one week by an anointed one. The logical question to ask at this point is: What covenant was introduced to the Jewish people in the year 27 C.E. and confirmed by an anointed one for one week afterwards? The remainder of this chapter will be devoted to identifying that covenant, and examining the six items set forth in verse 24 that preceded the covenant confirmation week.

The New Covenant

The key to identifying the covenant described in verse 27 is contained in verse 24, the opening verse of the prophecy of the seventy "weeks," which states *"Seventy weeks are determined upon thy people and upon thy holy city, to finish the transgression, and to make an end of sins, and to make reconciliation for iniquity, and to bring in everlasting righteousness, and to seal up the vision and prophecy, and to anoint the most Holy"* (KJV). In this verse, six items are described that must happen before the conclusion of the seventy "weeks" in 27 C.E. The first item, "to finish the transgression," was accomplished when Herod the Great captured Jerusalem from Antigonus in early 36 B.C.E., bringing the civil and religious revolt in Jerusalem and Judea to a close (see page 71). The next two items, "to make an end of sins" and "to make reconciliation for iniquity," identify the covenant in question by pointing to the Book of Jeremiah, chapter 31, verses 31-34, which say: *"Behold, the days come, saith the Lord, that I will make a new covenant with the house of Israel, and with the house of Judah: Not according to the covenant that I made with their fathers in the day that I took them by the hand to bring them out of the land of Egypt; which my covenant they brake, although I was an husband unto them, saith the Lord: But this shall be the covenant that I will make with the house of Israel; After those days, saith the Lord, I will put my law in their inward parts, and write it in their hearts; and will be their God, and they shall be my people. And they shall teach no more every man his neighbour, and every man his brother, saying, Know the Lord: for they shall all know me, from the least of them unto the greatest of them, saith the Lord; for I will forgive their iniquity, and I will remember their sin no more"* (KJV). Notice the promises at the end, "for I will forgive their iniquity" and "I will remember their sin no more." The wording of those phrases is almost identical to the first and second items of the six items listed as having to be accomplished during the seventy "weeks," namely, *"... to make an end of sins, and to make reconciliation for iniquity ..."* (KJV). The fact that this wording in Daniel, chapter 9, verse 24, mirrors the wording used in Jeremiah, chapter 31, verse 34, is the key to identifying the covenant in question. By using the same phraseology, the angel Gabriel identifies the covenant in Daniel's ninth chapter as being one and the same as the new covenant between Israel and God that was predicted by the prophet Jeremiah.

Some expositors object to this interpretation, saying that Jeremiah's "new covenant" was established with the nation of Israel when the Jews returned from Babylon. However, the history of that period indicates otherwise. The returning Jews rebuilt the Temple in Jerusalem and began observing the sacrificial system under the Mosaic covenant, exactly as before the exile, not under a new covenant that did not depend on the Temple system. They continued to do so until the Temple was destroyed in the year 70 C.E. Obviously, that interpretation cannot be what was meant. Other expositors claim that the new covenant was established by the rabbis after the Romans destroyed the Temple in 70 C.E., but that argument ignores the time frame for introducing and confirming the covenant set forth in verse 25 and verse 27, which verses taken together require that the anointed one begin confirming the new covenant no later than the year 27 C.E. So, according to the time line in Daniel, the introduction of the new covenant could not happen after the destruction of the Temple, as was claimed by many early Jewish expositors. As for most modern Jewish expositors, they interpret the reference to the new covenant in Jeremiah as referring to the original Mosaic covenant made at Sinai, but placed anew in the hearts of the Jewish people by the Messiah, usually assuming that will happen when a third Jewish Temple is rebuilt on the Temple Mount in the future. However, this is another wrong interpretation that ignores the time constraints of Daniel that require a new covenant beginning no later than the year 27 C.E.

The Book of the New Covenant

Since the *Tanakh* was completed sometime around 450 B.C.E., it will not contain the record of the introduction of the new covenant to Israel that occurred sometime after Pentecosts in 26 C.E. and before Pentecost in 27 C.E., nor will it record the fulfillment of the last five items in Daniel, chapter 9, verse 24, that must occur before the seventy "weeks" can come to a close. For that information, we must look to the *B'rit Hadashah*, which is the continuation of the *Tanakh*. The *B'rit Hadashah*, also called the Book of the New Covenant (New Testament), is a record of God's revelation to the Jewish people, and like the *Tanakh*, was recorded by Jews, making it an authentic and trustworthy testimony about the anointed one who confirmed the new covenant to Israel. The final five items of the six required items mentioned in verse 24, *"to make an end of sins, and to make reconciliation for iniquity, and to bring in everlasting righteousness, and to seal up the vision and prophecy, and to anoint the most Holy"* (KJV), have their fulfillments explained in its pages. Their fulfillments establish the time frame for the new covenant and identify the anointed one who confirmed the covenant for one week.

"to make an end of sins, and to make reconciliation for iniquity"

The first two items of the final five of the six required items from verse 24, "to make an end of sins, and to make reconciliation for iniquity," were shown in preceding paragraphs to be indicators that would identify the new covenant promised by Jeremiah. The introduction of the new covenant to Israel is described in the Gospels[1] of Matthew, Mark, and Luke, and it had to occur on or after Pentecost in the year 26 C.E. according to the chronological constraints spelled out in the prophecy of the seventy "weeks." This account is from the Gospel of Matthew, chapter 3, verses 1-12: *"In those days came John the Baptist, preaching in the wilderness of Judaea, And saying, Repent ye: for the kingdom of heaven is at hand. For this is he that was spoken of by the prophet Esaias, saying, The voice of one crying in the wilderness, Prepare ye the way of the Lord, make his paths straight. And the same John had his raiment of camel's hair, and a leathern girdle about his loins; and his meat was locusts and wild honey. Then went out to him Jerusalem, and all Judaea, and all the region round about Jordan, And were baptized of him in Jordan, confessing their sins. But when he saw many of the Pharisees and Sadducees come to his baptism, he said unto them, O generation of vipers, who hath warned you to flee from the wrath to come? Bring forth therefore fruits meet for repentance: And think not to say within yourselves, We have Abraham to our father: for I say unto you, that God is able of these stones[2] to raise up children unto Abraham. And now also the axe is laid unto the root of the trees: therefore every tree which bringeth not forth good fruit is hewn down, and cast into the fire. I indeed baptize you with water unto repentance: but he that cometh after me is mightier than I, whose shoes I am not worthy to bear: he shall baptize you with the Holy Ghost, and with fire: Whose fan is in his hand, and he will throughly purge his floor, and gather his wheat into the garner; but he will burn up the chaff with unquenchable fire"* (KJV).

John the Baptist was the messenger of the new covenant, sent by God to call the people of Israel to repentance for forgiveness of sins, and he did so without deference to the atonement achieved by the

---

[1] *Gospel* refers to the first four books of the *B'rit Hadashah*, Matthew, Mark, Luke, and John, which collectively testify about the life of *Yeshua Ha'Mashiach* (Jesus the Christ); the word itself is Middle English, derived from Old English *gōdspel* (a translation of Late Latin *evangelium*), meaning the "good news" about the kingdom of God and his salvation.

[2] John was possibly pointing to the twelve memorial stones, representing the tribes of Israel, which were placed in the bed of the Jordan River when the Israelites entered the land, as described in Joshua, chapter 4, verses 4-11.

annual Temple system of animal sacrifice required by the Mosaic covenant. His use of baptism by submersion in water, called a *mikvah* by Jews, was a ritual representing purification of the soul from most sins, a meaning that would have been well understood by the Jewish people who heard John's message. His use of the Jordan River for baptism—that is, using freely running water that Jews considered to be "living waters" having special powers of purification from all sins—made for a powerful message that challenged the established religious authorities and the efficacy of the Law under the Mosaic covenant. However, these same authorities were intimidated by John, who the masses considered to be the longed-awaited Messiah. Later, when John was baptizing at Bethabara, the Temple authorities sent priests and Levites to John, seeking to know who he was, as recorded in the Gospel of John, chapter 1, verses 19-28: *"And this is the record of John, when the Jews sent priests and Levites from Jerusalem to ask him, Who art thou? And he confessed, and denied not; but confessed, I am not the Christ. And they asked him, What then? Art thou Elias? And he saith, I am not. Art thou that prophet? And he answered, No. Then said they unto him, Who art thou? that we may give an answer to them that sent us. What sayest thou of thyself? He said, I am the voice of one crying in the wilderness, Make straight the way of the Lord, as said the prophet Esaias. And they which were sent were of the Pharisees. And they asked him, and said unto him, Why baptizest thou then, if thou be not that Christ, nor Elias, neither that prophet? John answered them, saying, I baptize with water: but there standeth one among you, whom ye know not; He it is, who coming after me is preferred before me, whose shoe's latchet I am not worthy to unloose. These things were done in Bethabara beyond Jordan, where John was baptizing"* (KJV). Thus, John stated emphatically that he was not the anointed one who would confirm the covenant after the seventy "weeks," but that the anointed one was that very day walking among the people of Israel. But, who was this anointed one who would confirm the new covenant? That question is answered by the fulfillment of the final three items of the six required items in Daniel, chapter 9, verse 24.

"to bring in everlasting righteousness"

The first of the final three items in verse 24 that were required to be fulfilled before the end of the seventy "weeks," *"to bring in everlasting righteousness"* (KJV), was fulfilled by the baptism of Jesus in the Jordan River by John the Baptist. This event is described in each of the Gospels of Matthew, Mark, and Luke, and had to occur after the Pentecost of 26 C.E. and on or before the Pentecost of 27 C.E. according to the chronological constraints spelled out in the prophecy of the seventy "weeks."

The account of the baptism that is most pertinent to verse 24, in that it identifies this event with the prophecy of the seventy "weeks," is given in the Gospel of Matthew, chapter 3, verses 1-17: *"Then cometh Jesus from Galilee to Jordan unto John, to be baptized of him. But John forbad him, saying, I have need to be baptized of thee, and comest thou to me? And Jesus answering said unto him, Suffer it to be so now: for thus it becometh us to fulfil all righteousness. Then he suffered him. And Jesus, when he was baptized, went up straightway out of the water: and, lo, the heavens were opened unto him, and he saw the Spirit of God descending like a dove, and lighting upon him: And lo a voice from heaven, saying, This is my beloved Son, in whom I am well pleased"* (KJV).

The Gospel of Mark contains a second account of the baptism of Jesus in chapter 1, verses 1-11: *"The beginning of the gospel of Jesus Christ, the Son of God; As it is written in the prophets, Behold, I send my messenger before thy face, which shall prepare thy way before thee. The voice of one crying in the wilderness, Prepare ye the way of the Lord, make his paths straight. John did baptize in the wilderness, and preach the baptism of repentance for the remission of sins. And there went out unto him all the land of Judaea, and they of Jerusalem, and were all baptized of him in the river of Jordan, confessing their sins. And John was clothed with camel's hair, and with a girdle of a skin about his loins; and he did eat locusts and wild honey; And preached, saying, There cometh one mightier than I after me, the latchet of whose shoes I am not worthy to stoop down and unloose. I indeed have baptized you with water: but he shall baptize you with the Holy Ghost. And it came to pass in those days, that Jesus came from Nazareth of Galilee, and was baptized of John in Jordan. And straightway coming up out of the water, he saw the heavens opened, and the Spirit like a dove descending upon him: And there came a voice from heaven, saying, Thou art my beloved Son, in whom I am well pleased"* (KJV).

A third account of the events surrounding the baptism of Jesus, along with some important chronological information, is given in the Gospel of Luke, chapter 3, verses 1-22: *"Now in the fifteenth year of the reign of Tiberius Caesar, Pontius Pilate being governor of Judaea, and Herod being tetrarch of Galilee, and his brother Philip tetrarch of Ituraea and of the region of Trachonitis, and Lysanias the tetrarch of Abilene, Annas and Caiaphas being the high priests, the word of God came unto John the son of Zacharias in the wilderness. And he came into all the country about Jordan, preaching the baptism of repentance for the remission of sins; As it is written in the book of the words of Esaias the prophet, saying, The voice of one crying in the wilderness, Prepare ye the way of the Lord, make his paths straight. Every valley shall be filled, and every mountain and hill shall be brought low; and the crooked shall be made straight, and the rough ways shall be made smooth; And all flesh shall see the salvation of God. Then said he to the multitude that came forth to be baptized of him, O generation of vipers, who hath warned you to flee from the wrath to come? Bring forth therefore fruits worthy of repentance, and begin not to say within yourselves, We have Abraham to our father: for I say unto you, That God is able of these stones to raise up children unto Abraham. And now also the axe is laid unto the root of the trees: every tree therefore which bringeth not forth good fruit is hewn down, and cast into the fire. And the people asked him, saying, What shall we do then? He answereth and saith unto them, He that hath two coats, let him impart to him that hath none; and he that hath meat, let him do likewise. Then came also publicans to be baptized, and said unto him, Master, what shall we do? And he said unto them, Exact no more than that which is appointed you. And the soldiers likewise demanded of him, saying,*

And what shall we do? And he said unto them, Do violence to no man, neither accuse any falsely; and be content with your wages. And as the people were in expectation, and all men mused in their hearts of John, whether he were the Christ, or not; John answered, saying unto them all, I indeed baptize you with water; but one mightier than I cometh, the latchet of whose shoes I am not worthy to unloose: he shall baptize you with the Holy Ghost and with fire: Whose fan is in his hand, and he will throughly purge his floor, and will gather the wheat into his garner; but the chaff he will burn with fire unquenchable. And many other things in his exhortation preached he unto the people. But Herod the tetrarch, being reproved by him for Herodias his brother Philip's wife, and for all the evils which Herod had done, Added yet this above all, that he shut up John in prison. Now when all the people were baptized, it came to pass, that Jesus also being baptized, and praying, the heaven was opened, And the Holy Ghost descended in a bodily shape like a dove upon him, and a voice came from heaven, which said, Thou art my beloved Son; in thee I am well pleased" (KJV).

In the Gospel accounts of the baptism of Jesus, there are two important pieces of information that are particularly useful for interpretive purposes, as follows:

(1) The first piece of information is found in the statement by Jesus in the Gospel of Matthew that his baptism was being done "to fulfil all righteousness." The Greek word πληρῶσαι (Strong's NT: 4137), rendered as "fulfil" in the King James text, is most often used to indicate fulfillment of Scripture, and that is the case in this instance. Over the years, countless expositors have questioned the need for Jesus to be baptized by John the Baptist. If indeed his life was sinless, as is taught in the Scriptures, why was it necessary for Jesus to submit to a baptism of repentance for remission of sins? The answer is quite simple. The baptism of Jesus by John was done to fulfill the prophecy about fulfilling all righteousness that was specified in Daniel, chapter 9, verse 24, and it served as a signal, a public announcement of the identity of the anointed one specified in verse 27 who would confirm the new covenant.

(2) The second piece of information is the chronologically rich statement in the Gospel of Luke that the ministry of John the Baptist began in the fifteenth year of the reign of Tiberius Caesar, when Pilate was governor of Judea, and so on. The stated purpose of Jesus' baptism by John the Baptist, "to fulfil all righteousness," had to occur before Pentecost in the year 27 C.E., the year that marked the end of the seventy "weeks," so the chronological information in Luke can be used to pinpoint the start of the ministry of John with accuracy and make sure a pre-Pentecost of 27 C.E. baptism was possible. Since Joseph Caiaphas was high priest from 18 C.E. until 36 C.E.,[1] Pontius Pilate was governor of Judea from 26 C.E. until 36 C.E., Herod Antipas was tetrarch of the Galilee from 4 B.C.E. until 39 C.E., Herod Philip II

---

[1] Luke also mentions Annas as high priest, which is unusual, since there was only one high priest at a time, and Caiaphas is confirmed to have been the high priest between 18 C.E. and 36 C.E. The mention of Annas can be explained by the fact that he was a high priest who preceded Caiaphas between 6 C.E. and 15 C.E., and was the father-in-law of Caiaphas, making him a *high priest emeritus*, so to speak. Also, Annas may have served as high priest when Caiaphas was ritually impure for some reason. No mention of Lysanias, tetrarch of Abilene, has been found outside of Luke, so no dating is possible.

was tetrarch of Ituraea and the region of Trachonitis from 4 B.C.E. until about 33/34 C.E., all of those dates taken together produce a time frame that occurs between 26 C.E. and 33/34 C.E. A baptism happening between the Pentecosts of 26 C.E. and 27 C.E. can be seen to fall within that time frame. So far, so good. Next, some portion of "the fifteenth year of the reign of Tiberius Caesar" must be shown to have happened before the Pentecost in 27 C.E., the time specified as the conclusion of the seventy "weeks" (see Table 6.1 on page 67). Traditional expositors usually assign the fifteenth year of Tiberius to the year 28 C.E., but that date is not as simple to fix with certainty as it would seem at first glance.

Scholars specializing in problems of biblical chronology have examined the possible years that could be identified as the fifteenth year of the reign of Tiberius. The possibilities depend on whether one counts the first year of Tiberius' reign as an accession year followed by numbered years or counts numbered years with no accession year, on whether the count begins with the year of his co-reign over the provinces with Augustus or with the year of his sole reign after Augustus died, and on the type of calendar used, either Roman, Syro-Macedonian, or Jewish. If Jewish, there is the added uncertainty about whether the new year started with Nisan, the first month, or Tishri, the seventh month. Sixteen different time periods have been identified by chronologists as the fifteenth year of the reign of Tiberius, the time period stipulated for the start of the ministry of John the Baptist. They range in real time from the year 26 C.E. to the year 30 C.E. Five of the sixteen configurations allow for the fifteenth year of Tiberius' reign to occur after Pentecost in the year 26 C.E. and before Pentecost in the year 27 C.E., which is the Pentecost that concluded the prophecy of the seventy "weeks."

The dates for the five possible time periods [1] for the fifteenth year of Tiberius' reign are as follows:

(1) If regnal years of Tiberius are counted from his joint rule of the provinces with Augustus, his fifteenth regnal year was October, 26 C.E. to October, 27 C.E.,

(2) If regnal years of Tiberius from his joint rule of the provinces are counted as Julian calendar years according to the accession-year system, his fifteenth regnal year was January 1-December 31, 27 C.E.,

(3) If regnal years of Tiberius from his joint rule of the provinces are counted as Syro-Macedonian calendar years according to the non-accession-year system, his fifteenth regnal year was October 1, 26 C.E. to September 30, 27 C.E.,

(4) If regnal years of Tiberius from his joint rule of the provinces are counted as Jewish calendar years according to the non-accession-year system, his fifteenth regnal year was March-April, 26 C.E. to September 30, 27 C.E.,

(5) If regnal years of Tiberius from his joint rule of the provinces are counted as Jewish calendar years according to the accession-year system, his fifteenth regnal year was March-April, 26 C.E. to March-April, 28 C.E.

---

[1] Jack Finegan, *Handbook of Biblical Chronology* (Peabody, Massachusetts: Hendrickson Publishers, Inc., 1998), *p.* 330-345.

It is probable that the Gospel of Luke was written by a Jew,[1] that is, a Jewish follower of Jesus who had the Greek-sounding name Luke, possibly as a formal presentation to the former high priest Theophilus[2] for the purpose of explaining the growing branch of Judaism that was built on recognition of Jesus as the Messiah of Israel. Thus, it seems reasonable to assume that a Jewish calendar system was used to calculate the fifteenth year of Tiberius as a reference in Luke, using one of the methods employed by calendars mentioned in numbers four and five on the preceding page. However, the calendar used is not really important. All that is needed in this exposition is to show that the "fifteenth year of the reign of Tiberius" could have been referring to a time period that occurred before Pentecost in the year 27 C.E., which marks the end of the seventy "weeks," and that has been shown fivefold.

Now that the ministry of John the Baptist has been located in time as beginning sometime after March-April of 26 C.E., can the year of Jesus' baptism be placed within the time frame defined by the start of John's ministry in early 26 C.E. and the end of the seventy "weeks" on the Pentecost of 27 C.E.? Yes, it can be, at least indirectly. The approximate age at which Jesus was baptized is given in the Gospel of Luke, chapter 3, verse 23: *"And Jesus himself began to be about thirty years of age"* (KJV). Since Jesus was born sometime before the death of Herod the Great, who died in March of 4 B.C.E., it can be easily confirmed by simple calculation (see Table 7.1 below) that Jesus would have been "about 30 years of age" in the time period between the Pentecost of 26 C.E., the sixty-ninth "week" of the prophecy of the seventy "weeks," and the Pentecost of 27 C.E., the seventieth "week."

Table 7.1 - Year of Jesus' Baptism					
1 year old - 4/3 B.C.E.	2 years old - 3/2 B.C.E.	3 years old - 2/1 B.C.E.	4 years old - 1 B.C.E./1 C.E.	5 years old - 1/2 C.E.	6 years old - 2/3 C.E.
7 years old - 3/4 C.E.	8 years old - 4/5 C.E.	9 years old - 5/6 C.E.	10 years old - 6/7 C.E.	11 years old - 7/8 C.E.	12 years old - 8/9 C.E.
13 years old - 9/10 C.E.	14 years old - 10/11 C.E.	15 years old - 11/12 C.E.	16 years old - 12/13 C.E.	17 years old - 13/14 C.E.	18 years old - 14/15 C.E.
19 years old - 15/16 C.E..	20 years old - 16/17 C.E.	21 years old - 17/18 C.E.	22 years old - 18/19 C.E.	23 years old - 19/20 C.E.	24 years old - 20/21 C.E.
25 years old - 21/22 C.E.	26 years old - 22/23 C.E.	27 years old - 23/24 C.E.	28 years old - 24/25 C.E.	29 years old - 25/26 C.E.	30 years old - 26/27 C.E.

So far, four of the six items that were required to happen before the seventy "weeks" ended in the year 27 C.E., have now been demonstrated to have happened exactly in the order predicted. The new covenant was introduced by John the Baptist in early 26 C.E., and the baptism of Jesus by John, which identified Jesus as the anointed one who would confirm the new covenant to Israel, happened sometime after John began his ministry in 26 C.E. and before the seventy "weeks" came to their end on Pentecost

---

[1] Based on the fact that the rest of the Bible (*Tanakh* and *B'rit Hadashah*) was written by Jews, it seems only logical to assume that the entire Bible, including the Gospel of Luke, was written by Jews. That is the assumption used in this book.

[2] Theophilus, high priest from 37-41 C.E., was the son of the high priest Annas, brother of the high priest Caiaphas, both mentioned in Luke, and grandfather of a woman named Johanna, possibly the one mentioned in Luke, chapter 8, verse 3.

of 27 C.E. That leaves just the fifth and sixth items, *"to seal up the vision and prophecy"* (KJV) and *"to anoint the most Holy"* (KJV). These last two items will now be shown to have been fulfilled at the time of the baptism of Jesus, setting the stage for his public ministry.

"to seal up the vision and prophecy"

The fifth of the six items set forth in verse 24, *"to seal up the vision and prophecy,"* (a strict translation of the Masoretic Text yields: *"to seal up the vision and prophet"*) was fulfilled at the time of the baptism of Jesus. After his baptism, in the Gospel of John, chapter 6, verse 27, Jesus revealed to his disciples that God had previously sealed him, saying: *"... for him* [*i.e.,* for the Son of Man, a term Jesus used to describe himself] *hath God the Father sealed"* (KJV). Jesus was revealing to them that his messiahship and his role as "The Prophet" had been attested by God, but sealed away from the understanding of the leadership and people of Israel (all except those Israelites who were chosen by God to understand Jesus' message). God had warned Israel through Moses about what would happen if the nation did not keep the commandments. Daniel himself called attention to Moses' warning in his prayer (see page 67), and Isaiah, repeating Moses, had foretold that the nation of Israel would be given spiritual blindness, as recorded in Isaiah, chapter 6, verses 9-10: *"In the year that king Uzziah died I saw also the Lord sitting upon a throne, high and lifted up, and his train filled the temple. Above it stood the seraphims ... And one cried unto another, and said, Holy, holy, holy, is the Lord of hosts: the whole earth is full of his glory. And the posts of the door moved at the voice of him that cried, and the house was filled with smoke. Then said I, Woe is me! for I am undone; because I am a man of unclean lips, and I dwell in the midst of a people of unclean lips: for mine eyes have seen the King, the Lord of hosts. Then flew one of the seraphims unto me, having a live coal in his hand, which he had taken with the tongs from off the altar: And he laid it upon my mouth, and said, Lo, this hath touched thy lips; and thine iniquity is taken away, and thy sin purged. Also I heard the voice of the Lord, saying, Whom shall I send, and who will go for us? Then said I, Here am I; send me. And he said, Go, and tell this people, Hear ye indeed, but understand not; and see ye indeed, but perceive not. Make the heart of this people fat, and make their ears heavy, and shut their eyes; lest they see with their eyes, and hear with their ears, and understand with their heart, and convert, and be healed"* (KJV). Note the phrases "thine iniquity is taken away, and thy sin purged," which use the same terminology used in verse 24 to signal the new covenant.

The theme of the spiritual blindness of Israel is further clarified in Isaiah, chapter 29, verses 10-14: *"For the Lord hath poured out upon you the spirit of deep sleep, and hath closed your eyes: the prophets and your rulers, the seers hath he covered. And the vision of all is become unto you as the words of a book that is sealed, which men deliver to one that is learned, saying, Read this, I pray thee: and he saith, I cannot; for it is sealed: And the book is delivered to him that is not learned, saying, Read this, I pray thee: and he saith, I am not learned. Wherefore the Lord said, Forasmuch as this people draw near me with their mouth, and with their lips do honour me, but have removed their heart far from me, and their fear toward me is taught by the precept of men: Therefore, behold, I will proceed to do a marvellous work among this people, even a marvellous work and a wonder: for the wisdom of their wise men shall perish, and the understanding of their prudent men shall be hid"* (KJV). This latter passage from Isaiah makes clear that the vision of Isaiah was not the only vision that was sealed away from Israel, but that the blindness of Israel would be extended to include the wisdom of their wise men and the understanding of their prudent men about the entire testimony of Moses and the prophets, all of this to occur in the future, after the time of Isaiah, when God would do a marvellous work and wonder among the people.

Jesus was restrained by the spiritual blindness that was imposed by God on the religious leadership and people of Israel, as indicated in the Gospel of Matthew, chapter 13, verses 10-17, where he specifically invokes the words of Isaiah: *"And the disciples came, and said unto him, Why speakest thou unto them in parables? He answered and said unto them. ... Therefore speak I to them in parables: because they seeing see not; and hearing they hear not, neither do they understand. And in them is fulfilled the prophecy of Esaias, which saith, By hearing ye shall hear, and shall not understand; and seeing ye shall see, and shall not perceive: For this people's heart is waxed gross, and their ears are dull of hearing, and their eyes they have closed; lest at any time they should see with their eyes, and hear with their ears, and should understand with their heart, and should be converted, and I should heal them. But blessed are your eyes, for they see: and your ears, for they hear. For verily I say unto you, That many prophets and righteous men have desired to see those things which ye see, and have not seen them; and to hear those things which ye hear, and have not heard them"* (KJV).

Isaiah had specifically predicted the blindness of Israel with respect to the ministry of Jesus. In Isaiah, chapter 53, the prophet wrote: *"Who hath believed our report? and to whom is the arm of the Lord revealed? For he shall grow up before him as a tender plant, and as a root out of a dry ground: he hath no form nor comeliness; and when we shall see him, there is no beauty that we should desire him. He is despised and rejected of men; a man of sorrows, and acquainted with grief: and we hid as it were our faces from him; he was despised, and we esteemed him not. Surely he hath borne our griefs, and carried our sorrows: yet we did esteem him stricken, smitten of God, and afflicted. But he was wounded for our transgressions, he was bruised for our iniquities: the chastisement of our peace was upon him; and with his stripes we are healed. All we like sheep have gone astray; we have turned every one to his own way; and the Lord hath laid on him the iniquity of us all. He was oppressed, and he was afflicted, yet he opened not his mouth: he is brought as a lamb to the slaughter, and as a sheep before her shearers is dumb, so he openeth not his mouth. He was taken from prison and from judgment: and who shall declare his generation? for he was cut off out of the land of the living: for the transgression of my people was he stricken. And he made his grave with the wicked, and with the rich in his death; because he had done no violence, neither was any deceit in his mouth. Yet it pleased the Lord to bruise him; he hath put him to grief: when thou shalt make his soul an offering for sin, he shall see his seed, he shall prolong his days, and the pleasure of the Lord shall prosper in his hand. He shall see of the travail of his soul, and shall be satisfied: by his knowledge shall my righteous servant justify many; for he shall bear their iniquities. Therefore will I divide him a portion with the great, and he shall divide the spoil with the strong; because he hath poured out his soul unto death: and he was numbered with the transgressors; and he bare the sin of many, and made intercession for the transgressors"* (KJV).

"to anoint the most Holy"

The last of the six items that had to be accomplished before the end of the seventy "weeks," *"to anoint the most Holy"* as specified in verse 24, was accomplished by the baptism of Jesus. This event involved an anointing that would signify a Holy One being given as a covenant to Israel (or "cut off" according to verse 26, see discussion of the word יִכָּרֵת on page 72). The covenant was the "new covenant" that was prophesied in Jeremiah, chapter 31, verses 31-34, as explained at the beginning of this chapter. In addition, viewing the baptism in the context of Isaiah, chapter 41, verses 1-8a, which says, *"Behold my servant, whom I uphold; mine elect, in whom my soul delighteth; I have put my spirit upon him: he shall bring forth judgment to the Gentiles. He shall not cry, nor lift up, nor cause his voice to be heard in the street. A bruised reed shall he not break, and the smoking flax shall he not quench: he shall bring forth judgment unto truth. He shall not fail nor be discouraged, till he have set judgment in the earth: and the isles shall wait for his law. Thus saith God the Lord, he that created the heavens, and stretched them out; he that spread forth the earth, and that which cometh out of it; he that giveth breath unto the people upon it, and spirit to them that walk therein: I the Lord have called thee in righteousness, and will hold thine hand, and will keep thee, and give thee for a covenant of the people, for a light of the Gentiles; To open the blind eyes, to bring out the prisoners from the prison, and them that sit in darkness out of the prison house. I am the Lord: that is my name"* (KJV), it can be understood that Jesus' anointing by the Spirit of God at his baptism was his identification as the suffering servant in Isaiah, chapter 53, who would bear the iniquities of and justify many. By the very act of his being baptized by immersion of his body in the living waters of the Jordan River, his death, burial, and resurrection to eternal life, which would take place at the end of his ministry, was portrayed for all to see. His anointing in 27 C.E. set the stage for his ministry of confirmation to begin, a ministry that would be completed by the arrival of the Holy Spirit to dwell in the hearts and minds of all who believed in him after his resurrection.[1]

---

[1] The baptism of Jesus re-introduced and clarified the trinitarian concept of the One God, with the Father, Son, and Holy Spirit appearing together at the same time as distinct personalities of the Godhead. This trinitarian concept was first introduced in the *Tanakh*, in the Book of Genesis, chapter 18, verses 1-18, when Abraham was visited by the Lord, who made an appearance in the form of three men who gave Abraham the promise of the son out of Sarah through whom all nations would be blessed. During his baptism by John the Baptist in the Jordan River (probably at the same place where the stones were placed in the bed of the river when the Children of Israel crossed into the promised land), God the Father recognized Jesus as the son of promise, the seed of Abraham who would be a light to the nations and the glory of Israel.

John the Baptist explained the meaning of the baptism of Jesus, as recorded in the Gospel of John, chapter 1, verses 29-36: *"The next day John seeth Jesus coming unto him, and saith, Behold the Lamb of God, which taketh away the sin of the world. This is he of whom I said, After me cometh a man which is preferred before me: for he was before me. And I knew him not: but that he should be made manifest to Israel, therefore am I come baptizing with water. And John bare record, saying, I saw the Spirit descending from heaven like a dove, and it abode upon him. And I knew him not: but he that sent me to baptize with water, the same said unto me, Upon whom thou shalt see the Spirit descending, and remaining on him, the same is he which baptizeth with the Holy Ghost. And I saw, and bare record that this is the Son of God. Again the next day after John stood, and two of his disciples; And looking upon Jesus as he walked, he saith, Behold the Lamb of God!"* (KJV).[1] Thus, the baptism of Jesus, which was ratified by the Holy Spirit (as prophesied in Isaiah, chapter 41), was accomplished, and the sixth and final item required to be accomplished during the seventy "weeks," *"to anoint the most Holy"* (KJV) as specified in Daniel, chapter 9, verse 24, was accomplished. Immediately afterwards, Jesus was led into the Judean wilderness, where he was tempted by Satan for forty days and forty nights. Soon thereafter, the seventy "weeks" were brought to a close by the Feast of Weeks, which ended on the Day of Pentecost in 27 C.E.

With the close of the seventy "weeks," verse 27 continues the prophecy in Daniel, chapter 9, by specifying what will happen next: *"And he shall confirm the covenant with many for one week: and in the midst of the week he shall cause the sacrifice and oblation to cease. And the people of the prince that shall come shall destroy the city and the sanctuary, and the end thereof shall be with a flood, and unto the end of the war desolations are determined, and for the overspreading of abominations he shall make it desolate, even until the consummation, and that determined shall be poured upon the desolate"* (KJV). Jesus began confirming the new covenant by proclaiming the kingdom of heaven to his Jewish brethren, as recorded in the Gospel of Luke, chapter 4, verses 13-21: *"And when the devil had ended all the temptation, he departed from him for a season. And Jesus returned in the power of the Spirit into Galilee: and there went out a fame of him through all the region round about. And he taught in their synagogues, being glorified of all. And he came to Nazareth, where he had been brought up: and, as his custom was, he went into the synagogue on the sabbath day, and stood up for to read. And there was delivered unto him the book of the prophet Esaias. And when he had opened the book, he found the place where it was written, The Spirit of the Lord is upon me, because he hath anointed me to preach the gospel to the poor; he hath sent me to heal the brokenhearted, to preach deliverance to the captives, and recovering of sight to the blind, to set at liberty them that are bruised, To preach the acceptable year of the Lord.[2] And he closed the book, and he gave it again to the minister, and sat down. And the eyes of all them that were in the synagogue were fastened on him. And he began to say unto them, This day is this scripture fulfilled*

---

[1] Based on John's emphatic identification of Jesus as the "Lamb of God," it seems probable that the baptism of Jesus by John the Baptist took place during the week of Passover, 27 C.E., and that is the assumption made in this exposition.
[2] See Isaiah 61:1-2a.

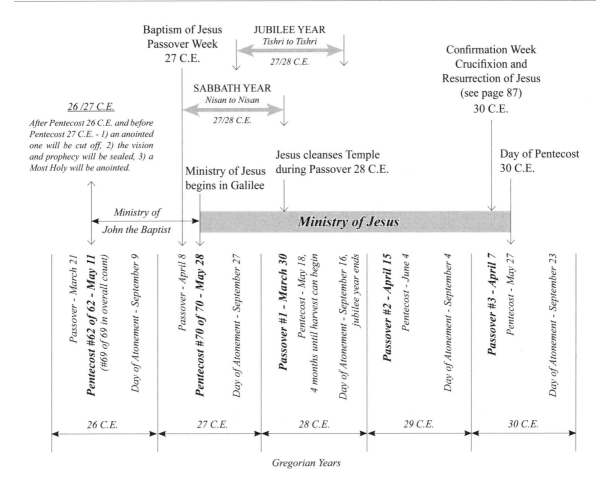

Diagram 7.1 - The Ministry of Jesus

in your ears" (KJV). For the next three years, Jesus preached his new-covenant message in Judea, Samaria, Galilee, and other parts of Israel, including Jerusalem. A time line for the three-year ministry of Jesus, based on the "three-Passover" chronology in the Gospel of John,[1] is shown in Diagram 7.1 above.

---

[1] The Gospel of John mentions three Passovers, in chapters 2, 6, and 11. Some chronologists speculate that a fourth Passover is alluded to in chapter 4, verse 35, when Jesus tells his disciples, *"Say not ye, There are yet four months, and then cometh harvest? behold, I say unto you, Lift up your eyes, and look on the fields; for they are white already to harvest"* (KJV). When he made this statement, Jesus had recently celebrated Passover, as mentioned in chapter 2, verse 12, which had occurred on March 30, 28 C.E. (the year can be derived from the reference in John, chapter 2, verse 20, to Herod's Temple, begun in the year 19 B.C.E., having been under construction for 46 years). Since the fields were white (ripe), that would make the time of the statement to be sometime in late April or May, harvest time for barley and wheat in ancient Israel. Jesus would soon thereafter celebrate the next feast, Pentecost, as mentioned in chapter 5, verse 1. Thus, it can be deduced that Jesus made his statement between Passover and Pentecost in 28 C.E., and it seems logical to assume that Jesus made it fairly close to the Day of Pentecost since the fields were turning white (ripe) for harvest. But, because 27/28 C.E. was a jubilee year in which harvesting was prohibited, there could be no harvesting done until the Jubilee ended on September 16, four months later. This is what Jesus was talking about in chapter 4, verse 35. An extra Passover there is unnecessary, and impossible chronologically.

Jesus' authority as mediator of the new covenant was not understood by the Jewish religious and political leadership of that time, and, as a result of the spiritual blindness Isaiah had predicted would eventually happen to Israel, his simple message of justification through repentance and faith was almost universally rejected by the Temple authorities, Pharisees, Sadducees, scribes, and rabbis of his time.[1] On the other hand, many Jewish people in the countryside, and even many non-elites in Jerusalem—those who were no doubt enlightened by exposure to the gospel of the coming kingdom preached beforehand by John the Baptist—responded to Jesus' message of salvation and were baptized into the new covenant, as recorded in the Gospel of John, chapter 3, verse 26: *"And they came unto John* [the Baptist]*, and said unto him, Rabbi, he that was with thee beyond Jordan, to whom thou barest witness, behold, the same baptizeth,*[2] *and all men come to him. John answered and said, A man can receive nothing, except it be given him from heaven. Ye yourselves bear me witness, that I said, I am not the Christ, but that I am sent before him. He that hath the bride is the bridegroom: but the friend of the bridegroom, which standeth and heareth him, rejoiceth greatly because of the bridegroom's voice: this my joy therefore is fulfilled. He must increase, but I must decrease. He that cometh from above is above all: he that is of the earth is earthly, and speaketh of the earth: he that cometh from heaven is above all. And what he hath seen and heard, that he testifieth; and no man receiveth his testimony. He that hath received his testimony hath set to his seal that God is true. For he whom God hath sent speaketh the words of God: for God giveth not the Spirit by measure unto him. The Father loveth the Son, and hath given all things into his hand. He that believeth on the Son hath everlasting life: and he that believeth not the Son shall not see life; but the wrath of God abideth on him"* (KJV).

The Confirmation of the Covenant

The ministry of Jesus reached its climax during Passover week in the year 30 C.E. (see time line shown in Diagram 7.2 on the next page), during which the first part of verse 27, *"And he shall confirm the covenant with many for one week: and in the midst of the week he shall cause the sacrifice and oblation to cease,"* was fulfilled. Jesus began the week by entering Jerusalem as the King of Israel, as recorded in the Gospel of Luke, chapter 19, verses 29-38: *"And it came to pass, when he was come nigh to Bethphage and Bethany, at the mount called the mount of Olives, he sent two of his disciples, Saying, Go ye into the village over against you; in the which at your entering ye shall find a colt tied, whereon yet never man sat: loose him, and bring him hither. And if any man ask you, Why do ye loose him? thus shall ye say unto him, Because the Lord hath need of him. And they that were sent went their way, and*

---

[1] Much harm has been done by those who have used the rejection of Jesus' ministry by the Jewish leadership that is recorded in the *B'rit Hadashah* (New Testament) to justify anti-Semitic views and actions against Jewish people, individually and collectively, over the centuries. A careful reading and correct interpretation of the Bible, both the *Tanakh* and *B'rit Hadashah*, will show that there is absolutely no theological justification whatsoever for anti-Semitic/anti-Jewish views or actions.
[2] See John 4:2: *"Though Jesus himself baptized not, but his disciples"* [did the baptizing] (KJV).

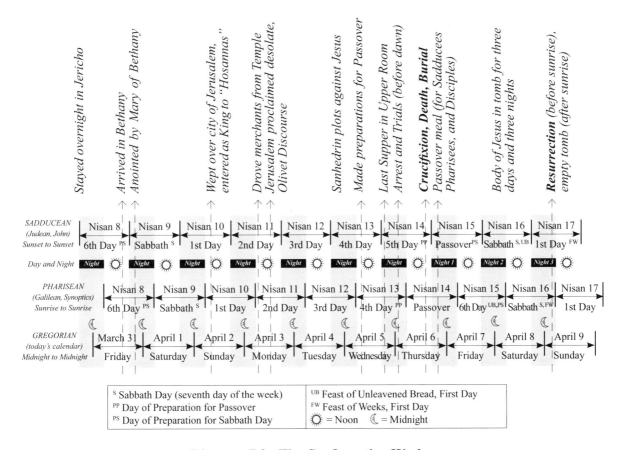

Diagram 7.2 - The Confirmation Week

(showing Sadducean, Pharisean, and Gregorian days)

found even as he had said unto them. And as they were loosing the colt, the owners thereof said unto them, Why loose ye the colt? And they said, The Lord hath need of him. And they brought him to Jesus: and they cast their garments upon the colt, and they set Jesus thereon.[1] *And as he went, they spread their clothes in the way. And when he was come nigh, even now at the descent of the mount of Olives, the whole multitude of the disciples began to rejoice and praise God with a loud voice for all the mighty works that they had seen; Saying, Blessed be the King that cometh in the name of the Lord: peace in heaven, and glory in the highest"* (KJV). The kingship of Jesus was rejected by official Judaism from the beginning. During his entry into Jerusalem, the Gospel of Luke, chapter 19, verses 39-44, records this exchange: *"And some of the Pharisees from among the multitude said unto him, Master, rebuke thy disciples. And he answered and said unto them, I tell you that, if these should hold their peace, the stones would immediately cry out. And when he was come near, he beheld the city, and wept over it, Saying, If thou hadst known, even thou, at least in this thy day, the things which belong unto thy peace! but*

---

[1] This act was an intentional fulfillment of the regal prophecy in Zechariah, chapter 9, verse 9.

now they are hid from thine eyes. For the days shall come upon thee, that thine enemies shall cast a trench about thee, and compass thee round, and keep thee in on every side, And shall lay thee even with the ground, and thy children within thee; and they shall not leave in thee one stone upon another; because thou knewest not the time of thy visitation" (KJV). It is significant that Jesus' entry into Jerusalem occurred on Nisan 10, the day designated for selecting the Passover lamb, thus pointing toward his crucifixion four days later, on Nisan 14, the eve of Passover when the Pascal lamb was to be slain. At a supper with his disciples just hours before his arrest and trials by Jewish and Roman authorities, Jesus made it plain that the blood of his life that would be shed by his impending sacrifice on the cross was the blood that confirmed the new covenant, as recorded in the Gospel of Matthew, chapter 26, verses 26-28: *"And as they were eating, Jesus took bread, and blessed it, and brake it, and gave it to the disciples, and said, Take, eat; this is my body. And he took the cup, and gave thanks, and gave it to them, saying, Drink ye all of it; For this is my blood of the new testament* [covenant]*, which is shed for many for the remission of sins"* (KJV). The week of confirming the new covenant was completed by the burial of Jesus in a tomb for three days and three nights, and then by his bodily resurrection to life on the third day, Nisan 17 by Sadducean reckoning (or Nisan 16 by Pharisean), in both cases the resurrection occurring on the first day of the Feast of Weeks (First Fruits). Forty days later, after appearing to many of his followers to create witnesses to his resurrection, Jesus ascended from the Mount of Olives to sit at the right hand of God. Ten days later on Pentecost, the followers of Jesus were gathered in Jerusalem as he had commanded, where the Holy Spirit was given to each of them as he had promised before he ascended. From a theological standpoint, Jesus' crucifixion on Nisan 14 in the year 30 C.E., in the midst of the week, confirmed the new covenant with blood and brought to an end the efficacy of Temple sacrifices under the Mosaic Covenant. The cessation of the sacrificial system had been predicted in verse 27b, *"and in the midst of the week he shall cause the sacrifice and oblation to cease"* (KJV), and the cessation was attested by ominous signs[1] and subsequent history. The priests continued to offer sacrifices in the Temple for another forty years, until it was destroyed by the Romans in 70 C.E. (*"And the people of the prince that shall come shall destroy the city and the sanctuary"*), an event that brought to a close the work of the Levitical priesthood. Verse 27c goes on to prophesy, *"and the end thereof shall be with a flood, and unto the end of the war desolations are determined, and for the overspreading of abominations he shall make it desolate, even until the consummation, and that determined shall be poured upon the desolate"* (KJV),[2] in this way foretelling the state of spiritual desolation that would afflict Jerusalem and the Temple Mount for centuries to come.

---

[1] *Jerusalem Talmud*, Tractate Yoma 6:3 [33b]: "It has been taught: For forty years before the destruction of the Temple the western menorah light darkened, the crimson thread did not turn white, and the lot for the Lord always came up in the left hand. The priests would close the gates of the Temple at night and get up in the morning and find them open" (AP).

[2] See previous exposition of verse 27 on *p. 72*.

THE WISE SHALL UNDERSTAND

The capture of the Temple Mount by Israel during the Six-Day War in 1967 was the key that unsealed the Danielic prophecies for understanding by this generation. Seven years later, on a spring day in 1974, I questioned whether that event might be the fulfillment of the prophecy set forth in Daniel, chapter 8. Ever since that day, the chrono-specific prophecies in the Book of Daniel have been uppermost in my thoughts. I still recall the excitement I experienced when I finally dared to believe that a modern-day fulfillment of an ancient Bible prophecy had indeed occurred in my lifetime. For days afterwards my spirit was buoyed by the knowledge that God was once again making his presence obvious in history, that he had demonstrated his Lordship over human events by ensuring that the "good guys" were victorious, and, most astounding of all, that he had chosen to reveal the meaning of his latest handiwork in history to me. Still, my faith was weak and my belief eventually slipped back into uncertainty. It took additional years of Bible study and prayer before I believed beyond doubt that God had actually revealed to me the key that would unseal the Danielic prophecies. Over the years that followed, as I sought more understanding from the Bible, and then meditated on the meanings of the prophecies as my understanding increased, I came to realize that one day I would be called upon to share my understanding of Daniel with others. This book is the result of my obedience to that calling.

Now that you have read this exposition of the Danielic prophecies for yourself, you will no doubt agree that the interpretations set forth herein are non-traditional,[1] so much so that many of you may still be having trouble accepting that they are correct. I can sympathize. Like you, I was raised with a healthy respect for the traditional commentaries produced by expositors whose works have become the accepted expositions of the Danielic prophecies in this day and age. So, taking a new look at Daniel did not come easy for me, either. I had to summon the courage to set aside my long-standing allegiance to the old interpretations before I could begin to see the new. That is why I chose the method used in this book to explain the prophecies. Instead of discussing all previous expositions as a prelude to a lucubrated presentation showing that the new interpretations are better, I preferred to offer the interpretations in as simple and direct a manner as possible, recounting the path of understanding that I traveled to arrive at them, then leaving it to the reader to follow that path as God opens the heart and mind to do so.

Like many past expositors who have struggled to explain the chrono-specific prophecies in Daniel to others, I have been made constantly aware of my own compositional limitations, and living day after

---

[1] Some have even objected that this book often reads more like a technical manual than a Bible commentary. I respond: "Technical, yes, absolutely. That's because the prophecies deal with a technical subject, time, and were written by Daniel, who understood time not only as an observant Jew but also as a Chaldean-trained astronomer and mathematician!" (see Daniel 2:48).

day with the prospect and responsibility of rightly dividing the word of truth for publication has been one of the most humbling experiences of my life. At the same time, I have experienced a rare intimacy and fellowship with God as he has patiently worked within me to bring forth this book. When all is said and done, I realize just how privileged and blessed I am to have been found useful in the process of making these new interpretations of the chrono-specific prophecies in Daniel known to this generation.

As you consider the interpretations of the Danielic prophecies set forth in this book, two final points should be kept in mind. First, it is important to remember that all of the fulfillment events used to formulate the interpretations of the prophecies herein had already occurred in history by the time I began to study them. I did not have to look into the future to understand any of the prophecies in the Book of Daniel, nor does anyone else. Second, the fulfillment of every chrono-specific prophecy set forth in Daniel has been fully explained in this book. This means that there are no end-time events in Daniel that are waiting to happen in the future, apart from the resurrection of Daniel himself that is implied in chapter 12. Everything else prophesied in Daniel is now a part of history. This latter point is important for the field of biblical eschatology, which will henceforth need to re-examine its traditional understanding of end-time chronology, and it will have to do so without using Daniel to identify and explain future events. No doubt, the process of re-examining the end time without a future chronology from Daniel to build upon will be a troubling journey for many traditional Bible expositors, especially when they realize that some of their long-held eschatological assumptions may have to be adjusted, or perhaps even discarded, along the way. On the other hand, the process of re-evaluating eschatological assumptions will be a grand adventure for the more daring expositors among us, both Christian and Jewish, leading them on an exciting spiritual journey that will eventually give us a more complete understanding of the end time in which we are living, and of God's plan for the end of the age.

In concluding, I express my hope that this exposition of the chrono-specific Danielic prophecies has been a blessing to you, and that, in some small way, it will stimulate you to hasten your own journey of spiritual discovery. Time is short, and there is much to learn and share!

Daniel

"Blessed be the name of God for ever and ever: for wisdom and might are his:
and he changeth the times and the seasons: he removeth kings, and setteth up kings:
he giveth wisdom unto the wise, and knowledge to them that know understanding:
he revealeth the deep and secret things: he knoweth what is in the darkness,
and the light dwelleth with him." – DANIEL 2:20-22 (KJV)

∞

SUPPLEMENTARY MATERIAL

BACKGROUND NOTES
on the Book of Daniel

The Book of Daniel is one of the most debated books of the Bible. Scholars and theologians seem unable to agree about who wrote it, when it was written, and what it means. For the purposes of this book, the things that the Book of Daniel says about itself are taken at face value.[1]

Author: The Book of Daniel, chapters 1-12, was written by Daniel, a Jewish man of possibly noble birth who was carried away as a captive from Judea to Babylon by Nebuchadnezzar, almost certainly in the year 605 B.C.E. In his book, Daniel records the revelation given to him by God through visions, dreams, and angels. Interestingly, he never refers to himself as a prophet, and his book is not included in the "Prophets" section of the *Tanakh*, being placed in the "Writings" section instead. In the *B'rit Hadashah,* Jesus specifically refers to him as "Daniel the prophet" (see Matthew 24:15, Mark 13:14), and his book is placed among those of the major prophets in most Christian Bibles. Although not stated, it can be inferred that Daniel was in his early teen years when taken to Babylon. There he lived and was schooled in the king's palace, and eventually held high office in the Babylonian Empire. Daniel spent most of his life removed from Jerusalem and Judea, but remained faithful to his Jewish religion and upbringing for all of his days. Daniel lived to see the fall of Babylon to Cyrus the Great of Persia, but nothing is known about his life thereafter. His death is assumed to have occurred soon after 536 B.C.E., with his place of burial unknown. In Hebrew, the name Daniel means "God is my judge."

Date: It is not known whether the chapters in the Book of Daniel were recorded individually at the time they were revealed, as a collection of several chapters at a time, or perhaps even as one continuous work, although it is certain that all were written down after the author was carried to Babylon in the year 605 B.C.E. Of the visions and dreams interpreted in this book, the following chronology of Daniel is assumed: chapter 7 was written in the first year of King Belshazzar, *c.* 553 B.C.E., chapter 8 in the third year of King Belshazzar, *c.* 551 B.C.E., chapter 9 in the first year of Darius the Mede, son of Ahasuerus, *c.* 538 B.C.E., chapters 10-12 in the third year of King Cyrus of Persia, *c.* 536 B.C.E.

Language: Biblical Hebrew was used for Daniel, chapter 1, verse 1, through chapter 2, verse 3, and in chapter 8, verse 1, through chapter 12, verse 13. Aramaic, the *lingua franca* of the Mesopotamian region in the 6th century B.C.E., was used for Daniel, chapters 2, verse 4, through chapter 7, verse 28. No expositor has come up with a good explanation for Daniel's use of two languages to write his book.

---

[1] In the opinion of your author, the accuracy of the prophecies set forth in the Book of Daniel, when correctly interpreted and diligently compared to the historical record, gives ample testimony to the trustworthiness of the entire work.

Historical context: Daniel was born in the reign of King Josiah (*r.* 640-609 B.C.E.), who presided over a period of religious revival in the kingdom of Judah. Josiah restored the Temple and its priesthood to purity and re-instituted the festivals. This return to righteousness followed the extreme wickedness of King Manasseh (*r.* 697-642 B.C.E.), who had provoked God to say in 2 Kings, chapter 21, verses 10-15: *"Because Manasseh king of Judah hath done these abominations, and hath done wickedly above all that the Amorites did, which were before him, and hath made Judah also to sin with his idols: Therefore thus saith the Lord God of Israel, Behold, I am bringing such evil upon Jerusalem and Judah, that whosoever heareth of it, both his ears shall tingle. And I will stretch over Jerusalem the line of Samaria, and the plummet of the house of Ahab: and I will wipe Jerusalem as a man wipeth a dish, wiping it, and turning it upside down. And I will forsake the remnant of mine inheritance, and deliver them into the hand of their enemies; and they shall become a prey and a spoil to all their enemies; Because they have done that which was evil in my sight, and have provoked me to anger, since the day their fathers came forth out of Egypt, even unto this day"* (KJV). However, God was so pleased with Josiah that he promised him that he would not see the wrath to come. During Josiah's reign, Egypt was the great power to the south. To the north, the power of Assyria was on the wane and that of Babylon on the rise. In 609 B.C.E., Josiah, in an attempt to block an Egyptian army that was passing through his territory to aid their Assyrians allies, who were under attack by Babylon, was killed in battle. As a consequence, the countdown to judgement against Judah that God had paused during Josiah's lifetime was resumed. In 605 B.C.E., the Egyptians clashed with the Babylonians in the Battle of Carchemish. The Babylonians under Nebuchadnezzar were victorious. After the battle, Nebuchadnezzar moved south to capture and subjugate cities in Judah. It was at this time that Daniel and many Hebrew nobles were taken captive to Babylon, and Judah came under the Babylonian hegemony. In 597 B.C.E., after a short rebellion by King Jehoiachin of Judah, Nebuchadnezzar captured Jerusalem and led the king and the prophet Ezekiel, and many of the people, into exile in Babylon. Eleven years later, Nebuchadnezzar returned for a third time, capturing Jerusalem in August of 586 B.C.E. It was at this time that Solomon's Temple and the walls of Jerusalem were destroyed, and the rest of the people taken into captivity. During the seventy years of the Exile (605-536 B.C.E.), a new power arrived on the scene which would challenge the supremacy of Babylon. As predicted in Isaiah, chapter 44, verse 28, and chapter 45, verse 1, Cyrus the Great unified the Medes and Persians, and in 539 B.C.E. conquered Babylon as King of Persia. Cyrus was an enlightened ruler who tolerated and even encouraged retention of the customs and religions of conquered peoples and territories. Not too long after conquering Babylon, Cyrus decreed that the Jews should return to their ancestral lands in Judah and rebuild their Temple. The first Jews returned in 536 B.C.E. and began to rebuild Jerusalem and the Temple. Thus, the seventy years of Exile that had been predicted by the prophet Jeremiah came to an end. Prior to the return from Babylon, God had revealed to Daniel the history of the Jewish people from the end of the Exile until the end of days.

THE HEBREW CALENDAR
in Ancient Times

The earliest description of a calendar in the Bible is found in Genesis, chapter 1, verse 14: *"And God said, Let there be lights in the firmament of the heaven to divide the day from the night; and let them be for signs, and for seasons, and for days, and years"* (KJV). As this verse demonstrates, timekeeping was related to astronomy from the very beginning. Unfortunately, the Bible does not describe the actual calendar used by the ancients, so we can only guess about its structure and accuracy.

The first calendar component mentioned by name in the Bible is found in the Book of Exodus, when God commanded that the Passover be observed in the first month, which was called Abib. The early books of the Bible mention only four months by name: Abib, the first month in Exodus, chapter 12, verse 2 and chapter 13, verse 4; Zif, the second month in 1 Kings, chapter 6, verse 1; Ethanim, the seventh month in 1 Kings, chapter 8, verse 2; and Bul, the eighth month in 1 Kings, chapter 6, verse 38. From these mentions, it has been assumed that the early Hebrew calendar was a strict lunar calendar. There is evidence, however, that the movement of the sun was also taken into account by the early Hebrews. The *Gezer Calendar*, dating from the 10th century B.C.E., the earliest written example of a Hebrew calendar found so far, clearly shows a year of twelve months which are correlated with agricultural seasons (olive harvest, early grain planting, late grain planting, hoeing of flax, barley harvest, wheat harvest, *etc.*). This correlation of months to seasons confirms that the early Hebrew calendar was not exclusively lunar, but was instead lunisolar in practice, coordinated in some manner with the seasons as well as the movement of the moon, so as to keep the calendar aligned with the seasons year after year.

As can best be determined, the months in the Hebrew calendar, prior to the Exodus, alternated between lengths of 29 and 30 days as a way of averaging the months to take into account the actual length of the lunar month, which is approximately 29½ days. The resulting year was composed of 354 days. Since this 354-day lunar year was approximately eleven days shorter than the actual solar year of 365¼ days, an adjustment by calculation (probably a leap month added every three or four years, but the exact method is still unknown) was made to keep the seasons in synch with the sun. The Egyptians coped with the discrepancy between the lunar and solar year by adopting a civil calendar of twelve months, each month having 30 days, so as to make a year of 360 days, then they added five leap days at the beginning of each year to prevent calendar creep. The Hebrews may have followed this civil calendar for secular purposes while captive in Egypt, but there is no evidence that they ever used a calendar with a 360-day year for sacred purposes. Some expositors of biblical prophecy have postulated a 360-day "prophetic year" that they claim can be used for interpreting the chrono-specific prophecies in Daniel and other books of the Bible, but the Bible itself does not mention or support such a calendar system.

Until the Exodus, the basic components of the Hebrew calendar were all derived astronomically from physical observations of the heavens—the day from the rising and setting of the sun, the month from the crescent of the new moon, and the year from the equinoxes and solstices of the sun as they related to agricultural events. After the Exodus, the new nation of Israel was given a non-astronomical time unit to add to its basic system. God gave them the sabbath (seventh) day to observe as a reminder of their deliverance from bondage, as recorded in Deuteronomy, chapter 5, verses 12-15: *"Keep the sabbath day to sanctify it, as the Lord thy God hath commanded thee. Six days thou shalt labour, and do all thy work: But the seventh day is the sabbath of the Lord thy God: in it thou shalt not do any work, thou, nor thy son, nor thy daughter, nor thy manservant, nor thy maidservant, nor thine ox, nor thine ass, nor any of thy cattle, nor thy stranger that is within thy gates; that thy manservant and thy maidservant may rest as well as thou. And remember that thou wast a servant in the land of Egypt, and that the Lord thy God brought thee out thence through a mighty hand and by a stretched out arm: therefore the Lord thy God commanded thee to keep the sabbath day"* (KJV). Thus, the seven-day week became a unit of time.

In addition to the sabbath day and week, a sabbath year and a jubilee year were added to the calendar by Moses, as well as a system of festivals and religious days to be observed throughout the year. The Jewish new year was originally celebrated in the first month, as God had commanded, but when Israel became a kingdom there is evidence that a civil year was instituted with its new year observed in the seventh month. In later times, the religious and civil new years were combined into one Jewish new-year observance on the first day of the seventh month. Other changes were to happen over time as well. The Exile in Babylon that began in 605 B.C.E. resulted in major changes to the Hebrew calendar. The most obvious change was that the names of the Babylonian months were adopted, and those names are still being used today. The first month Abib became Nisan, the seventh month Ethanim became Tishri, and so on (see list of names of Jewish months on the sabbath-jubilee diagram on page 97). More important for accuracy, the 19-year cycle of calendar synchronization (later called the Metonic cycle), with its schedule for adding leap months to seven specified years in every nineteen-year cycle, became standard, and it is reflected in the chronology of the Book of Daniel.

The ancient Hebrew calendar had a high degree of accuracy. Before 70 C.E., it was based on priestly observations from Jerusalem, the sighting of the new moon being the most important event. After the Temple priesthood ceased to function, the calendar was maintained by rabbis in various locations. Since observations from the Temple were no longer possible, and since the Jewish people were becoming so widely dispersed that timely dissemination of calendar information was impossible from one central location, a new Hebrew calendar, one based solely on calculations, was developed by Rabbi Hillel II in the 4th century C.E. A derivative of that calendar is still being used by many Jews today.

∞

CALENDAR OF SABBATH AND JUBILEE YEARS

God commanded the Israelites to begin observing sabbath and jubilee years once they had entered the promised land of Canaan. The instructions are recorded in Leviticus, chapter 25. The observance of the first sabbath year began in the year 1,388 B.C.E., and the observance of the first jubilee year began in the year 1,346 B.C.E. In the sabbath and jubilee tables in this section, sabbath years begin in the spring, on the 1st of Nisan, and extend until the next 1st of Nisan, whereas jubilee years begin in the fall, on the 10th of Tishri in the forty-ninth year of a 49-year cycle, and continue until the 10th of Tishri in the first year of the next 49-year cycle. Thus, the jubilee year is not a separate year unto itself, but overlaps the last months of one 49-year cycle and the first months in the next 49-year cycle, as follows:

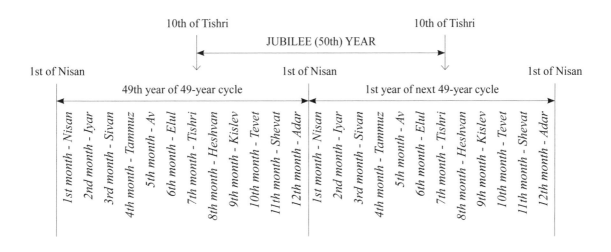

Sabbath and Jubilee Years from 1,602 C.E. to 2,037 C.E.

(year to right indicates starting year)

Jubilee Year	7th Sabbath	6th Sabbath	5th Sabbath	4th Sabbath	3rd Sabbath	2nd Sabbath	1st Sabbath
2037/2036	2037/2036	2030/2029	2023/2022	2016/2015	2009/2008	2002/2001	1995/1994
1988/1987	1988/1987	1981/1980	1974/1973	1967/1966	1960/1959	1953/1952	1946/1945
1939/1938	1939/1938	1932/1931	1925/1924	1918/1917	1911/1910	1904/1903	1897/1896
1890/1889	1890/1889	1883/1882	1876/1875	1869/1868	1862/1861	1855/1854	1848/1847
1841/1840	1841/1840	1834/1833	1827/1826	1820/1819	1813/1812	1806/1805	1799/1798
1792/1791	1792/1791	1785/1784	1778/1777	1771/1770	1764/1763	1757/1756	1750/1749
1743/1742	1743/1742	1736/1735	1729/1728	1722/1721	1715/1714	1708/1707	1701/1700
1694/1693	1694/1693	1687/1686	1680/1679	1673/1672	1666/1665	1659/1658	1652/1651
1645/1644	1645/1644	1638/1637	1631/1630	1624/1623	1617/1616	1610/1609	1603/1602

Sabbath and Jubilee Years from 1 C.E. to 1,596 C.E.

(year to right indicates starting year)

Jubilee Year	7th Sabbath	6th Sabbath	5th Sabbath	4th Sabbath	3rd Sabbath	2nd Sabbath	1st Sabbath
1596/1595	1596/1595	1589/1588	1582/1581	1575/1574	1568/1567	1561/1560	1554/1553
1547/1546	1547/1546	1540/1539	1533/1532	1526/1525	1519/1518	1512/1511	1505/1504
1498/1497	1498/1497	1491/1490	1484/1483	1477/1476	1470/1469	1463/1462	1456/1455
1449/1448	1449/1448	1442/1441	1435/1434	1428/1427	1421/1420	1414/1413	1407/1406
1400/1399	1400/1399	1393/1392	1386/1385	1379/1378	1372/1371	1365/1364	1358/1357
1351/1350	1351/1350	1344/1343	1337/1336	1330/1329	1323/1322	1316/1315	1309/1308
1302/1301	1302/1301	1295/1294	1288/1287	1281/1280	1274/1273	1267/1266	1260/1259
1253/1252	1253/1252	1246/1245	1239/1238	1232/1231	1225/1224	1218/1217	1211/1210
1204/1203	1204/1203	1197/1196	1190/1189	1183/1182	1176/1175	1169/1168	1162/1161
1155/1154	1155/1154	1148/1147	1141/1140	1134/1133	1127/1126	1120/1119	1113/1112
1106/1105	1106/1105	1099/1098	1092/1091	1085/1084	1078/1077	1071/1069	1064/1063
1057/1056	1057/1056	1050/1049	1043/1042	1036/1035	1029/1028	1022/1021	1015/1014
1008/1007	1008/1007	1001/1000	994/993	987/986	980/979	973/972	966/965
959/958	959/958	952/951	945/944	938/937	931/930	924/923	917/916
910/909	910/909	903/902	896/895	889/888	882/881	875/874	868/867
861/860	861/860	854/853	847/846	840/839	833/832	826/825	819/818
812/811	812/811	805/804	798/797	791/790	784/783	777/776	770/769
763/762	763/762	756/755	749/748	742/741	735/734	728/727	721/720
714/713	714/713	707/706	700/699	693/692	686/685	679/678	672/671
665/664	665/664	658/657	651/650	644/643	637/636	630/629	623/622
616/615	616/615	609/608	602/601	595/594	588/587	581/580	574/573
567/566	567/566	560/559	553/552	546/545	539/538	532/531	525/524
518/517	518/517	511/510	504/503	497/496	490/489	483/482	476/475
469/468	469/468	462/461	455/454	448/447	441/440	434/433	427/426
420/419	420/419	413/412	406/405	399/398	392/391	385/384	378/377
371/370	371/370	364/363	357/356	350/349	343/342	336/335	329/328
322/321	322/321	315/314	308/307	301/300	294/293	287/286	280/279
273/272	273/272	266/265	259/258	252/251	245/244	238/237	231/230
224/223	224/223	217/216	210/209	203/202	196/195	189/188	182/181
175/174	175/174	168/167	161/160	154/153	147/146	140/139	133/132
126/125	126/125	119/118	112/111	105/104	98/97	92/91	85/84
77/76	77/76	70/69	63/62	56/55	49/48	42/41	35/34
28/27	28/27	21/20	14/13	7/6	---	---	---

Sabbath and Jubilee Years from 1 B.C.E. to 1,388 B.C.E.

(year to right indicates starting year)

Jubilee Year	7th Sabbath	6th Sabbath	5th Sabbath	4th Sabbath	3rd Sabbath	2nd Sabbath	1st Sabbath
- - -	- - -	- - -	- - -	- - -	1 /2	8/9	15/16
22/23	22/23	29/30	36/37	43/44	50/51	57/58	64/65
71/72	72/73	79/80	86/87	93/94	100/101	107/108	114/115
120/121	120/121	127/128	134/135	141/142	148/149	155/156	162/163
169/170	169/170	176/177	183/184	190/191	197/198	204/205	211/212
218/219	218/219	225/226	232/233	239/240	246/247	253/254	260/261
267/268	267/268	274/275	281/282	288/289	295/296	302/303	309/310
316/317	316/317	323/324	330/331	337/338	344/345	351/352	358/359
365/366	365/366	372/373	379/380	386/387	393/394	400/401	407/408
414/415	414/415	421/422	428/429	435/436	442/443	449/450	456/457
463/464	463/464	470/471	477/478	484/485	491/492	498/499	505/506
512/513	512/513	519/520	526/527	533/534	540/541	547/548	554/555
561/562	561/562	568/569	575/576	582/583	589/590	596/597	603/604
610/611	610/611	617/618	624/625	631/632	638/639	645/646	652/653
659/660	659/660	666/667	673/674	680/681	687/688	694/695	701/702
708/709	708/709	715/716	722/723	729/730	736/737	743/744	750/751
757/758	757/758	764/765	771/772	778/779	785/786	792/793	799/800
806/807	806/807	813/814	820/821	827/828	834/835	841/842	848/849
855/856	855/856	862/863	869/870	876/877	883/884	890/891	897/898
904/905	904/905	911/912	918/919	925/926	932/933	939/940	946/947
953/954	953/954	960/963	967/968	974/975	981/982	988/989	995/996
1002/1003	1002/1003	1009/1010	1016/1017	1023/1024	1030/1031	1037/1038	1044/1045
1051/1052	1051/1052	1058/1059	1065/1066	1072/1073	1079/1080	1086/1087	1093/1094
1100/1101	1100/1101	1107/1108	1114/1115	1121/1122	1128/1129	1135/1136	1142/1143
1149/1150	1149/1150	1156/1157	1163/1164	1170/1171	1177/1178	1184/1185	1191/1192
1198/1199	1198/1199	1205/1206	1212/1213	1219/1220	1226/1227	1233/1234	1240/1241
1247/1248	1247/1248	1254/1255	1261/1262	1268/1269	1275/1276	1282/1283	1289/1290
1296/1297	1296/1297	1303/1304	1310/1311	1317/1318	1323/1324	1331/1332	1338/1339
1345/1346	1345/1346	1352/1353	1359/1360	1366/1367	1373/1374	1380/1381	1387/1388

In the table for years B.C.E. above, note that the year that started the sabbath cycle in the land of Canaan, 1393/1394 B.C.E., and the next five years in that first sabbath cycle after the land was settled (1392/1393 B.C.E., 1391/1392 B.C.E., 1390/1391 B.C.E., 1389/1390 B.C.E., 1388/1389 B.C.E.) are not shown. Also, note that there was no year "0" (zero) when going from years B.C.E. on this chart to years C.E. on the chart on the opposite page; the year 1 B.C.E. is followed by the year 1 C.E. as time moves forward in history.

Using the Sabbath and Jubilee Tables

The sabbath and jubilee tables for the years 1,388 B.C.E. to 2,037 C.E. on the three preceding pages were generated by identifying the year 954/953 B.C.E. as the jubilee year Solomon used for dedication of his Temple (see discussion on page 64). The accuracy of the data was confirmed by its alignment with the year 27/28 C.E., which was proclaimed as a jubilee year by Jesus in the Gospel of Luke, chapter 4, verses 18-19. The sabbath and jubilee tables can sometimes be used to help interpret and/or validate other chronological data in the Bible. A good example of such use can be demonstrated by applying the tables to resolve the conflict in the chronology of the reign of Hezekiah, king of Judah.

Example 1 - The Reign of Hezekiah: The details of his reign are set forth in 2 Kings, chapters 18-20; 2 Chronicles, chapters 29-32; and Isaiah, chapters 36-39. Traditional interpretation assumes that the "sign," described in Isaiah, chapter 37, verse 30, *"And this shall be a sign unto thee, Ye shall eat this year such as groweth of itself; and the second year that which springeth of the same: and in the third year sow ye, and reap, and plant vineyards, and eat the fruit thereof"* (KJV), was a sabbath-jubilee observance during which no crops were harvested for two years, followed by a third year in which crops were harvested. It is also assumed that the observance of that two-year sabbath-jubilee cycle coincided with the invasion of Judah by Sennecherib of Assyria, which the Bible says took place in Hezekiah's fourteenth year. Since the invasion can be pinpointed to the year 701 B.C.E. from the Assyrian *limmu* list, which is anchored precisely in time by the solar eclipse that took place on June 15, 763 B.C.E., Hezekiah seemingly had to begin his reign fourteen years earlier in the year 715 B.C.E. However, the Bible states that Hezekiah began his reign in the third year of the reign of Hoshea, king of Israel, which can be identified as the year 729 B.C.E. Obviously, something is wrong with the traditional interpretation. Fortunately, this is where having accurate tables of sabbath and jubilee years comes in handy. The tables show that the jubilee year during the reign of Hezekiah began in the year 709 B.C.E., not in the year 701 B.C.E. as is traditionally assumed. That discrepancy means that there has to be another explanation besides the sabbath-jubilee cycle for why there would have been two successive years without crops, and there is. From the tables, it can be seen that the year preceding the invasion, namely 702 B.C.E., was a sabbath year. That sabbath year can be assumed to account for the first "no crop" year in the three-year-long "sign" about no-crop and harvest years given to Hezekiah by God. The following year, 701 B.C.E., was a year with no crops because the invasion of Judah by Sennecherib and his Assyrian army would have prevented both planting and harvesting from being carried out normally that year. The third year was to be a normal harvest year, which meant that Sennecherib had to be neutralized so that crops could be planted, and that is what happened. God sent an angel to destroy the Assyrians surrounding Jerusalem. Overnight, 185,000 Assyrians were killed, whereupon Sennecherib packed up and went home. After two years with no crops, the land was at peace in the third year, and crops were planted and harvested. The "sign" given to Hezekiah was fulfilled exactly as promised. But,

Chronology of King Hezekiah's Reign

Year B.C.E.		*King Hezekiah of Judah* *(Tishri to Tishri regnal years)*	*King Hoshea of Israel* *(Nisan to Nisan regnal years)*
729	Hezekiah becomes king (729/728) – – – – →		
728		Accession Year – – – – – – – →	3rd year of Hoshea
727	Temple sanctified (first month) – – – – → Passover celebrated (second month)	1st year of reign	
726		2nd year of reign	
725		3rd year of reign	
724	Siege of Samaria begins – – – – – – – –	4th year of reign – – – – – –	7th year of Hoshea
723		5th year of reign	
722	Fall of Samaria to Assyria – – – – – – –	6th year of reign – – – – – – →	9th year of Hoshea
721		7th year of reign	
720		8th year of reign	
719		9th year of reign	
718		10th year of reign	
717		11th year of reign	
716		12th year of reign	
715	Hezekiah's illness – – – – – – – – – –	13th year of reign	*Hezekiah's extra 15 years*
714		14th year of reign	1st extra year
713		15th year of reign	2nd extra year
712	*b.* Manasseh, Hezekiah's son	16th year of reign	3rd extra year
711		17th year of reign	4th extra year
710		18th year of reign	5th extra year
709	Sabbath and Jubilee year (709/708) *(observance not mentioned in Scripture)*	19th year of reign	6th extra year
708		20th year of reign	7th extra year
707		21st year of reign	8th extra year
706		22nd year of reign	9th extra year
705		23rd year of reign	10th extra year
704		24th year of reign	11th extra year
703		25th year of reign	12th extra year
702	Sabbath year (702/701) - ***1st year, no crops***	26th year of reign	13th extra year
701	Sennecherib's invasion - ***2nd year, no crops*** –	27th year of reign – – – – – →	14th extra year
700	Hezekiah's Sign - ***3rd year, crops harvested*** *d.* Hezekiah – – – – – – – – – – –	28th year of reign	15th extra year
		29th year of reign	

this explanation creates another chronological problem. If Hezekiah began his reign in 729 B.C.E. and was invaded by Sennecherib twenty-eight years later in 701 B.C.E., how could the invasion have taken place in the fourteenth year of Hezekiah's reign? This apparent conflict is easy to explain. The Masoretic Text does not say *fourteenth year of reign*. It says only that Sennecherib invaded in the *fourteenth year* of Hezekiah. Remember, God had previously extended Hezekiah's life by fifteen years. The invasion of Sennecherib came in the fourteenth year of the fifteen-year extension, not in the fourteenth year of his reign. The chronology of the reign of Hezekiah can thus be reconciled to incorporate all of the data given in the Bible, as shown on the previous page.

Example 2 - The Year of the Exodus: The year of the Exodus can be calculated from the chronological information given in 1 Kings, chapter 6, verse 1, *"And it came to pass in the four hundred and eightieth year after the children of Israel were come out of the land of Egypt, in the fourth year of Solomon's reign over Israel, in the month Zif, which is the second month, that he began to build the house of the Lord"* (KJV), and then verified by using the sabbath and jubilee tables as a crosscheck. Applying the definition of a "time" (228 years, which was defined in Chapter Three, see page 25) to the "seven times" in Daniel, chapter 4, the fourth year of King Solomon's reign can be calculated to have been the year 961 B.C.E., as shown on Diagram 6.1 on page 65. Adding 480 years to that date gives the year 1,441 B.C.E. as the date of the Exodus from Egypt. *Crosschecking the Result:* Using the year from the table denoting the observance of the first sabbath year, 1,388 B.C.E., calculate backwards seven years to find the year when the land was first at rest and the sabbath-jubilee count began:

> 7th year in the first sabbath cycle was ... 1,388 B.C.E.
>
> 6th year in the first sabbath cycle was ... 1,389 B.C.E.
>
> 5th year in the first sabbath cycle was ... 1,390 B.C.E.
>
> 4th year in the first sabbath cycle was ... 1,391 B.C.E.
>
> 3rd year in the first sabbath cycle was ... 1,392 B.C.E.
>
> 2nd year in the first sabbath cycle was ... 1,393 B.C.E.
>
> 1st year in the first sabbath cycle was ... 1,394 B.C.E = the year when land was first at rest.

In the year when the land was first at rest, Caleb was eighty-five years old according to Joshua, chapter 14, verses 7-10, and forty years old when he was sent by Moses from Kadesh-Barnea into the land of Canaan as a spy. That means there were forty-five years from the first year in the sabbath cycle back to the time the spies were sent forth, which takes us back to the year 1,394 B.C.E. + 45 years = 1,439 B.C.E. Then, from Numbers, chapter 1, verse 1, it can be seen that the spies were sent into Canaan sometime late in the second year after leaving Egypt, so two more years can be added to the 1,439 B.C.E. date on which the spies were sent, yielding the year 1,441 B.C.E. as the date of the Exodus. This result matches the year of the Exodus derived from the calculation based on the year Solomon started building the Temple.

∽

COMPLEMENTARY CHRONOLOGY
in the Book of Ezekiel

An important chrono-specific prophecy is set forth in Ezekiel, chapter 4, verses 5-6: *"Also for your part lie on your left side and place the iniquity of the house of Israel on it. For the number of days you lie on your side you will bear their iniquity. I have determined that the number of the years of their iniquity are to be the number of days for you, 390 days. So bear the iniquity of the house of Israel. When you have completed these days, then lie down a second time, but on your right side, and bear the iniquity of the house of Judah 40 days. I have assigned one day for each year"* (KJV). This prophecy specifies a period of 430 days during which the prophet Ezekiel was to bear the iniquity of Israel and Judah by laying on his right and left sides, a task that represented a "siege of Jerusalem" that would last for a period of 430 years. Since Ezekiel usually dated events from the time when King Jehoiachin was taken into exile,[1] it seemed logical to me that the count for the 430 years would use the same starting point. Thus, it was necessary to identify the year when the exile of Jehoiachin began so as to correctly interpret the prophecy.

Ezekiel gives chronological clues that help determine the year of Jehoiachin's exile. In chapter 40, verse 1, he writes: *"In the five and twentieth year of our captivity, in the beginning of the year ... in the fourteenth year after that the city was smitten"* (KJV). This equates the twenty-fifth year of the exile of Jehoiachin with the fourteenth year after the destruction of Jerusalem, which was destroyed on August 14, 586 B.C.E.[2] Since Jewish years at the time of Ezekiel were reckoned from the first month of the year in accordance with the command given in Exodus 12, verse 2, *"This month* [Nisan, the month of the Passover] *shall be unto you the beginning of months: it shall be the first month of the year to you"* (KJV), the observance of the Passover was a way of keeping track of the passage of years, as demonstrated in Daniel, chapter 8, verses 13-14. This method of using Passovers to keep track of years seems to apply to the chronological references in Ezekiel as well. Thus, Ezekiel's reference to the "fourteenth year" after the destruction of Jerusalem in chapter 40, verse 1, would mean that fourteen Passovers had occurred after that event, and his reference to the "twenty-fifth year" after the beginning of the exile of Jehoiachin would mean that twenty-five Passovers had occurred after that event.

Table A (on next page) demonstrates how the Passovers that indicate the passage of years in Ezekiel, chapter 40, verse 1, should be counted. Each Passover in the table is denoted as "P#" (where "#" is its number in the count), followed by its corresponding Gregorian year. The table should be read backwards, starting with the cell on the bottom row labeled "Ezekiel 40:1," representing the time when Ezekiel

---

[1] See examples of such dating in Ezekiel 1:2; 8:1; 20:1; 24:1; 26:1; 29:1, 17; 30:20; 31:1; 32:1, 17; 33:21; 40:1.
[2] Jack Finegan, *Handbook of Biblical Chronology* (Peabody, Massachusetts: Hendrickson Publishers, Inc., 1998), *p.* 259.

wrote that verse. The cell labeled "Jerusalem," representing the date of the destruction of Jerusalem, August 14, 586 B.C.E., is reached by counting back fourteen Passovers (P1-P14). Counting back eleven more Passovers (P15-P25) reveals that the twenty-fifth Passover occurred in the year 596 B.C.E.

Table A - How to count the Passovers in Ezekiel 40:1									
Begin Exile	P25 - 596 B.C.E.	P24 - 595 B.C.E.	P23 - 594 B.C.E.	P22 - 593 B.C.E.	P21 - 592 B.C.E.	P20 - 591 B.C.E.	P19 - 590 B.C.E.	P18 - 589 B.C.E.	P17 - 588 B.C.E.
P16 - 587 B.C.E.	P15 - 586 B.C.E.	Jerusalem	P14 - 585 B.C.E.	P13 - 584 B.C.E.	P12 - 583 B.C.E.	P11 - 582 B.C.E.	P10 - 581 B.C.E.	P9 - 580 B.C.E.	P8 - 579 B.C.E.
P7 - 578 B.C.E.	P6 - 577 B.C.E.	P5 - 576 B.C.E.	P4 - 575 B.C.E.	P3 - 574 B.C.E.	P2 - 573 B.C.E.	P1 - 572 B.C.E.	Ezekiel 40:1	- - -	- - -

As the above table shows,[1] the exile of Jehoiachin had to begin **before** the Passover in 596 B.C.E. It also had to happen **after** the surrender of Jerusalem on March 16, 597 B.C.E., which the Babylonian Chronicle (on British Museum tablet number 21946) records as occurring on the second day of the month Addaru, just before the new year began. Adding yet another clue, II Chronicles, chapter 36, verse 10, says that Jehoiachin was ordered brought to Babylon *"when the year was expired"* (KJV), just after the new year had begun. These time constraints indicate that Jehoiachin was exiled sometime after the Passover in 597 B.C.E. So, now that the time of the exile has been identified, the 430 Passovers can be counted to reveal the time span specified in Ezekiel, chapter 4, verses 5-6. Table B (below) demonstrates how to count the Passovers. Note that the count begins with the Passover in 596 B.C.E., the first Passover after the arrival of Jehoiachin in Babylon. Each Passover in the table is denoted as "P#" (where "#" is its number in the count), followed by its corresponding Gregorian year. After the initial ten Passovers (P1 through P10), which are shown on the top line, Passovers are shown in ten-year increments (so that you can verify the count on your fingers). The final year is revealed as 167 B.C.E.

Table B - How to count the 430 Passovers in Ezekiel 4:5-6									
P1 - 596 B.C.E.	P2 - 595 B.C.E.	P3 - 594 B.C.E.	P4 - 593 B.C.E.	P5 - 592 B.C.E.	P6 - 591 B.C.E.	P7 - 590 B.C.E.	P8 - 589 B.C.E.	P9 - 588 B.C.E.	P10 - 587 B.C.E.
1-10 see above	P20 - 577 B.C.E.	P30 - 567 B.C.E.	P40 - 557 B.C.E.	P50 - 547 B.C.E.	P60 - 537 B.C.E.	P70 - 527 B.C.E.	P80 - 517 B.C.E.	P90 -507 B.C.E.	P100 - 497 B.C.E.
P110 - 487 B.C.E.	P120 - 477 B.C.E.	P130 - 467 B.C.E.	P140 - 457 B.C.E.	P150 - 447 B.C.E.	P160 - 437 B.C.E.	P170 - 427 B.C.E.	P180 - 417 B.C.E.	P190 - 407 B.C.E.	P200 - 397 B.C.E.
P210 - 387 B.C.E.	P220 - 377 B.C.E.	P230 - 367B.C.E.	P240 - 357 B.C.E.	P250 - 347 B.C.E.	P260 - 337 B.C.E.	P270 - 327 B.C.E.	P280 - 317 B.C.E.	P290 - 307 B.C.E.	P300 - 297 B.C.E.
P310 - 287 B.C.E.	P320 - 277 B.C.E.	P330 - 267 B.C.E.	P340 - 257 B.C.E.	P350 - 247 B.C.E.	P360 - 237 B.C.E.	P370 - 227 B.C.E.	P380 - 217 B.C.E.	P390 - 207 B.C.E.	P400 - 197 B.C.E.
P410 - 187 B.C.E.	P420 - 177 B.C.E.	P430 - 167 B.C.E.	- - -	- - -	- - -	- - -	- - -	- - -	- - -

---

[1] Table A can also be used to interpret the reference to *"the thirtieth year"* (KJV) in Ezekiel, chapter 1, verses 1-2, noting that verse 2 equates the thirtieth year with the fifth year of Jehoiachin's captivity. The fifth year of Jehoiachin's captivity is the year that falls between the Passovers of 593 B.C.E. and 592 B.C.E. (denoted as "P21" in the table). The thirtieth year back from there would be the year bounded by the Passovers in 622 B.C.E. and 621 B.C.E. This indicates that Ezekiel counted the thirty years in verses 1-2 from the Great Passover celebrated by King Josiah of Judah in 622 B.C.E. (see II Kings 22:8, 23:1-23).

THE MODERN NATION OF ISRAEL
Is it Biblical?

The modern nation of Israel and how it came into being is a remarkable story. That story began in earnest in the year 1897, when the first Zionist Congress was convened in Basel, Switzerland, with the announced purpose of achieving a political homeland in Palestine for the Jewish people. The Zionist movement immediately gained traction and several attempts to create a Jewish homeland were proposed, the most famous being the 1903 proposal by Great Britain offering land for a Jewish state in Uganda in East Africa, a proposal rejected by Jewish leaders. In 1917, the focus turned back to the Middle East when Great Britain, which had captured Palestine from the Ottomans, issued the Balfour Declaration favoring a homeland there (see page 113). Five years later, the League of Nations endorsed the idea of a Jewish homeland in Palestine by passing the Mandate of 1922, and made Great Britain the administrator of the mandated territory (see page 114). After WWII, when the horror of the Holocaust once again focused world attention on the need for a Jewish homeland, the United Nations passed Resolution 181 in 1947, partitioning Palestine between Arabs and Jews (see page 117). The Arabs rejected the resolution, but, when the mandate expired on May 14, 1948, the Jews in Palestine proclaimed the modern nation of Israel (see page 128). Two years later, in 1950, the Knesset (Israel's parliament) passed the Law of Return (see page 130) which, for all practical purposes, brought to an end the involuntary *Diaspora* of Jews among the nations of the world that had begun with the Roman destruction of Judea in 70 C.E. Henceforth, any Jewish person living in any nation could come to the new nation of Israel and find a haven in their ancient ancestral homeland. Still, the meaning of this modern-day Jewish rebirth was questioned by many people, who asked: Is the modern ingathering of Jews to *Eretz-Israel* a fulfillment of Bible prophecy, or is it just a remarkable secular phenomenon with no biblical basis?

The Patriarchal Covenants

To understand any biblical reference to the modern nation of Israel, the foundational promises and covenants made by God to the patriarchs must be understood. The first promise God gave to Abram in Ur of the Chaldees is recorded in Genesis, chapter 12, verses 1-3: *"Now the Lord had said unto Abram, Get thee out of thy country, and from thy kindred, and from thy father's house, unto a land that I will shew thee: And I will make of thee a great nation, and I will bless thee, and make thy name great; and thou shalt be a blessing: And I will bless them that bless thee, and curse him that curseth thee: and in thee shall all families of the earth be blessed"* (KJV). Abram obeyed God, left Ur, and traveled to the land of Canaan, where he remained until famine forced him to seek food in Egypt. When conditions improved, Abram returned to the land of Canaan, where God renewed the promises, as recorded in Genesis, chapter 13, verses 14-15: *"And the Lord said unto Abram, ... , Lift up now thine eyes, and look from the place where thou art northward, and southward, and eastward, and westward: For all the land which thou seest, to thee will I give it, and to thy seed for ever"* (KJV). God confirmed his promises by making a covenant with Abram, as recorded in Genesis, chapter 15, verses 1-18: *"After these things the word of the Lord came unto Abram in a vision, saying, Fear not, Abram: I am thy shield, and thy exceeding great reward. And Abram said, Lord God, what wilt thou give me, seeing I go childless, and the steward of my house is this Eliezer of Damascus? And Abram said, Behold, to me thou hast given no seed: and, lo, one born in my house is mine heir. And, behold, the word of the Lord came unto him, saying, This shall not be thine heir; but he that shall come forth out of thine own bowels shall be thine heir. And he brought him forth abroad, and said, Look now toward heaven, and tell the stars, if thou be able to number them: and he said unto him, So shall thy seed be. And he believed in the Lord; and he counted it to him for righteousness. And he said unto him, I am the Lord that brought thee out of Ur of the Chaldees, to give thee this land to inherit it. And he said, Lord God, whereby shall I know that I shall inherit it? And he said unto him, Take me an heifer of three years old, and a she goat of three years old, and a ram of three years old, and a turtledove, and a young pigeon. And he took unto him all these, and divided them in the midst, and laid each piece one against another: but the birds divided he not. And when the fowls came down upon the carcases, Abram drove them away. And when the sun was going down, a deep sleep fell upon Abram; and, lo, an horror of great darkness fell upon him. And he said unto Abram, Know of a surety that thy seed shall be a stranger in a land that is not theirs, and shall serve them; and they shall afflict them four hundred years; And also that nation, whom they shall serve, will I judge: and afterward shall they come out with great substance. And thou shalt go to thy fathers in peace; thou shalt be buried in a good old age. But in the fourth generation they shall come hither again: for the iniquity of the Amorites is not yet full. And it came to pass, that, when the sun went down, and it was dark, behold a smoking furnace, and a burning lamp that passed between those pieces. In the same day the Lord made a covenant with Abram, saying, Unto thy seed have I given this land, from the river of Egypt unto the great river, the river Euphrates"* (KJV).

Some years later, God reiterated his covenant with Abraham, and designated that the blessings of the covenant would apply to future generations through Abraham's seed (descendants), as recorded in Genesis, chapter 17, verses 1-13, : *"And when Abram was ninety years old and nine, the Lord appeared to Abram, and said unto him, I am the Almighty God; walk before me, and be thou perfect. And I will make my covenant between me and thee, and will multiply thee exceedingly. And Abram fell on his face: and God talked with him, saying, As for me, behold, my covenant is with thee, and thou shalt be a father of many nations. Neither shall thy name any more be called Abram, but thy name shall be Abraham; for a father of many nations have I made thee. And I will make thee exceeding fruitful, and I will make nations of thee, and kings shall come out of thee. And I will establish my covenant between me and thee and thy seed after thee in their generations for an everlasting covenant, to be a God unto thee, and to thy seed after thee. And I will give unto thee, and to thy seed after thee, the land wherein thou art a stranger, all the land of Canaan, for an everlasting possession; and I will be their God. And God said unto Abraham, Thou shalt keep my covenant therefore, thou, and thy seed after thee in their generations. This is my covenant, which ye shall keep, between me and you and thy seed after thee; Every man child among you shall be circumcised. And ye shall circumcise the flesh of your foreskin; and it shall be a token of the covenant betwixt me and you ... and my covenant shall be in your flesh for an everlasting covenant"* (KJV).

After Abraham died, the blessings of the covenant God had made with him were passed on and confirmed to Isaac, the "seed of Abraham" designated by God, as recorded in Genesis, chapter 26, verses 1-5. Then, just prior his death, Isaac confirmed the blessings of the Abrahamic covenant to his son Jacob, as recorded in Genesis, chapter 28, verses 1-4. However, because he had obtained the blessing through deceit, fooling his father Isaac to give him the blessing that should have gone to his older brother Esau, Jacob was forced by fear of retribution to avoid the wrath of his brother by fleeing from the promised covenant land of Canaan. As he was leaving, Jacob had a dream at Bethel in which God gave him assurances that the covenant would still be still binding, as recorded in Genesis, chapter 28, verses 10-15: *"And Jacob went out from Beer-sheba, and went toward Haran. And he lighted upon a certain place, and tarried there all night, because the sun was set; and he took of the stones of that place, and put them for his pillows, and lay down in that place to sleep. And he dreamed, and behold a ladder set up on the earth, and the top of it reached to heaven: and behold the angels of God ascending and descending on it. And, behold, the Lord stood above it, and said, I am the Lord God of Abraham thy father, and the God of Isaac: the land whereon thou liest, to thee will I give it, and to thy seed; And thy seed shall be as the dust of the earth, and thou shalt spread abroad to the west, and to the east, and to the north, and to the south: and in thee and in thy seed shall all the families of the earth be blessed. And, behold, I am with thee, and will keep thee in all places whither thou goest, and will bring thee again into this land; for I will not leave thee, until I have done that which I have spoken to thee of"* (KJV). On his return to the land of Canaan twenty years later, Jacob was met once again by God, who reminded him of the covenant, as recorded in Genesis, chapter 35, verses 9-15: *"And God appeared unto Jacob again, when he came out of Padan-aram, and blessed him. And God said unto him, Thy name is Jacob: thy name shall not be called any more Jacob, but Israel shall be thy name: and he called his name Israel. And God said unto him, I am God Almighty: be fruitful and multiply; a nation and a company of nations shall be of thee, and kings shall come out of thy loins; And the land which I gave Abraham and Isaac, to thee I will give it, and to thy seed after thee will I give the land. And God went up from him in the place where he talked with him. And Jacob set up a pillar in the place where he talked with him, even a pillar of stone: and he poured a drink offering thereon, and he poured oil thereon. And Jacob called the name of the place where God spake with him, Bethel"* (KJV). Thus, Jacob became Israel, and his descendants would become the Children of Israel, rightful heirs to the covenant promises of land and nationhood made by God to their fathers.

The National Covenant

Jacob and his family prospered in the land of Canaan until a famine caused all of them to seek relief in Egypt, as their father Abraham had done in a previous time of famine. There the Israelites grew into a multitude so numerous that the Egyptians began to fear them. Eventually they enslaved them. Then, after four-hundred years of affliction at the hand of the Egyptians, as God had told Abraham would happen, God called Moses to lead the Children of Israel out of Egypt and into the desert of the Sinai, where he would make them into a nation. The Book of Exodus recounts the story of Israel's deliverance and its call to be God's chosen people at Mount Horeb, as recorded in Exodus, chapter 19, verses 1-8: *"In the third month, when the children of Israel were gone forth out of the land of Egypt, the same day came they into the wilderness of Sinai. For they were departed from Rephidim, and were come to the desert of Sinai, and had pitched in the wilderness; and there Israel camped before the mount. And Moses went up unto God, and the Lord called unto him out of the mountain, saying, Thus shalt thou say to the house of Jacob, and tell the children of Israel; Ye have seen what I did unto the Egyptians, and how I bare you on eagles' wings, and brought you unto myself. Now therefore, if ye will obey my voice indeed, and keep my covenant, then ye shall be a peculiar treasure unto me above all people: for all the earth is mine: And ye shall be unto me a kingdom of priests, and an holy nation. These are the words which thou shalt speak unto the children of Israel. And Moses came and called for the elders of the people, and laid before their faces all these words which the Lord commanded him. And all the people answered together, and said, All that the Lord hath spoken we will do. And Moses returned the words of the people unto the Lord"* (KJV).

Unlike the covenant with Abraham, Isaac, and Jacob, the national covenant with the Children of Israel was conditional. It required that they do something, namely, that they obey God's voice and keep his covenant. To achieve this end, God gave them *Torah* with its commandments and teachings, the Tabernacle with its high priest who had access to Urim and Thummin,[1] and later the judges and prophets. Unfortunately, when it came time to go up to possess the promised land of Canaan, the Children of Israel who had come out of Egypt were overcome by fear. God judged their lack of faith harshly, decreeing that they would not see the promised land. All except Joshua and Caleb, who were spared because of their faith, died during the next forty years of wandering in the wilderness while God raised up a new generation that would go in to possess the land in faith. In Moab, just before they crossed the Jordan to take possession of the land, God made a covenant with the new generation of Israelites, as recorded in Deuteronomy, chapter 29, verses 1-29: *"These are the words of the covenant, which the Lord commanded Moses to make with the children of Israel in the land of Moab, beside the*

---

[1] Urim and Thummin and how they functioned are not fully explained in the Bible. They were objects that fit into a special pocket on the breastplate that was worn by the high priest. They apparently provided the high priest with a means of receiving direct counsel from God on various matters (see Exodus 28:30, Leviticus 8:8, Numbers 27:21).

covenant which he made with them in Horeb. And Moses called unto all Israel, and said unto them, Ye have seen all that the Lord did before your eyes in the land of Egypt unto Pharaoh, and unto all his servants, and unto all his land; The great temptations which thine eyes have seen, the signs, and those great miracles: Yet the Lord hath not given you an heart to perceive, and eyes to see, and ears to hear, unto this day. And I have led you forty years in the wilderness: your clothes are not waxen old upon you, and thy shoe is not waxen old upon thy foot. Ye have not eaten bread, neither have ye drunk wine or strong drink: that ye might know that I am the Lord your God. And when ye came unto this place, Sihon the king of Heshbon, and Og the king of Bashan, came out against us unto battle, and we smote them: And we took their land, and gave it for an inheritance unto the Reubenites, and to the Gadites, and to the half tribe of Manasseh. Keep therefore the words of this covenant, and do them, that ye may prosper in all that ye do. Ye stand this day all of you before the Lord your God; your captains of your tribes, your elders, and your officers, with all the men of Israel, Your little ones, your wives, and thy stranger that is in thy camp, from the hewer of thy wood unto the drawer of thy water: That thou shouldest enter into covenant with the Lord thy God, and into his oath, which the Lord thy God maketh with thee this day: That he may establish thee to day for a people unto himself, and that he may be unto thee a God, as he hath said unto thee, and as he hath sworn unto thy fathers, to Abraham, to Isaac, and to Jacob. Neither with you only do I make this covenant and this oath; But with him that standeth here with us this day before the Lord our God, and also with him that is not here with us this day: (For ye know how we have dwelt in the land of Egypt; and how we came through the nations which ye passed by; And ye have seen their abominations, and their idols, wood and stone, silver and gold, which were among them:) Lest there should be among you man, or woman, or family, or tribe, whose heart turneth away this day from the Lord our God, to go and serve the gods of these nations; lest there should be among you a root that beareth gall and wormwood; And it come to pass, when he heareth the words of this curse, that he bless himself in his heart, saying, I shall have peace, though I walk in the imagination of mine heart, to add drunkenness to thirst: The Lord will not spare him, but then the anger of the Lord and his jealousy shall smoke against that man, and all the curses that are written in this book shall lie upon him, and the Lord shall blot out his name from under heaven. And the Lord shall separate him unto evil out of all the tribes of Israel, according to all the curses of the covenant that are written in this book of the law: So that the generation to come of your children that shall rise up after you, and the stranger that shall come from a far land, shall say, when they see the plagues of that land, and the sicknesses which the Lord hath laid upon it; And that the whole land thereof is brimstone, and salt, and burning, that it is not sown, nor beareth, nor any grass groweth therein, like the overthrow of Sodom, and Gomorrah, Admah, and Zeboim, which the Lord overthrew in his anger, and in his wrath: Even all nations shall say, Wherefore hath the Lord done thus unto this land? what meaneth the heat of this great anger? Then men shall say, Because they have forsaken the covenant of the Lord God of their fathers, which he made with them when he brought them forth out of the land of Egypt: For they went and served other gods, and worshipped them, gods whom they knew not, and whom he had not given unto them: And the anger of the Lord was kindled against this land, to bring upon it all the curses that are written in this book: And the Lord rooted them out of their land in anger, and in wrath, and in great indignation, and cast them into another land, as it is this day. The secret things belong unto the Lord our God: but those things which are revealed belong unto us and to our children for ever, that we may do all the words of this law" (KJV).

The Hebrew Scriptures—everything after the five Books of Moses—are a record of the struggle of the nation of Israel to keep the covenant and stay in the land. Repeatedly through the period of the judges and under king after king, the people of Israel (and then Judah) were increasingly unfaithful. Prophet after prophet warned the people that they would be removed from the land if they did not repent, to no avail. Time and again God was forced to discipline the people until they would ask for forgiveness, allowing him to show his mercy by retaining them as a nation in the promised land. Finally, as a judgement and example to the southern kingdom of Judah, God permanently removed the northern kingdom of Israel from the land in 722 B.C.E., by the hand of the Assyrians. Judah did not seem to take heed and failed to correct its ways, except for a brief period of faithfulness under king Josiah, who sought to do the will of God with all his heart. After his death in 609 B.C.E., though, the decline began again and continued until 605 B.C.E., when God began a three-staged exile of Judah from the land for seventy years, by the hand of the Babylonians. In 536 B.C.E., using Cyrus the Great of Persia, God fulfilled his promise to restore the people to the land if they repented (see Daniel's prayer on page 67). Still, over the next six centuries, the Jewish nation grew increasingly unfaithful to the covenant, causing God to eventually remove them from the land once again, this time at the hand of the Romans. For more than 1,800 years afterwards, the Jewish people would remain nationless in the *Diaspora*, dispersed among Gentiles.

The Modern Nation of Israel - Is it Biblical?

Today, the involuntary *Diaspora* of Jews among the nations has ended. This is obvious to any student of modern history. In recent years, there has been an unprecedented influx of Jews from around the world into the nation of Israel. The Bible predicted that this would happen. However, most of the references that speak of the ingathering, such as those in Ezekiel, are not specific as to the exact time. They say that it will happen in the latter days, but not specifically when. To find such a chrono-specific prophecy that involves the modern nation of Israel and the subsequent end of the involuntary dispersal of Jews among the nations, one has to look to the words of Jesus in the Book of the New Covenant, the *B'rit Hadashah*. Just before his crucifixion in 30 C.E., Jesus was walking in the Temple with his disciples, who were marveling at the buildings. The Gospel of Luke, chapter 21, verses 5-24, recounts this conversation: *"And as some spake of the temple, how it was adorned with goodly stones and gifts, he said, As for these things which ye behold, the days will come, in the which there shall not be left one stone upon another, that shall not be thrown down. And they asked him, saying, Master, but when shall these things be? and what sign will there be when these things shall come to pass? And he said, Take heed that ye be not deceived: for many shall come in my name, saying, I am Christ; and the time draweth near: go ye not therefore after them. But when ye shall hear of wars and commotions, be not terrified: for these things must first come to pass; but the end is not by and by. Then said he unto them, Nation shall rise against nation, and kingdom against kingdom: And great earthquakes shall be in divers places, and famines, and pestilences; and fearful sights and great signs shall there be from heaven. But before all these, they shall lay their hands on you, and persecute you, delivering you up to the synagogues, and into prisons, being brought before kings and rulers for my name's sake. And it shall turn to you for a testimony ... And when ye shall see Jerusalem compassed with armies, then know that the desolation thereof is nigh. Then let them which are in Judaea flee to the mountains; and let them which are in the midst of it depart out; and let not them that are in the countries enter thereinto. For these be the days of vengeance, that all things which are written may be fulfilled. But woe unto them that are with child, and to them that give suck, in those days! for there shall be great distress in the land, and wrath upon this people. And they shall fall by the edge of the sword, and shall be led away captive into all nations: and Jerusalem shall be trodden down of the Gentiles, until the times of the Gentiles be fulfilled"* (KJV).

Here is how I interpreted the above Scripture reference to confirm that the modern nation of Israel is foretold in the Bible. First, I noted that the phrase "times of the Gentiles" mentioned in the last sentence is a chrono-specific reference used in the same way that Daniel used the word "time" as a chronological marker in his prophecies. Second, I recalled that a "time" was defined as 228 Passovers (see page 25), so this reference by Jesus to the "times" (plural) must mean a time period with a duration of at least 2 x 228 Passovers = 456 Passovers, or possibly even higher multiples. Third, I ventured that the method of interpretation that I had used to understand the chrono-specific prophecy in Daniel, chapter 8 (see Chapter One, on page 7) that foretold restoration of the Temple Mount, an event pertaining to modern Israel, might be useful in understanding the "times of the Gentiles." Since the Battle of Granicus, the first time Alexander the Great defeated the Persians, had been the starting point for calculating the restoration of the Temple Mount, I began with the starting date for that prophecy, May/June 334 B.C.E., and began counting forward in multiples of "times" (*i.e.*, in increments of 228 Passovers) from the first Passover after the battle (the Passover in 333 B.C.E.), looking for a match with a modern event in Jewish history. To my surprise, ten "times" (2,280 Passovers) forward in time from that Passover brought the count to the Passover in 1947. I knew that shortly thereafter, the United Nations had passed Resolution 1501, which partitioned Palestine and established international authority for establishing a Jewish homeland in *Eretz-Israel*. Continuing to look for another match, I began counting from the second battle won by Alexander against Persia, the Battle of Issus in 333 B.C.E., and did the same calculation, using ten "times" as before, which brought the count to the Passover in 1948. I knew that shortly after that Passover, the nation of Israel had been proclaimed. Continuing in the same manner, I calculated ten "times" from the third and final battle against the Persians won by Alexander, the Battle of Gaugamela which was fought in 331 B.C.E. This third calculation brought the count to the

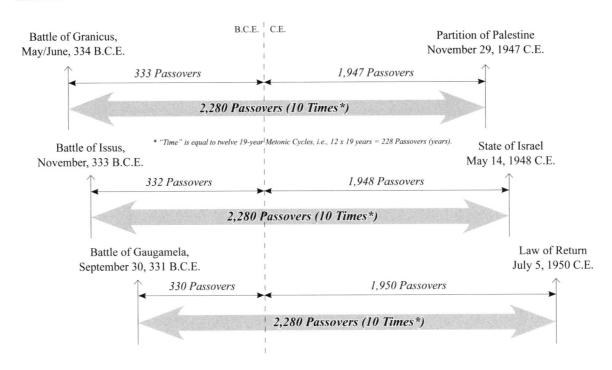

Diagram 6A - The Times of the Gentiles

Passover in 1950. I knew that shortly thereafter the Israeli Knesset had passed the Law of Return, an act bringing the involuntary *Diaspora* to an official end after more than 1,800 years. With the passage of the Law of Return in 1950, no Jewish person was forced to live anywhere else besides *Eretz-Israel*.

The prophecy spoken by Jesus in the Gospel of Luke, chapter 21, verse 24, contains the only reference in the Bible to the "times of the Gentiles." Traditionally, the phrase has been interpreted to refer to the time when non-Jewish nations would be dominant in history, but the viewpoint of Jesus is really more from Jewish history. Perhaps a better rendering might be "times among the Gentiles." By using the phrase "times of the Gentiles," Jesus was referring to the involuntary *Diaspora*—the period when the Jews would be, in his words, "led away captive into all nations" as a result of the Jewish-Roman wars of 66-135 C.E., where they would remain dispersed until the "times among the Gentiles" had been fulfilled. The three-stage fulfillment of the prophecy of Jesus (see Diagram 6A above), with each stage highlighting an important event in modern Jewish history, is verification that modern Israel is predicted in the Bible, with the time of its rebirth foretold exactly. Thus, the modern nation of Israel is indeed biblical, and the ingathering of the Jewish people to Israel is a clear indicator that the "times of the Gentiles" have been completed, and are being followed by the time of the end that is now underway.

∞

Important Documents

in Modern Jewish History

The Balfour Declaration - November 2, 1917

> Foreign Office,
> November 2nd, 1917.
>
> Dear Lord Rothschild.
>
> I have much pleasure in conveying to you, on behalf of His Majesty's Government, the following declaration of sympathy with Jewish Zionist aspirations which has been submitted to, and approved by, the Cabinet
>
> "His Majesty's Government view with favour the establishment in Palestine of a national home for the Jewish people, and will use their best endeavors to facilitate the achievement of this object, it being clearly understood that nothing shall be done which may prejudice the civil and religious rights of existing non-Jewish communities in Palestine, or the rights and political status enjoyed by Jews in any other country".
>
> I should be grateful if you would bring this declaration to the knowledge of the Zionist Federation.
>
> Arthur James Balfour

Facsimile based on original letter in the British Library

The Palestine Mandate - July 24, 1922

The Council of the League of Nations:

Whereas the Principal Allied Powers have agreed, for the purpose of giving effect to the provisions of Article 22 of the Covenant of the League of Nations, to entrust to a Mandatory selected by the said Powers the administration of the territory of Palestine, which formerly belonged to the Turkish Empire, within such boundaries as may be fixed by them; and

Whereas the Principal Allied Powers have also agreed that the Mandatory should be responsible for putting into effect the declaration originally made on November 2nd, 1917, by the Government of His Britannic Majesty, and adopted by the said Powers, in favor of the establishment in Palestine of a national home for the Jewish people, it being clearly understood that nothing should be done which might prejudice the civil and religious rights of existing nonJewish communities in Palestine, or the rights and political status enjoyed by Jews in any other country; and

Whereas recognition has thereby been given to the historical connection of the Jewish people with Palestine and to the grounds for reconstituting their national home in that country; and

Whereas the Principal Allied Powers have selected His Britannic Majesty as the Mandatory for Palestine; and

Whereas the mandate in respect of Palestine has been formulated in the following terms and submitted to the Council of the League for approval; and

Whereas His Britannic Majesty has accepted the mandate in respect of Palestine and undertaken to exercise it on behalf of the League of Nations in conformity with the following provisions; and

Whereas by the aforementioned Article 22 (paragraph 8), it is provided that the degree of authority, control or administration to be exercised by the Mandatory, not having been previously agreed upon by the Members of the League, shall be explicitly defined by the Council of the League Of Nations; confirming the said Mandate, defines its terms as follows:

ARTICLE 1. The Mandatory shall have full powers of legislation and of administration, save as they may be limited by the terms of this mandate.

ARTICLE 2. The Mandatory shall be responsible for placing the country under such political, administrative and economic conditions as will secure the establishment of the Jewish national home, as laid down in the preamble, and the development of self-governing institutions, and also for safeguarding the civil and religious rights of all the inhabitants of Palestine, irrespective of race and religion.

ARTICLE 3. The Mandatory shall, so far as circumstances permit, encourage local autonomy.

ARTICLE 4. An appropriate Jewish agency shall be recognised as a public body for the purpose of advising and cooperating with the Administration of Palestine in such economic, social and other matters as may affect the establishment of the Jewish national home and the interests of the Jewish population in Palestine, and, subject always to the control of the Administration to assist and take part in the development of the country. The Zionist organization, so long as its organization and constitution are in the opinion of the Mandatory appropriate, shall be recognised as such agency. It shall take steps in consultation with His Britannic Majesty's Government to secure the cooperation of all Jews who are willing to assist in the establishment of the Jewish national home.

ARTICLE 5. The Mandatory shall be responsible for seeing that no Palestine territory shall be ceded or leased to, or in any way placed under the control of the Government of any foreign Power.

ARTICLE 6. The Administration of Palestine, while ensuring that the rights and position of other sections of the population are not prejudiced, shall facilitate Jewish immigration under suitable conditions and shall encourage, in cooperation with the Jewish agency referred to in Article 4, close settlement by Jews on the land, including State lands and waste lands not required for public purposes.

ARTICLE 7. The Administration of Palestine shall be responsible for enacting a nationality law. There shall be included in this law provisions framed so as to facilitate the acquisition of Palestinian citizenship by Jews who take up their permanent residence in Palestine.

ARTICLE 8. The privileges and immunities of foreigners, including the benefits of consular jurisdiction and protection as formerly enjoyed by Capitulation or usage in the Ottoman Empire, shall not be applicable in Palestine.

Unless the Powers whose nationals enjoyed the aforementioned privileges and immunities on August 1st, 1914, shall have previously renounced the right to their reestablishment, or shall have agreed to their nonapplication for a specified period, these privileges and immunities shall, at the expiration of the mandate, be immediately reestablished in their entirety or with such modifications as may have been agreed upon between the Powers concerned.

ARTICLE 9. The Mandatory shall be responsible for seeing that the judicial system established in Palestine shall assure to foreigners, as well as to natives, a complete guarantee of their rights. Respect for the personal status of the various peoples and communities and for their religious interests shall be fully guaranteed.

ARTICLE 11. The Administration of Palestine shall take all necessary measures to safeguard the interests of the community in connection with the development of the country, and, subject to any international obligations accepted by the Mandatory, shall have full power to provide for public ownership or control of any of the natural resources of the country or of the public works, services and utilities established or to be established therein. It shall introduce a land system appropriate to the needs of the country, having regard, among other things, to the desirability of promoting the close settlement and intensive cultivation of the land. The Administration may arrange with the Jewish agency mentioned in Article 4 to construct or operate, upon fair and equitable terms, any public works, services and utilities, and to develop any of the natural resources of the country, in so far as these matters are not directly undertaken by the Administration. Any such arrangements shall provide that no profits distributed by such agency, directly or indirectly, shall exceed a reasonable rate of interest on the capital, and any further profits shall be utilised by it for the benefit of the country in a manner approved by the Administration.

ARTICLE 12. The Mandatory shall be entrusted with the control of the foreign relations of Palestine and the right to issue exequaturs to consuls appointed by foreign Powers. He shall also be entitled to afford diplomatic and consular protection to citizens of Palestine when outside its territorial limits.

ARTICLE 13. All responsibility in connection with the Holy Places and religious buildings or sites in Palestine, including that of preserving existing rights and of securing free access to the Holy Places, religious buildings and sites and the free exercise of worship, while ensuring the requirements of public order and decorum, is assumed by the Mandatory, who shall be responsible solely to the League of Nations in all matters connected herewith, provided that nothing in this article shall prevent the Mandatory from entering into such arrangements as he may deem reasonable with the Administration for the purpose of carrying the provisions of this article into effect; and provided also that nothing in this mandate shall be construed as conferring upon the Mandatory authority to interfere with the fabric or the management of purely Moslem sacred shrines, the immunities of which are guaranteed.

ARTICLE 14. A special commission shall be appointed by the Mandatory to study, define and determine the rights and claims in connection with the Holy Places and the rights and claims relating to the different religious communities in Palestine. The method of nomination, the composition and the functions of this Commission shall be submitted to the Council of the League for its approval, and the Commission shall not be appointed or enter upon its functions without the approval of the Council.

ARTICLE 15. The Mandatory shall see that complete freedom of conscience and the free exercise of all forms of worship, subject only to the maintenance of public order and morals, are ensured to all. No discrimination of any kind shall be made between the inhabitants of Palestine on the ground of race, religion or language. No person shall be excluded from Palestine on the sole ground of his religious belief. The right of each community to maintain its own schools for the education of its own members in its own language, while conforming to such educational requirements of a general nature as the Administration may impose, shall not be denied or impaired.

ARTICLE 16. The Mandatory shall be responsible for exercising such supervision over religious or eleemosynary bodies of all faiths in Palestine as may be required for the maintenance of public order and good government. Subject to such supervision, no measures shall be taken in Palestine to obstruct or interfere with the enterprise of such bodies or to discriminate against any representative or member of them on the ground of his religion or nationality.

ARTICLE 17. The Administration of Palestine may organist on a voluntary basis the forces necessary for the preservation of peace and order, and also for the defence of the country, subject, however, to the supervision of the Mandatory, but shall not use them for purposes other than those above specified save with the consent of the Mandatory. Except for such purposes, no military, naval or air forces shall be raised or maintained by the Administration of Palestine. Nothing in this article shall preclude the Administration of Palestine from contributing to the cost of the maintenance of the forces of the Mandatory in Palestine. The Mandatory shall be entitled at all times to use the roads, railways and ports of Palestine for the movement of armed forces and the carriage of fuel and supplies.

ARTICLE 18. The Mandatory shall see that there is no discrimination in Palestine against the nationals of any State Member of the League of Nations (including companies incorporated under its laws) as compared with those of the Mandatory or of any foreign State in matters concerning taxation, commerce or navigation, the exercise of industries or professions, or in the treatment of merchant vessels or civil aircraft. Similarly, there shall be no discrimination in Palestine against goods originating in or destined for any of the said States, and there shall be freedom of transit under equitable conditions across the mandated area. Subject as aforesaid and to the other provisions of this mandate, the Administration of Palestine may, on the advice of the Mandatory, impose such taxes and customs duties as it may consider necessary, and take such steps as it may think best to promote the development of the natural resources of the country and to safeguard the interests of the population. It may also, on the advice of the Mandatory, conclude a special customs agreement with any State the territory of which in 1914 was wholly included in Asiatic Turkey or Arabia.

ARTICLE 19. The Mandatory shall adhere on behalf of the Administration of Palestine to any general international conventions already existing, or which may be concluded hereafter with the approval of the League of Nations, respecting the slave traffic, the traffic in arms and ammunition, or the traffic in drugs, or relating to commercial equality, freedom of transit and navigation, aerial navigation and postal, telegraphic and wireless communication or literary, artistic or industrial property.

ARTICLE 20. The Mandatory shall cooperate on behalf of the Administration of Palestine, so far as religious, social and other conditions may permit, in the execution of any common policy adopted by the League of Nations for preventing and combating disease, including diseases of plants and animals.

ARTICLE 21. The Mandatory shall secure the enactment within twelve months from this date, and shall ensure the execution of a Law of Antiquities based on the following rules. This law shall ensure equality of treatment in the matter of excavations and archaeological research to the nationals of all States Members of the League of Nations.

(1) "Antiquity" means any construction or any product of human activity earlier than the year 1700 A. D.

(2) The law for the protection of antiquities shall proceed by encouragement rather than by threat.

Any person who, having discovered an antiquity without being furnished with the authorization referred to in paragraph 5, reports the same to an official of the competent Department, shall be rewarded according to the value of the discovery.

(3) No antiquity may be disposed of except to the competent Department, unless this Department renounces the acquisition of any such antiquity.

No antiquity may leave the country without an export licence from the said Department.

(4) Any person who maliciously or negligently destroys or damages an antiquity shall be liable to a penalty to be fixed.

(5) No clearing of ground or digging with the object of finding antiquities shall be permitted, under penalty of fine, except to persons authorised by the competent Department.

(6) Equitable terms shall be fixed for expropriation, temporary or permanent, of lands which might be of historical or archaeological interest.

(7) Authorization to excavate shall only be granted to persons who show sufficient guarantees of archaeological experience. The Administration of Palestine shall not, in granting these authorizations, act in such a way as to exclude scholars of any nation without good grounds.

(8) The proceeds of excavations may be divided between the excavator and the competent Department in a proportion fixed by that Department. If division seems impossible for scientific reasons, the excavator shall receive a fair indemnity in lieu of a part of the find.

ARTICLE 22. English, Arabic and Hebrew shall be the official languages of Palestine. Any statement or inscription in Arabic on stamps or money in Palestine shall be repeated in Hebrew and any statement or inscription in Hebrew shall be repeated in Arabic.

ARTICLE 23. The Administration of Palestine shall recognise the holy days of the respective communities in Palestine as legal days of rest for the members of such communities.

ARTICLE 24. The Mandatory shall make to the Council of the League of Nations an annual report to the satisfaction of the Council as to the measures taken during the year to carry out the provisions of the mandate. Copies of all laws and regulations promulgated or issued during the year shall be communicated with the report.

ARTICLE 25. In the territories lying between the Jordan and the eastern boundary of Palestine as ultimately determined, the Mandatory shall be entitled, with the consent of the Council of the League of Nations, to postpone or withhold application of such provisions of this mandate as he may consider inapplicable to the existing local conditions, and to make such provision for the administration of the territories as he may consider suitable to those conditions, provided that no action shall be taken which is inconsistent with the provisions of Articles 15, 16 and 18.

ARTICLE 26. The Mandatory agrees that, if any dispute whatever should arise between the Mandatory and another member of the League of Nations relating to the interpretation or the application of the provisions of the mandate, such dispute, if it cannot be settled by negotiation, shall be submitted to the Permanent Court of International Justice provided for by Article 14 of the Covenant of the League of Nations.

ARTICLE 27. The consent of the Council of the League of Nations is required for any modification of the terms of this mandate.

ARTICLE 28. In the event of the termination of the mandate hereby conferred upon the Mandatory, the Council of the League of Nations shall make such arrangements as may be deemed necessary for safeguarding in perpetuity, under guarantee of the League, the rights secured by Articles 13 and 14, and shall use its influence for securing, under the guarantee of the League, that the Government of Palestine will fully honour the financial obligations legitimately incurred by the Administration of Palestine during the period of the mandate, including the rights of public servants to pensions or gratuities.

The present instrument shall be deposited in original in the archives of the League of Nations and certified copies shall be forwarded by the SecretaryGeneral of the League of Nations to all members of the League.

Done at London the twentyfourth day of July, one thousand nine hundred and twentytwo.

Text courtesy of The Avalon Project at Yale Law School

The League of Nations Palestine Mandate of 1922 gave administration of that territory to Great Britain, the nation that had gained possession of Palestine from the Ottoman Empire during WWI. After WWII, the League of Nations was superseded by the United Nations. United Nations General Assembly Resolution 181 called for the partition of the British-ruled Palestine Mandate into a Jewish state and an Arab state. It was approved on November 29, 1947 with 33 votes in favor, 13 against, 10 abstentions and one absent. The resolution was accepted by the Jews in Palestine, yet rejected by the Arabs in Palestine and the Arab states.

U.N. General Assembly Resolution 181 (Partition of Palestine)
November 29, 1947

The General Assembly,

Having met in special session at the request of the mandatory Power to constitute and instruct a Special Committee to prepare for the consideration of the question of the future Government of Palestine at the second regular session;

Having constituted a Special Committee and instructed it to investigate all questions and issues relevant to the problem of Palestine, and to prepare proposals for the solution of the problem, and

Having received and examined the report of the Special Committee (document A/364)(1) including a number of unanimous recommendations and a plan of partition with economic union approved by the majority of the Special Committee,

Considers that the present situation in Palestine is one which is likely to impair the general welfare and friendly relations among nations;

Takes note of the declaration by the mandatory Power that it plans to complete its evacuation of Palestine by 1 August 1948;

Recommends to the United Kingdom, as the mandatory Power for Palestine, and to all other Members of the United Nations the adoption and implementation, with regard to the future Government of Palestine, of the Plan of Partition with Economic Union set out below;

Requests that

The Security Council take the necessary measures as provided for in the plan for its implementation;

The Security Council consider, if circumstances during the transitional period require such consideration, whether the situation in Palestine constitutes a threat to the peace. If it decides that such a threat exists, and in order to maintain international peace and security, the Security Council should supplement the authorization of the General Assembly by taking measures, under Articles 39 and 41 of the Charter, to empower the United Nations Commission, as provided in this resolution, to exercise in Palestine the functions which are assigned to it by this resolution;

The Security Council determine as a threat to the peace, breach of the peace or act of aggression, in accordance with Article 39 of the Charter, any attempt to alter by force the settlement envisaged by this resolution;

The Trusteeship Council be informed of the responsibilities envisaged for it in this plan;

Calls upon the inhabitants of Palestine to take such steps as may be necessary on their part to put this plan into effect;

Appeals to all Governments and all peoples to refrain from taking any action which might hamper or delay the carrying out of these recommendations, and

Authorizes the Secretary-General to reimburse travel and subsistence expenses of the members of the Commission referred to in Part 1, Section B, Paragraph I below, on such basis and in such form as he may determine most appropriate in the circumstances, and to provide the Commission with the necessary staff to assist in carrying out the functions assigned to the Commission by the General Assembly.*

The General Assembly,

Authorizes the Secretary-General to draw from the Working Capital Fund a sum not to exceed 2,000,000 dollars for the purposes set forth in the last paragraph of the resolution on the future government of Palestine.

Plan of Partition with Economic Union

Part I. Future Constitution and Government of Palestine

A. TERMINATION OF MANDATE, PARTITION AND INDEPENDENCE

The Mandate for Palestine shall terminate as soon as possible but in any case not later than 1 August 1948.

The armed forces of the mandatory Power shall be progressively withdrawn from Palestine, the withdrawal to be completed as soon as possible but in any case not later than 1 August 1948.

The mandatory Power shall advise the Commission, as far in advance as possible, of its intention to terminate the mandate and to evacuate each area.

The mandatory Power shall use its best endeavours to ensure that an area situated in the territory of the Jewish State, including a seaport and hinterland adequate to provide facilities for a substantial immigration, shall be evacuated at the earliest possible date and in any event not later than 1 February 1948.

Independent Arab and Jewish States and the Special International Regime for the City of Jerusalem, set forth in Part III of this Plan, shall come into existence in Palestine two months after the evacuation of the armed forces of the mandatory Power has been completed but in any case not later than 1 October 1948. The boundaries of the Arab State, the Jewish State, and the City of Jerusalem shall be as described in Parts II and III below.

The period between the adoption by the General Assembly of its recommendation on the question of Palestine and the establishment of the independence of the Arab and Jewish States shall be a transitional period.

B. STEPS PREPARATORY TO INDEPENDENCE

A Commission shall be set up consisting of one representative of each of five Member States. The Members represented on the Commission shall be elected by the General Assembly on as broad a basis, geographically and otherwise, as possible.

The administration of Palestine shall, as the mandatory Power withdraws its armed forces, be progressively turned over to the Commission, which shall act in conformity with the recommendations of the General Assembly, under the guidance of the Security Council. The mandatory Power shall to the fullest possible extent coordinate its plans for withdrawal with the plans of the Commission to take over and administer areas which have been evacuated.

In the discharge of this administrative responsibility the Commission shall have authority to issue necessary regulations and take other measures as required.

The mandatory Power shall not take any action to prevent, obstruct or delay the implementation by the Commission of the measures recommended by the General Assembly.

On its arrival in Palestine the Commission shall proceed to carry out measures for the establishment of the frontiers of the Arab and Jewish States and the City of Jerusalem in accordance with the general lines of the recommendations of the General Assembly on the partition of Palestine. Nevertheless, the boundaries as described in Part II of this Plan are to be modified in such a way that village areas as a rule will not be divided by state boundaries unless pressing reasons make that necessary.

The Commission, after consultation with the democratic parties and other public organizations of the Arab and Jewish States, shall select and establish in each State as rapidly as possible a Provisional Council of Government. The activities of both the Arab and Jewish Provisional Councils of Government shall be carried out under the general direction of the Commission.

If by 1 April 1948 a Provisional Council of Government cannot be selected for either of the States, or, if selected, cannot carry out its functions, the Commission shall communicate that fact to the Security Council for such action with respect to that State as the Security Council may deem proper, and to the Secretary-General for communication to the Members of the United Nations.

Subject to the provisions of these recommendations, during the transitional period the Provisional Councils of Government, acting under the Commission, shall have full authority in the areas under their control including authority over matters of immigration and land regulation.

The Provisional Council of Government of each State, acting under the Commission, shall progressively receive from the Commission full responsibility for the administration of that State in the period between the termination of the Mandate and the establishment of the State's independence.

The Commission shall instruct the Provisional Councils of Government of both the Arab and Jewish States, after their formation, to proceed to the establishment of administrative organs of government, central and local.

The Provisional Council of Government of each State shall, within the shortest time possible, recruit an armed militia from the residents of that State, sufficient in number to maintain internal order and to prevent frontier clashes.

This armed militia in each State shall, for operational purposes, be under the command of Jewish or Arab officers resident in that State, but general political and military control, including the choice of the militia's High Command, shall be exercised by the Commission.

The Provisional Council of Government of each State shall, not later than two months after the withdrawal of the armed forces of the mandatory Power, hold elections to the Constituent Assembly which shall be conducted on democratic lines.

The election regulations in each State shall be drawn up by the Provisional Council of Government and approved by the Commission. Qualified voters for each State for this election shall be persons over eighteen years of age who are (a) Palestinian citizens residing in that State; and (b) Arabs and Jews residing in the State, although not Palestinian citizens, who, before voting, have signed a notice of intention to become citizens of such State.

Arabs and Jews residing in the City of Jerusalem who have signed a notice of intention to become citizens, the Arabs of the Arab State and the Jews of the Jewish State, shall be entitled to vote in the Arab and Jewish States respectively.

Women may vote and be elected to the Constituent Assemblies.

During the transitional period no Jew shall be permitted to establish residence in the area of the proposed Arab State, and no Arab shall be permitted to establish residence in the area of the proposed Jewish State, except by special leave of the Commission.

The Constituent Assembly of each State shall draft a democratic constitution for its State and choose a provisional government to succeed the Provisional Council of Government appointed by the Commission.

The Constitutions of the States shall embody Chapters 1 and 2 of the Declaration provided for in section C below and include, inter alia, provisions for:

Establishing in each State a legislative body elected by universal suffrage and by secret ballot on the basis of proportional representation, and an executive body responsible to the legislature;

Settling all international disputes in which the State may be involved by peaceful means in such a manner that international peace and security, and justice, are not endangered;

Accepting the obligation of the State to refrain in its international relations from the threat or use of force against the territorial integrity or political independence of any State, or in any other manner inconsistent with the purpose of the United Nations;

Guaranteeing to all persons equal and non-discriminatory rights in civil, political, economic and religious matters and the enjoyment of human rights and fundamental freedoms, including freedom of religion, language, speech and publication, education, assembly and association;

Preserving freedom of transit and visit for all residents and citizens of the other State in Palestine and the City of Jerusalem, subject to considerations of national security, provided that each State shall control residence within its borders.

The Commission shall appoint a preparatory economic commission of three members to make whatever arrangements are possible for economic co-operation, with a view to establishing, as soon as practicable, the Economic Union and the Joint Economic Board, as provided in section D below.

During the period between the adoption of the recommendations on the question of Palestine by the General Assembly and the termination of the Mandate, the mandatory Power in Palestine shall maintain full responsibility for administration in areas from which it has not withdrawn its armed forces. The Commission shall assist the mandatory Power in the carrying out of these functions. Similarly the mandatory Power shall co-operate with the Commission in the execution of its functions.

With a view to ensuring that there shall be continuity in the functioning of administrative services and that, on the withdrawal of the armed forces of the mandatory Power, the whole administration shall be in the charge of the Provisional Councils and the Joint Economic Board, respectively, acting under the Commission, there shall be a progressive transfer, from the mandatory Power to the Commission, of responsibility for all the functions of government, including that of maintaining law and order in the areas from which the forces of the mandatory Power have been withdrawn.

The Commission shall be guided in its activities by the recommendations of the General Assembly and by such instructions as the Security Council may consider necessary to issue.

The measures taken by the Commission, within the recommendations of the General Assembly, shall become immediately effective unless the Commission has previously received contrary instructions from the Security Council.

The Commission shall render periodic monthly progress reports, or more frequently if desirable, to the Security Council.

The Commission shall make its final report to the next regular session of the General Assembly and to the Security Council simultaneously.

C. DECLARATION

A declaration shall be made to the United Nations by the Provisional Government of each proposed State before independence. It shall contain, inter alia, the following clauses:

General Provision - The stipulations contained in the Declaration are recognized as fundamental laws of the State and no law, regulation or official action shall conflict or interfere with these stipulations, nor shall any law, regulation or official action prevail over them.

Chapter I: Holy Places, Religious Buildings and Sites

Existing rights in respect of Holy Places and religious buildings or sites shall not be denied or impaired.

In so far as Holy Places are concerned, the liberty of access, visit, and transit shall be guaranteed, in conformity with existing rights, to all residents and citizen of the other State and of the City of Jerusalem, as well as to aliens, without distinction as to nationality, subject to requirements of national security, public order and decorum.

Similarly, freedom of worship shall be guaranteed in conformity with existing rights, subject to the maintenance of public order and decorum.

Holy Places and religious buildings or sites shall be preserved. No act shall be permitted which may in an way impair their sacred character. If at any time it appears to the Government that any particular Holy Place, religious, building or site is in need of urgent repair, the Government may call upon the community or communities concerned to carry out such repair. The Government may carry it out itself at the expense of the community or community concerned if no action is taken within a reasonable time.

No taxation shall be levied in respect of any Holy Place, religious building or site which was exempt from taxation on the date of the creation of the State.

No change in the incidence of such taxation shall be made which would either discriminate between the owners or occupiers of Holy Places, religious buildings or sites, or would place such owners or occupiers in a position less favourable in relation to the general incidence of taxation than existed at the time of the adoption of the Assembly's recommendations.

The Governor of the City of Jerusalem shall have the right to determine whether the provisions of the Constitution of the State in relation to Holy Places, religious buildings and sites within the borders of the State and the religious rights appertaining thereto, are being properly applied and respected, and to make decisions on the basis of existing rights in cases of disputes which may arise between the different religious communities or the rites of a religious community with respect to such places, buildings and sites. He shall receive full co-operation and such privileges and immunities as are necessary for the exercise of his functions in the State.

Chapter 2: Religious and Minority Rights

Freedom of conscience and the free exercise of all forms of worship, subject only to the maintenance of public order and morals, shall be ensured to all.

No discrimination of any kind shall be made between the inhabitants on the ground of race, religion, language or sex.

All persons within the jurisdiction of the State shall be entitled to equal protection of the laws.

The family law and personal status of the various minorities and their religious interests, including endowments, shall be respected.

Except as may be required for the maintenance of public order and good government, no measure shall be taken to obstruct or interfere with the enterprise of religious or charitable bodies of all faiths or to discriminate against any representative or member of these bodies on the ground of his religion or nationality.

The State shall ensure adequate primary and secondary education for the Arab and Jewish minority, respectively, in its own language and its cultural traditions.

The right of each community to maintain its own schools for the education of its own members in its own language, while conforming to such educational requirements of a general nature as the State may impose, shall not be denied or impaired. Foreign educational establishments shall continue their activity on the basis of their existing rights.

No restriction shall be imposed on the free use by any citizen of the State of any language in private intercourse, in commerce, in religion, in the Press or in publications of any kind, or at public meetings.

No expropriation of land owned by an Arab in the Jewish State (by a Jew in the Arab State)(4) shall be allowed except for public purposes. In all cases of expropriation full compensation as fixed by the Supreme Court shall be said previous to dispossession.

Chapter 3: Citizenship, International Conventions and Financial Obligations

1. Citizenship

Palestinian citizens residing in Palestine outside the City of Jerusalem, as well as Arabs and Jews who, not holding Palestinian citizenship, reside in Palestine outside the City of Jerusalem shall, upon the recognition of independence, become citizens of the State in which they are resident and enjoy full civil and political rights. Persons over the age of eighteen years may opt, within one year from the date of recognition of independence of the State in which they reside, for citizenship of the other State, providing that no Arab residing in the area of the proposed Arab State shall have the right to opt for citizenship in the proposed Jewish State and no Jew residing in the proposed Jewish State shall have the right to opt for citizenship in the proposed Arab State. The exercise of this right of option will be taken to include the wives and children under eighteen years of age of persons so opting.

Arabs residing in the area of the proposed Jewish State and Jews residing in the area of the proposed Arab State who have signed a notice of intention to opt for citizenship of the other State shall be eligible to vote in the elections to the Constituent Assembly of that State, but not in the elections to the Constituent Assembly of the State in which they reside.

2. International conventions

The State shall be bound by all the international agreements and conventions, both general and special, to which Palestine has become a party. Subject to any right of denunciation provided for therein, such agreements and conventions shall be respected by the State throughout the period for which they were concluded.

Any dispute about the applicability and continued validity of international conventions or treaties signed or adhered to by the mandatory Power on behalf of Palestine shall be referred to the International Court of Justice in accordance with the provisions of the Statute of the Court.

3. Financial obligations

The State shall respect and fulfil all financial obligations of whatever nature assumed on behalf of Palestine by the mandatory Power during the exercise of the Mandate and recognized by the State. This provision includes the right of public servants to pensions, compensation or gratuities.

These obligations shall be fulfilled through participation in the Joint Economic Board in respect of those obligations applicable to Palestine as a whole, and individually in respect of those applicable to, and fairly apportionable between, the States.

A Court of Claims, affiliated with the Joint Economic Board, and composed of one member appointed by the United Nations, one representative of the United Kingdom and one representative of the State concerned, should be established. Any dispute between the United Kingdom and the State respecting claims not recognized by the latter should be referred to that Court.

Commercial concessions granted in respect of any part of Palestine prior to the adoption of the resolution by the General Assembly shall continue to be valid according to their terms, unless modified by agreement between the concession-holders and the State.

Chapter 4: Miscellaneous Provisions

The provisions of chapters 1 and 2 of the declaration shall be under the guarantee of the United Nations, and no modifications shall be made in them without the assent of the General Assembly of the United Nations. Any Member of the United Nations shall have the right to bring to the attention of the General Assembly any infraction or danger of infraction of any of these stipulations, and the General Assembly may thereupon make such recommendations as it may deem proper in the circumstances.

Any dispute relating to the application or interpretation of this declaration shall be referred, at the request of either party, to the International Court of Justice, unless the parties agree to another mode of settlement.

D. ECONOMIC UNION AND TRANSIT

The Provisional Council of Government of each State shall enter into an undertaking with respect to Economic Union and Transit. This undertaking shall be drafted by the Commission provided for in section B, paragraph 1, utilizing to the greatest possible extent the advice and cooperation of representative organizations and bodies from each of the proposed States. It shall contain provisions to establish the Economic Union of Palestine and provide for other matters of common interest. If by 1 April 1948 the Provisional Councils of Government have not entered into the undertaking, the undertaking shall be put into force by the Commission.

The Economic Union of Palestine

The objectives of the Economic Union of Palestine shall be:

A customs union;

A joint currency system providing for a single foreign exchange rate;

Operation in the common interest on a non-discriminatory basis of railways inter-State highways; postal, telephone and telegraphic services and ports and airports involved in international trade and commerce;

Joint economic development, especially in respect of irrigation, land reclamation and soil conservation;

Access for both States and for the City of Jerusalem on a non-discriminatory basis to water and power facilities.

There shall be established a Joint Economic Board, which shall consist of three representatives of each of the two States and three foreign members appointed by the Economic and Social Council of the United Nations. The foreign members shall be appointed in the first instance for a term of three years; they shall serve as individuals and not as representatives of States.

The functions of the Joint Economic Board shall be to implement either directly or by delegation the measures necessary to realize the objectives of the Economic Union. It shall have all powers of organization and administration necessary to fulfil its functions.

The States shall bind themselves to put into effect the decisions of the Joint Economic Board. The Board's decisions shall be taken by a majority vote.

In the event of failure of a State to take the necessary action the Board may, by a vote of six members, decide to withhold an appropriate portion of the part of the customs revenue to which the State in question is entitled under the Economic Union. Should the State persist in its failure to cooperate, the Board may decide by a simple majority vote upon such further sanctions, including disposition of funds which it has withheld, as it may deem appropriate.

In relation to economic development, the functions of the Board shall be planning, investigation and encouragement of joint development projects, but it shall not undertake such projects except with the assent of both States and the City of Jerusalem, in the event that Jerusalem is directly involved in the development project.

In regard to the joint currency system, the currencies circulating in the two States and the City of Jerusalem shall be issued under the authority of the Joint Economic Board, which shall be the sole issuing authority and which shall determine the reserves to be held against such currencies.

So far as is consistent with paragraph 2(b) above, each State may operate its own central bank, control its own fiscal and credit policy, its foreign exchange receipts and expenditures, the grant of import licences, and may conduct international financial operations on its own faith and credit. During the first two years after the termination of the Mandate, the Joint Economic Board shall have the authority to take such measures as may be necessary to ensure that - to the extent that the total foreign exchange revenues of the two States from the export of goods and services permit, and provided that each State takes appropriate measures to conserve its own foreign exchange resources - each State shall have available, in any twelve months' period, foreign exchange sufficient to assure the supply of quantities of imported goods and services for consumption in its territory equivalent to the quantities of such goods and services consumed in that territory in the twelve months' period ending 31 December 1947.

All economic authority not specifically vested in the Joint Economic Board is reserved to each State.

There shall be a common customs tariff with complete freedom of trade between the States, and between the States and the City of Jerusalem.

The tariff schedules shall be drawn up by a Tariff Commission, consisting of representatives of each of the States in equal numbers, and shall be submitted to the Joint Economic Board for approval by a majority vote. In case of disagreement in the Tariff Commission, the Joint Economic Board shall arbitrate the points of difference. In the event that the Tariff Commission fails to draw up any schedule by a date to be fixed, the Joint Economic Board shall determine the tariff schedule.

The following items shall be a first charge on the customs and other common revenue of the Joint Economic Board:

The expenses of the customs service and of the operation of the joint services;

The administrative expenses of the Joint Economic Board;

The financial obligations of the Administration of Palestine, consisting of:

The service of the outstanding public debt;

The cost of superannuation benefits, now being paid or falling due in the future, in accordance with the rules and to the extent established by paragraph 3 of chapter 3 above.

After these obligations have been met in full, the surplus revenue from the customs and other common services shall be divided in the following manner: not less than 5 per cent and not more than 10 per cent to the City of Jerusalem; the residue shall be allocated to each State by the Joint Economic Board equitably, with the objective of maintaining a sufficient and suitable level of government and social services in each State, except that the share of either State shall not exceed the amount of that State's contribution to the revenues of the Economic Union by more than approximately four million pounds in any year. The amount granted may be adjusted by the Board according to the price level in relation to the prices prevailing at the time of the establishment of the Union. After five years, the principles of the distribution of the joint revenue may be revised by the Joint Economic Board on a basis of equity.

All international conventions and treaties affecting customs tariff rates, and those communications services under the jurisdiction of the Joint Economic Board, shall be entered into by both States. In these matters, the two States shall be bound to act in accordance with the majority of the Joint Economic Board.

The Joint Economic Board shall endeavour to secure for Palestine's exports fair and equal access to world markets.

All enterprises operated by the Joint Economic Board shall pay fair wages on a uniform basis.

Freedom of Transit and Visit

The undertaking shall contain provisions preserving freedom of transit and visit for all residents or citizens of both States and of the City of Jerusalem, subject to security considerations; provided that each State and the City shall control residence within its borders.

Termination, Modification and Interpretation of the Undertaking

The undertaking and any treaty issuing therefrom shall remain in force for a period of ten years. It shall continue in force until notice of termination, to take effect two years thereafter, is given by either of the parties.

During the initial ten-year period, the undertaking and any treaty issuing therefrom may not be modified except by consent of both parties and with the approval of the General Assembly.

Any dispute relating to the application or the interpretation of the undertaking and any treaty issuing therefrom shall be referred, at the request of either party, to the International Court Of Justice, unless the parties agree to another mode of settlement.

E. ASSETS

The movable assets of the Administration of Palestine shall be allocated to the Arab and Jewish States and the City of Jerusalem on an equitable basis. Allocations should be made by the United Nations Commission referred to iii section B, paragraph 1, above. Immovable assets shall become the property of the government of the territory in which they are situated.

During the period between the appointment of the United Nations Commission and the termination of the Mandate, the mandatory Power shall, except in respect of ordinary operations, consult with the Commission on any measure which it may contemplate involving the liquidation, disposal or encumbering of the assets of the Palestine Government, such as the accumulated treasury surplus, the proceeds of Government bond issues, State lands or any other asset.

F. ADMISSION TO MEMBERSHIP IN THE UNITED NATIONS

When the independence of either the Arab or the Jewish State as envisaged in this plan has become effective and the declaration and undertaking, as envisaged in this plan, have been signed by either of them, sympathetic consideration should be given to its application for admission to membership in the United Nations in accordance with article 4 of the Charter of the United Nations.

Part II. Boundaries

A. THE ARAB STATE

The area of the Arab State in Western Galilee is bounded on the west by the Mediterranean and on the north by the frontier of the Lebanon from Ras en Naqura to a point north of Saliha. From there the boundary proceeds southwards, leaving the built-up area of Saliha in the Arab State, to join the southernmost point of this village. There it follows the western boundary line of the villages of 'Alma, Rihaniya and Teitaba, thence following the northern boundary line of Meirun village to join the Acre-Safad Sub-District boundary line. It follows this line to a point west of Es Sammu'i village and joins it again at the northernmost point of Farradiya. Thence it follows the sub-district boundary line to the Acre-Safad main road. From here it follows the western boundary of Kafr-I'nan village until it reaches the Tiberias-Acre Sub-District boundary line, passing to the west of the junction of the Acre-Safad and Lubiya-Kafr-I'nan roads. From the south-west corner of Kafr-I'nan village the boundary line follows the western boundary of the Tiberias Sub-District to a point close to the boundary line between the villages of Maghar and 'Eilabun, thence bulging out to the west to include as much of the eastern part of the plain of Battuf as is necessary for the reservoir proposed by the Jewish Agency for the irrigation of lands to the south and east.

The boundary rejoins the Tiberias Sub-District boundary at a point on the Nazareth-Tiberias road south-east of the built-up area of Tur'an; thence it runs southwards, at first following the sub-district boundary and then passing between the Kadoorie Agricultural School and Mount Tabor, to a point due south at the base of Mount Tabor. From here it runs due west, parallel to the horizontal grid line 230, to the north-east corner of the village lands of Tel Adashim. It then runs to the northwest corner of these lands, whence it turns south and west so as to include in the Arab State the sources of the Nazareth water supply in Yafa village. On reaching Ginneiger it follows the eastern, northern and western boundaries of the lands of this village to their south-west comer, whence it proceeds in a straight line to a point on the Haifa-Afula railway on the boundary between the villages of Sarid and El-Mujeidil. This is the point of intersection. The south-western boundary of the area of the Arab State in Galilee takes a line from this point, passing northwards along the eastern boundaries of Sarid and Gevat to the north-eastern corner of Nahalal, proceeding thence across the land of Kefar ha Horesh to a central point on the southern boundary of the village of 'Ilut, thence westwards along that village boundary to the eastern boundary of Beit Lahm, thence northwards and north-eastwards along its western boundary to the north-eastern corner of Waldheim and thence north-westwards across the village lands of Shafa 'Amr to the southeastern corner of Ramat Yohanan. From here it runs due north-north-east to a point on the Shafa 'Amr-Haifa road, west of its junction with the road of I'billin. From there it proceeds north-east to a point on the southern boundary of I'billin situated to the west of the I'billin-Birwa road. Thence along that boundary to its westernmost point, whence it turns to the north, follows across the village land of Tamra to the north-westernmost corner and along the western boundary of Julis until it reaches the Acre-Safad road. It then runs westwards along the southern side of the Safad-Acre road to the Galilee-Haifa District boundary, from which point it follows that boundary to the sea.

The boundary of the hill country of Samaria and Judea starts on the Jordan River at the Wadi Malih south-east of Beisan and runs due west to meet the Beisan-Jericho road and then follows the western side of that road in a north-westerly direction to the junction of the boundaries of the Sub-Districts of Beisan, Nablus, and Jenin. From that point it follows the Nablus-Jenin sub-District boundary westwards for a distance of about three kilometres and then turns north-westwards, passing to the east of the built-up areas of the villages of Jalbun and Faqqu'a, to the boundary of the Sub-Districts of Jenin and Beisan at a point northeast of Nuris. Thence it proceeds first northwestwards to a point due north of the built-up area of Zie'in and then westwards to the Afula-Jenin railway, thence north-westwards along the District boundary line to the point of intersection on the Hejaz railway. From here the boundary runs southwestwards, including the built-up area and some of the land of the village of Kh. Lid in the Arab State to cross the Haifa-Jenin road at a point on the district boundary between Haifa and Samaria west of El- Mansi. It follows this boundary to the southernmost point of the village of El-Buteimat. From here it follows the northern and eastern boundaries of the village of Ar'ara rejoining the Haifa-Samaria district boundary at Wadi 'Ara, and thence proceeding south-south-westwards in an approximately straight line joining up with the western boundary of Qaqun to a point east of the railway line on the eastern boundary of Qaqun village. From here it runs along the railway line some distance to the east of it to a point just east of the Tulkarm railway station. Thence the boundary follows a line half-way between the railway and the Tulkarm-Qalqiliya-Jaljuliya and Ras El-Ein road to a point just east of Ras El-Ein station, whence it proceeds along the railway some distance to the east of it to the point on the railway line south of the junction of the Haifa-Lydda and Beit Nabala lines, whence it proceeds along the southern border of Lydda airport to its south-west corner, thence in a south-westerly direction to a point just west of the built-up area of Sarafand El 'Amar, whence it turns south, passing just to the west of the built-up area of Abu El-Fadil to the north-east corner of the lands of Beer Ya'aqov. (The boundary line should be so demarcated as to allow direct access from the Arab State to the airport.) Thence the boundary line follows the western and southern boundaries of Ramle village, to the north-east corner of El Na'ana village, thence in a straight line to the southernmost point of El Barriya, along the eastern boundary of that village and the southern boundary of 'Innaba village. Thence it turns north to follow the southern side of the Jaffa-Jerusalem road until El-Qubab, whence it follows the road to the boundary of Abu-Shusha. It runs along the eastern boundaries of Abu Shusha, Seidun, Hulda to the southernmost point of Hulda, thence westwards in a straight line to the north-eastern corner of Umm Kalkha, thence following the northern boundaries of Umm Kalkha, Qazaza and the northern and western boundaries of Mukhezin to the Gaza District boundary and thence runs across the village lands of El-Mismiya El-Kabira, and Yasur to the southern point of intersection, which is midway between the built-up areas of Yasur and Batani Sharqi.

From the southern point of intersection the boundary lines run north-westwards between the villages of Gan Yavne and Barqa to the sea at a point half way between Nabi Yunis and Minat El-Qila, and south-eastwards to a point west of Qastina, whence it turns in a south-westerly direction, passing to the east of the built-up areas of Es Sawafir Esh Sharqiya and 'Ibdis. From the south-east corner of 'Ibdis village it runs to a point southwest of the built-up area of Beit 'Affa, crossing the Hebron-El-Majdal road just to the west of the built-up area of 'Iraq Suweidan. Thence it proceeds southward along the western village boundary of El-Faluja to the Beersheba Sub-District boundary. It then runs across the tribal lands of 'Arab El-Jubarat to a point on the boundary between the Sub-Districts of Beersheba and Hebron north of Kh. Khuweilifa, whence it proceeds in a south-westerly direction to a point on the Beersheba-Gaza main road two kilometres to the north-west of the town. It then turns south-eastwards to reach Wadi Sab' at a point situated one kilometer to the west of it. From here it turns north-eastwards and proceeds along Wadi Sab' and along the Beersheba-Hebron road for a distance of one kilometer, whence it turns eastwards and runs in a straight line to Kh. Kuseifa to join the Beersheba-Hebron Sub-District boundary. It then follows the Beersheba-Hebron boundary eastwards to a point north of Ras Ez-Zuweira, only departing from it so as to cut across the base of the indentation between vertical grid lines 150 and 160.

About five kilometres north-east of Ras Ez-Zuweira it turns north, excluding from the Arab State a strip along the coast of the Dead Sea not more than seven kilometres in depth, as far as 'Ein Geddi, whence it turns due east to join the Transjordan frontier in the Dead Sea.

The northern boundary of the Arab section of the coastal plain runs from a point between Minat El-Qila and Nabi Yunis, passing between the built-up areas of Gan Yavne and Barqa to the point of intersection. From here it turns south-westwards, running across the lands of Batani Sharqi, along the eastern boundary of the lands of Beit Daras and across the lands of Julis, leaving the built-up areas of Batani Sharqi and Julis to the westwards, as far as the north-west corner of the lands of Beit-Tima. Thence it runs east of El-Jiya across the village lands of El-Barbara along the eastern boundaries of the villages of Beit Jirja, Deir Suneid and Dimra. From the south-east corner of Dimra the boundary passes across the lands of Beit Hanun, leaving the Jewish lands of Nir-Am to the eastwards. From the south-east corner of Beit Hanun the line runs south-west to a point south of the parallel grid line 100, then turns north-west for two kilometres, turning again in a southwesterly direction and continuing in an almost straight line to the north-west corner of the village lands of Kirbet Ikhza'a. From there it follows the boundary line of this village to its southernmost point. It then runs in a southerly direction along the vertical grid line 90 to its junction with the horizontal grid line 70. It then turns south-eastwards to Kh. El-Ruheiba and then proceeds in a southerly direction to a point known as El-Baha, beyond which it crosses the Beersheba-El 'Auja main road to the west of Kh. El-Mushrifa. From there it joins Wadi El-Zaiyatin just to the west of El-Subeita. From there it turns to the north-east and then to the south-east following this Wadi and passes to the east of 'Abda to join Wadi Nafkh. It then bulges to the south-west along Wadi Nafkh, Wadi 'Ajrim and Wadi Lassan to the point where Wadi Lassan crosses the Egyptian frontier.

The area of the Arab enclave of Jaffa consists of that part of the town-planning area of Jaffa which lies to the west of the Jewish quarters lying south of Tel-Aviv, to the west of the continuation of Herzl street up to its junction with the Jaffa-Jerusalem road, to the south-west of the section of the Jaffa-Jerusalem road lying south-east of that junction, to the west of Miqve Yisrael lands, to the northwest of Holon local council area, to the north of the line linking up the north-west corner of Holon with the northeast corner of Bat Yam local council area and to the north of Bat Yam local council area. The question of Karton quarter will be decided by the Boundary Commission, bearing in mind among other considerations the desirability of including the smallest possible number of its Arab inhabitants and the largest possible number of its Jewish inhabitants in the Jewish State.

B. THE JEWISH STATE

The north-eastern sector of the Jewish State (Eastern Galilee) is bounded on the north and west by the Lebanese frontier and on the east by the frontiers of Syria and Trans-jordan. It includes the whole of the Huleh Basin, Lake Tiberias, the whole of the Beisan Sub-District, the boundary line being extended to the crest of the Gilboa mountains and the Wadi Malih. From there the Jewish State extends north-west, following the boundary described in respect of the Arab State. The Jewish section of the coastal plain extends from a point between Minat El-Qila and Nabi Yunis in the Gaza Sub-District and includes the towns of Haifa and Tel-Aviv, leaving Jaffa as an enclave of the Arab State. The eastern frontier of the Jewish State follows the boundary described in respect of the Arab State.

The Beersheba area comprises the whole of the Beersheba Sub-District, including the Negeb and the eastern part of the Gaza Sub-District, but excluding the town of Beersheba and those areas described in respect of the Arab State. It includes also a strip of land along the Dead Sea stretching from the Beersheba-Hebron Sub-District boundary line to 'Ein Geddi, as described in respect of the Arab State.

C. THE CITY OF JERUSALEM

The boundaries of the City of Jerusalem are as defined in the recommendations on the City of Jerusalem. (See Part III, section B, below).

Part III. City of Jerusalem

A. SPECIAL REGIME

The City of Jerusalem shall be established as a corpus separatum under a special international regime and shall be administered by the United Nations. The Trusteeship Council shall be designated to discharge the responsibilities of the Administering Authority on behalf of the United Nations.

B. BOUNDARIES OF THE CITY

The City of Jerusalem shall include the present municipality of Jerusalem plus the surrounding villages and towns, the most eastern of which shall be Abu Dis; the most southern, Bethlehem; the most western, 'Ein Karim (including also the built-up area of Motsa); and the most northern Shu'fat, as indicated on the attached sketch-map (annex B).

C. STATUTE OF THE CITY

The Trusteeship Council shall, within five months of the approval of the present plan, elaborate and approve a detailed statute of the City which shall contain, inter alia, the substance of the following provisions:

1. Government machinery; special objectives.

The Administering Authority in discharging its administrative obligations shall pursue the following special objectives:

To protect and to preserve the unique spiritual and religious interests located in the city of the three great monotheistic faiths throughout the world, Christian, Jewish and Moslem; to this end to ensure that order and peace, and especially religious peace, reign in Jerusalem;

To foster cooperation among all the inhabitants of the city in their own interests as well as in order to encourage and support the peaceful development of the mutual relations between the two Palestinian peoples throughout the Holy Land; to promote the security, well-being and any constructive measures of development of the residents having regard to the special circumstances and customs of the various peoples and communities.

2. Governor and Administrative staff.

A Governor of the City of Jerusalem shall be appointed by the Trusteeship Council and shall be responsible to it. He shall be selected on the basis of special qualifications and without regard to nationality. He shall not, however, be a citizen of either State in Palestine.

The Governor shall represent the United Nations in the City and shall exercise on their behalf all powers of administration, including the conduct of external affairs. He shall be assisted by an administrative staff classed as international officers in the meaning of Article 100 of the Charter and chosen whenever practicable from the residents of the city and of the rest of Palestine on a non-discriminatory basis. A detailed plan for the organization of the administration of the city shall be submitted by the Governor to the Trusteeship Council and duly approved by it.

3. Local autonomy

The existing local autonomous units in the territory of the city (villages, townships and municipalities) shall enjoy wide powers of local government and administration.

The Governor shall study and submit for the consideration and decision of the Trusteeship Council a plan for the establishment of special town units consisting, respectively, of the Jewish and Arab sections of new Jerusalem. The new town units shall continue to form part the present municipality of Jerusalem.

4. Security measures

The City of Jerusalem shall be demilitarized; neutrality shall be declared and preserved, and no para-military formations, exercises or activities shall be permitted within its borders.

Should the administration of the City of Jerusalem be seriously obstructed or prevented by the non-cooperation or interference of one or more sections of the population the Governor shall have authority to take such measures as may be necessary to restore the effective functioning of administration.

To assist in the maintenance of internal law and order, especially for the protection of the Holy Places and religious buildings and sites in the city, the Governor shall organize a special police force of adequate strength, the members of which shall be recruited outside of Palestine.

The Governor shall be empowered to direct such budgetary provision as may be necessary for the maintenance of this force.

5. Legislative Organization.

A Legislative Council, elected by adult residents of the city irrespective of nationality on the basis of universal and secret suffrage and proportional representation, shall have powers of legislation and taxation. No legislative measures shall, however, conflict or interfere with the provisions which will be set forth in the Statute of the City, nor shall any law, regulation, or official action prevail over them.

The Statute shall grant to the Governor a right of vetoing bills inconsistent with the provisions referred to in the preceding sentence. It shall also empower him to promulgate temporary ordinances in case the Council fails to adopt in time a bill deemed essential to the normal functioning of the administration.

6. Administration of Justice.

The Statute shall provide for the establishment of an independent judiciary system, including a court of appeal. All the inhabitants of the city shall be subject to it.

7. Economic Union and Economic Regime.

The City of Jerusalem shall be included in the Economic Union of Palestine and be bound by all stipulations of the undertaking and of any treaties issued therefrom, as well as by the decisions of the Joint Economic Board. The headquarters of the Economic Board shall be established in the territory City. The Statute shall provide for the regulation of economic matters not falling within the regime of the Economic Union, on the basis of equal treatment and non-discrimination for all members of thc United Nations and their nationals.

8. Freedom of Transit and Visit: Control of residents.

Subject to considerations of security, and of economic welfare as determined by the Governor under the directions of the Trusteeship Council, freedom of entry into, and residence within the borders of the City shall be guaranteed for the residents or citizens of the Arab and Jewish States. Immigration into, and residence within, the borders of the city for nationals of other States shall be controlled by the Governor under the directions of the Trusteeship Council.

Relations with Arab and Jewish States. Representatives of the Arab and Jewish States shall be accredited to the Governor of the City and charged with the protection of the interests of their States and nationals in connection with the international administration of thc City.

9. Official languages.

Arabic and Hebrew shall be the official languages of the city. This will not preclude the adoption of one or more additional working languages, as may be required.

10. Citizenship.

All the residents shall become ipso facto citizens of the City of Jerusalem unless they opt for citizenship of the State of which they have been citizens or, if Arabs or Jews, have filed notice of intention to become citizens of the Arab or Jewish State respectively, according to Part 1, section B, paragraph 9, of this Plan.

The Trusteeship Council shall make arrangements for consular protection of the citizens of the City outside its territory.

11. Freedoms of citizens

Subject only to the requirements of public order and morals, the inhabitants of the City shall be ensured the enjoyment of human rights and fundamental freedoms, including freedom of conscience, religion and worship, language, education, speech and press, assembly and association, and petition.

No discrimination of any kind shall be made between the inhabitants on the grounds of race, religion, language or sex.

All persons within the City shall be entitled to equal protection of the laws.

The family law and personal status of the various persons and communities and their religious interests, including endowments, shall be respected.

Except as may be required for the maintenance of public order and good government, no measure shall be taken to obstruct or interfere with the enterprise of religious or charitable bodies of all faiths or to discriminate against any representative or member of these bodies on the ground of his religion or nationality.

The City shall ensure adequate primary and secondary education for the Arab and Jewish communities respectively, in their own languages and in accordance with their cultural traditions.

The right of each community to maintain its own schools for the education of its own members in its own language, while conforming to such educational requirements of a general nature as the City may impose, shall not be denied or impaired.

Foreign educational establishments shall continue their activity on the basis of their existing rights.

No restriction shall be imposed on the free use by any inhabitant of the City of any language in private intercourse, in commerce, in religion, in the Press or in publications of any kind, or at public meetings.

12. Holy Places

Existing rights in respect of Holy Places and religious buildings or sites shall not be denied or impaired.

Free access to the Holy Places and religious buildings or sites and the free exercise of worship shall be secured in conformity with existing rights and subject to the requirements of public order and decorum.

Holy Places and religious buildings or sites shall be preserved.

No act shall be permitted which may in any way impair their sacred character.

If at any time it appears to the Governor that any particular Holy Place, religious building or site is in need of urgent repair, the Governor may call upon the community or communities concerned to carry out such repair. The Governor may carry it out himself at the expense of the community or communities concerned if no action is taken within a reasonable time.

No taxation shall be levied in respect of any Holy Place, religious building or site which was exempt from taxation on the date of the creation of the City. No change in the incidence of such taxation shall be made which would either discriminate between the owners or occupiers of Holy Places, religious buildings or sites or would place such owners or occupiers in a position less favourable in relation to the general incidence of taxation than existed at the time of the adoption of the Assembly's recommendations.

Special powers of the Governor in respect of the Holy Places, religious buildings and sites in the City and in any part of Palestine.

The protection of the Holy Places, religious buildings and sites located in the City of Jerusalem shall be a special concern of the Governor.

With relation to such places, buildings and sites in Palestine outside the city, the Governor shall determine, on the ground of powers granted to him by the Constitution of both States, whether the provisions of the Constitution of the Arab and Jewish States in Palestine dealing therewith and the religious rights appertaining thereto are being properly applied and respected.

The Governor shall also be empowered to make decisions on the basis of existing rights in cases of disputes which may arise between the different religious communities or the rites of a religious community in respect of the Holy Places, religious buildings and sites in any part of Palestine.

In this task he may be assisted by a consultative council of representatives of different denominations acting in an advisory capacity.

D. DURATION OF THE SPECIAL REGIME

The Statute elaborated by the Trusteeship Council the aforementioned principles shall come into force not later than 1 October 1948. It shall remain in force in the first instance for a period of ten years, unless the Trusteeship Council finds it necessary to undertake a re-examination of these provisions at an earlier date. After the expiration of this period the whole scheme shall be subject to examination by the Trusteeship Council in the light of experience acquired with its functioning. The residents the City shall be then free to express by means of a referendum their wishes as to possible modifications of regime of the City.

Part IV. Capitulations

States whose nationals have in the past enjoyed in Palestine the privileges and immunities of foreigners, including the benefits of consular jurisdiction and protection, as formerly enjoyed by capitulation or usage in the Ottoman Empire, are invited to renounce any right pertaining to them to the re-establishment of such privileges and immunities in the proposed Arab and Jewish States and the City of Jerusalem.

Adopted at the 128th plenary meeting on November 29, 1947.

33 in favor, 13 opposed, 10 abstained

* * * * *

Results of vote on U.N. Resolution 181 (Partition of Palestine)

In favour: 33 - Australia, Belgium, Bolivia, Brazil, Byelorussian S.S.R., Canada, Costa Rica, Czechoslovakia, Denmark, Dominican Republic, Ecuador, France, Guatemala, Haiti, Iceland, Liberia, Luxemburg, Netherlands, New Zealand, Nicaragua, Norway, Panama, Paraguay, Peru, Philippines, Poland, Sweden, Ukrainian S.S.R., Union of South Africa, U.S.A., U.S.S.R., Uruguay, Venezuela.

Against: 13 - Afghanistan, Cuba, Egypt, Greece, India, Iran, Iraq, Lebanon, Pakistan, Saudi Arabia, Syria, Turkey, Yemen.

Abstained: 10 - Argentina, Chile, China, Colombia, El Salvador, Ethiopia, Honduras, Mexico, United Kingdom, Yugoslavia.

* * * * *

(1) See Official Records of the General Assembly, Second Session Supplement No. 11, Volumes I-IV.

At its hundred and twenty-eighth plenary meeting on 29 November 1947 the General Assembly, in accordance with the terms of the above resolution, elected the following members of the United Nations Commission on Palestine: Bolivia, Czechoslovakia, Denmark, Panama, and Philippines.

(2) This resolution was adopted without reference to a Committee.

(3) The following stipulation shall be added to the declaration concerning the Jewish State: "In the Jewish State adequate facilities shall be given to Arabic-speaking citizens for the use of their language, either orally or in writing, in the legislature, before the Courts and in the administration."

(4) In the declaration concerning the Arab State, the words "by an Arab in the Jewish State" should be replaced by the words "by a Jew in the Arab State."

(5) On the question of the internationalization of Jerusalem, see also General Assembly resolutions 185 (S-2) of 26 April 1948; 187 (S-2) of 6 May 1948, 303 (IV) of 9 December 1949, and resolutions of the Trusteeship Council (Section IV).

Text courtesy of the United Nations and the Ministry of Foreign Affairs, State of Israel

On May 14, 1948, on the day that the British Mandate over Palestine expired, the Jewish People's Council gathered at the Tel Aviv Museum, approved this declaration, and proclaimed the establishment of the State of Israel ...

The Declaration of the Establishment of the State of Israel
May 14, 1948

Eretz-Israel [the Land of Israel, Palestine] was the birthplace of the Jewish people. Here their spiritual, religious and political identity was shaped. Here they first attained to statehood, created cultural values of national and universal significance and gave to the world the eternal Book of Books.

After being forcibly exiled from their land, the people kept faith with it throughout their Dispersion and never ceased to pray and hope for their return to it and for the restoration in it of their political freedom.

Impelled by this historic and traditional attachment, Jews strove in every successive generation to re-establish themselves in their ancient homeland. In recent decades they returned in their masses. Pioneers, ma'pilim [(Hebrew) - immigrants coming to Eretz-Israel in defiance of restrictive legislation] and defenders, they made deserts bloom, revived the Hebrew language, built villages and towns, and created a thriving community controlling its own economy and culture, loving peace but knowing how to defend itself, bringing the blessings of progress to all the country's inhabitants, and aspiring towards independent nationhood.

In the year 5657 (1897), at the summons of the spiritual father of the Jewish State, Theodore Herzl, the First Zionist Congress convened and proclaimed the right of the Jewish people to national rebirth in its own country.

This right was recognized in the Balfour Declaration of the 2nd November, 1917, and re-affirmed in the Mandate of the League of Nations which, in particular, gave international sanction to the historic connection between the Jewish people and Eretz-Israel and to the right of the Jewish people to rebuild its National Home.

The catastrophe which recently befell the Jewish people - the massacre of millions of Jews in Europe - was another clear demonstration of the urgency of solving the problem of its homelessness by re-establishing in Eretz-Israel the Jewish State, which would open the gates of the homeland wide to every Jew and confer upon the Jewish people the status of a fully privileged member of the comity of nations.

Survivors of the Nazi holocaust in Europe, as well as Jews from other parts of the world, continued to migrate to Eretz-Israel, undaunted by difficulties, restrictions and dangers, and never ceased to assert their right to a life of dignity, freedom and honest toil in their national homeland.

In the Second World War, the Jewish community of this country contributed its full share to the struggle of the freedom- and peace-loving nations against the forces of Nazi wickedness and, by the blood of its soldiers and its war effort, gained the right to be reckoned among the peoples who founded the United Nations.

On the 29th November, 1947, the United Nations General Assembly passed a resolution calling for the establishment of a Jewish State in Eretz-Israel; the General Assembly required the inhabitants of Eretz-Israel to take such steps as were necessary on their part for the implementation of that resolution. This recognition by the United Nations of the right of the Jewish people to establish their State is irrevocable.

This right is the natural right of the Jewish people to be masters of their own fate, like all other nations, in their own sovereign State.

Accordingly, We, members of the People's Council, representatives of the Jewish Community in Eretz-Israel and of the Zionist movement, are here assembled on the day of the termination of the British Mandate over Eretz-Israel and, by virtue of our natural and historic right and on the strength of the resolution of the United Nations General Assembly, hereby declare the establishment of a Jewish state in Eretz-Israel, to be known as the State of Israel.

WE DECLARE that, with effect from the moment of the termination of the Mandate being tonight, the eve of Sabbath, the 6th Iyar, 5708 (15th May, 1948), until the establishment of the elected, regular authorities of the State in accordance with the Constitution which shall be adopted by the Elected Constituent Assembly not later than the 1st October 1948, the People's Council shall act as a Provisional Council of State, and its executive organ, the People's Administration, shall be the Provisional Government of the Jewish State, to be called "Israel."

THE STATE OF ISRAEL will be open for Jewish immigration and for the Ingathering of the Exiles; it will foster the development of the country for the benefit of all its inhabitants; it will be based on freedom, justice and peace as envisaged by the prophets of Israel; it will ensure complete equality of social and political rights to all its inhabitants irrespective of religion, race or sex; it will guarantee freedom of religion, conscience, language, education and culture; it will safeguard the Holy Places of all religions; and it will be faithful to the principles of the Charter of the United Nations.

THE STATE OF ISRAEL is prepared to cooperate with the agencies and representatives of the United Nations in implementing the resolution of the General Assembly of the 29th November, 1947, and will take steps to bring about the economic union of the whole of Eretz-Israel.

WE APPEAL to the United Nations to assist the Jewish people in the building-up of its State and to receive the State of Israel into the comity of nations.

WE APPEAL - in the very midst of the onslaught launched against us now for months - to the Arab inhabitants of the State of Israel to preserve peace and participate in the upbuilding of the State on the basis of full and equal citizenship and due representation in all its provisional and permanent institutions.

WE EXTEND our hand to all neighbouring states and their peoples in an offer of peace and good neighbourliness, and appeal to them to establish bonds of cooperation and mutual help with the sovereign Jewish people settled in its own land. The State of Israel is prepared to do its share in a common effort for the advancement of the entire Middle East.

WE APPEAL to the Jewish people throughout the Diaspora to rally round the Jews of Eretz-Israel in the tasks of immigration and upbuilding and to stand by them in the great struggle for the realization of the age-old dream - the redemption of Israel.

Placing out trust in the "Rock of Israel," we affix our signatures to this proclamation at this session of the Provisional Council of State, on the soil of the homeland, in the city of Tel-Aviv, on this Sabbath Eve, the 5th day of Iyar, 5708 (14th May, 1948).

David Ben-Gurion	Zerach Wahrhaftig	Aharon Zisling
Daniel Auster	Herzl Vardi Rachel Cohen	Moshe Kolodny
Mordekhai Bentov	Rabbi Kalman Kahana	Eliezer Kaplan
Yitzchak Ben Zvi	Saadia Kobashi	Abraham Katznelson
Eliyahu Berligne	Rabbi Yitzchak Meir Levin	Felix Rosenblueth
Fritz Bernstein	Meir David Loewenstein	David Remez
Rabbi Wolf Gold	Zvi Luria	Berl Repetur
Meir Grabovsky	Golda Myerson	Mordekhai Shattner
Yitzchak Gruenbaum	Nachum Nir	Ben Zion Sternberg
Dr. Abraham Granovsky	Zvi Segal	Bekhor Shitreet
Eliyahu Dobkin	Rabbi Yehuda Leib Hacohen Fishman	Moshe Shapira
Meir Wilner-Kovner	David Zvi Pinkas	Moshe Shertok

Published in the Official Gazette, No. 1 of the 5th, Iyar, 5708 (14th May, 1948).

Text courtesy of the Ministry of Foreign Affairs, State of Israel

The Law of Return, 5710-1950[1] - July 5, 1950

Right of aliyah[2]

1. Every Jew has the right to come to this country as an oleh.[3]

Oleh's visa

2. (a) Aliyah shall be by oleh's visa.

(b) An oleh's visa shall be granted to every Jew who has expressed his desire to settle in Israel, unless the Minister of Immigration is satisfied that the applicant

(1) is engaged in an activity directed against the Jewish people; or

(2) is likely to endanger public health or the security of the State.

Oleh's certificate

3. (a) A Jew who has come to Israel and subsequent to his arrival has expressed his desire to settle in Israel may, while still in Israel, receive an oleh's certificate.

(b) The restrictions specified in section 2(b) shall apply also to the grant of an oleh's certificate, but a person shall not be regarded as endangering public health on account of an illness contracted after his arrival in Israel.

Residents and persons born in this country

4. Every Jew who has immigrated into this country before the coming into force of this Law, and every Jew who was born in this country, whether before or after the coming into force of this Law, shall be deemed to be a person who has come to this country as an oleh under this Law.

Implementation and regulations

5. The Minister of Immigration is charged with the implementation of this Law and may make regulations as to any matter relating to such implementation and also as to the grant of oleh's visas and oleh's certificates to minors up to the age of 18 years.

DAVID BEN-GURION
Prime Minister
MOSHE SHAPIRA
Minister of Immigration

YOSEF SPRINZAK
Acting President of the State
Chairman of the Knesset

Text courtesy of the Ministry of Foreign Affairs, State of Israel

---

[1] Passed by the Knesset on the 20th Tammuz, 5710 (5th July, 1950) and published in Sefer Ha-Chukkim No. 51 of the 21st Tammuz, 5710 (5th July. 1950), *p.* 159; the Bill and an Explanatory Note were published in Hatza'ot Chok No. 48 of the 12th Tammuz, 5710 (27th June, 1950), *p.* 189.

[2] *Aliyah* means the immigration of Jews to the modern nation of Israel.

[3] *Oleh* (plural: *olim*) means a Jew who is immigrating to the modern nation of Israel.

Below is an English transcript of the Israel Defence Forces radio traffic recorded on the morning of June 7, 1967, as the 55th Paratroopers Brigade liberated the Temple Mount and Western Wall during the Six-Day War ...

Liberation of the Temple Mount and Western Wall - June 7, 1967

Colonel Motta Gur[1] **[on loudspeaker]:** All company commanders, we're sitting right now on the ridge [Mount of Olives] and we're seeing the Old City. Shortly we're going to go in to the Old City of Jerusalem, that all generations have dreamed about. We will be the first to enter the Old City. Eitan's tanks will advance on the left and will enter the Lion's Gate. The final rendezvous will be on the open square [of the Temple Mount] above. ... *Sound of applause by the soldiers ...* **Yossi Ronen:** We are now walking on one of the main streets of Jerusalem towards the Old City. The head of the force is about to enter the Old City. ... *Gunfire* ... There is still shooting from all directions; we're advancing towards the entrance of the Old City. ... *Sound of gunfire and soldiers' footsteps ... Yelling of commands to soldiers ... More soldiers' footsteps ...* The soldiers are keeping a distance of approximately five meters between them ... It's still dangerous to walk around here; there is still sniper shooting here and there. ... *Gunfire* ... We're all told to stop ... we're advancing towards the mountainside ... on our left is the Mount of Olives ... we're now in the Old City opposite the Russian church ... I'm right now lowering my head, we're running next to the mountainside. ... We can see the stone walls. ... They're still shooting at us. ... The Israeli tanks are at the entrance to the Old City, and we're going ahead, through the Lion's Gate. I'm with the first unit to break through into the Old City. ... There is a Jordanian bus next to me, totally burnt; it is very hot here. ... We're about to enter the Old City itself. We're standing below the Lion's Gate, the Gate is about to come crashing down, probably because of the previous shelling. Soldiers are taking cover next to the palm trees ... I'm also staying close to one of the trees. ... We're getting further and further into the City. ... *Gunfire* ... **Colonel Motta Gur [on the army wireless]:** The Temple Mount is in our hands! I repeat, the Temple Mount is in our hands! All forces, stop firing! This is the David Operations Room. All forces, stop firing! I repeat, all forces, stop firing! Over. **Commander 89:** Commander eight-nine here, is this Motta (Gur) talking? Over. ... *Inaudible response on the army wireless by Motta Gur ...* **Gen. Uzi Narkiss:** Motta, there isn't anybody like you. You're next to the Mosque of Omar. ... **Yossi Ronen:** I'm driving fast through the Lion's Gate all the way inside the Old City. ... **Command on the army wireless:** Comb the area, discover the source of the firing. Protect every building, in every way. Do not touch anything, especially in the holy places. ... *Lt.-Col. Uzi Eilam blows the Shofar ... soldiers are singing 'Jerusalem of Gold' ...* **Gen. Narkiss:** Tell me, where is the Western Wall? How do we get there? ... **Yossi Ronen:** I'm walking right now down the steps towards the Western Wall. I'm not a religious man, I never have been, but this is the Western Wall and I'm touching the stones of the Western Wall. **Soldiers [reciting the 'Shehechianu' blessing]:** Baruch ata Hashem, elokeinu melech haolam, she-hechianu ve-kiemanu ve-hegianu la-zman ha-zeh. [Translation: Blessed art Thou Lord God King of the Universe who has sustained us and kept us and has brought us to this day] ... **Rabbi Shlomo Goren:** Baruch ata Hashem, menachem tsion u-voneh Yerushalayim. [Translation: Blessed are thou, who comforts Zion and builds Jerusalem] ... **Soldiers:** Amen! ...

---

[1] Col. Motta Gur commanded the 55th (Reserve) Paratroopers Brigade, the primary military unit deployed for the capture of the Temple Mount and Western Wall; Gen. Uzi Narkiss commanded the Israel Defense Forces (IDF) Central Region, which included Jerusalem, and was charged with defending against Jordanian aggression during the Six-Day War; Yossi Ronen was an IDF radio reporter; Rabbi Gen. Shlomo Goren was the Orthodox Zionist (Ashkenazi) Chief Rabbi of the Israeli army.

Soldiers sing 'Hatikva' [Israel's national anthem]* *next to the Western Wall* ... **Rabbi Goren:** We're now going to recite the prayer for the fallen soldiers of this war against all of the enemies of Israel. ... *Soldiers weeping* ... El male rahamim, shohen ba-meromim. Hamtse menuha nahona al kanfei hashina, be-maalot kedoshim, giborim ve-tehorim, kezohar harakiya meirim u-mazhirim. Ve-nishmot halalei tsava hagana le-yisrael, she-naflu be-maaraha zot, neged oievei yisrael, ve-shnaflu al kedushat Hashem ha-am ve-ha'arets, ve-shichrur Beit Hamikdash, Har Habayit, Hakotel ha-ma'aravi veyerushalayim ir ha-elokim. Be-gan eden tehe menuhatam. Lahen ba'al ha-rahamim, yastirem beseter knafav le-olamim. Ve-yitsror be-tsror ha-hayim et nishmatam adoshem hu nahlatam, ve-yanuhu be-shalom al mishkavam [soldiers weeping loud]ve-ya'amdu le-goralam le-kets ha-yamim ve-nomar amen! [Translation: Merciful God in heaven, may the heroes and the pure, be under thy Divine wings, among the holy and the pure who shine bright as the sky, and the souls of soldiers of the Israeli army who fell in this war against the enemies of Israel, who fell for their loyalty to God and the land of Israel, who fell for the liberation of the Temple, the Temple Mount, the Western Wall and Jerusalem the city of the Lord. May their place of rest be in paradise. Merciful One, O keep their souls forever alive under Thy protective wings. The Lord being their heritage, may they rest in peace, for they shalt rest and stand up for their allotted portion at the end of the days, and let us say, Amen.] ... *Soldiers weeping.* ... *Rabbi Goren sounds the shofar* ... *Sound of gunfire in the background* ... **Rabbi Goren:** Le-shana HA-ZOT be-Yerushalayim ha-b'nuya, be-yerushalayim ha-atika! [Translation: This year in a rebuilt Jerusalem! In the Jerusalem of old!]

* *Hatikva*
As long as deep in the heart,
The soul of a Jew yearns,
And towards the East,
An eye looks to Zion,
Our hope is not yet lost,
The hope of two thousand years,
To be a free people in our land,
The land of Zion and Jerusalem.

English lyrics of "Hatikva" courtesy of the Ministry of Foreign Affairs, State of Israel

Bible Study Resources

The Bible interprets itself with respect to the story it tells about the relationship between God and man. No outside resources are required to study its core message. All one has to do is read the Bible with an open mind and heart to understand its simple message about God's love for man and his plan of redemption for mankind. On the other hand, the study of chronology associated with the Bible's predictive prophecies is an exception to the rule. Extra-biblical records must be employed to identify post-biblical historical events as fulfillments of events described in Bible prophecy. Some of the resources found helpful for that purpose during the preparation of this book for publication are listed below. Admittedly, the list is brief, mainly because the Bible itself was the primary resource used to arrive at the interpretations and expositions of the chrono-specific prophecies explained herein.

Books on Chronology

Finegan, Jack. *Handbook of Biblical Chronology* (Revised Edition). Peabody, Massachusetts: Hendrickson Publishers, Inc., 1998.

Hoehner, Harold W. *Chronological Aspects of the Life of Christ.* Grand Rapids, Michigan: Zondervan Publishing House, 1977.

Parker, Richard A. and Waldo H. Dubberstein. *Babylonian Chronology 626 B.C. - A.D. 75.* Eugene, Oregon: Wipf and Stock Publishers, 2007.

Reingold, E. M., and N. Dershowitz. *Calendrical Calculations: The Millennium Edition.* Cambridge, England: Cambridge University Press, 2001.

Thiele, Edwin R. *The Mysterious Numbers of the Hebrew Kings* (Revised Edition). Grand Rapids, Michigan: Kregal Publications, Inc., 1994.

Wacholder, Ben Zion. *Essays on Jewish Chronology and Chronography.* New York, New York: KTAV Publishing House, 1976.

Books on History

Gur, Lt. Gen. Mordechai. *The Battle for Jerusalem.* New York, New York: Popular Library, 1974.

_____. *Josephus, The Complete Works: Translated by William Whiston, A.M.* Nashville, Tennessee: Thomas Nelson Publishers, 1998.

Oren, Michael B. *Six Days of War: June 1967 and the Making of the Modern Middle East.* Novato, California: Presidio Press, 2003.

Rabinovich, Abraham. *The Battle for Jerusalem: June 5-7, 1967.* Philadelphia, Pennsylvania: The Jewish Publication Society, 1972.

Articles on Chronology

Wacholder, Ben Zion. "The Calendar of Sabbatical Cycles During the Second Temple and the Early Rabbinic Period," Hebrew Union College Annual 44 (1973), *p.* 153-196.

Wacholder, Ben Zion. "Chronomessianism, The Timing of Messianic Movements and the Calendar of Sabbatical Cycles," Hebrew Union College Annual 46 (1975), *p.* 202-204.

Wacholder, Ben Zion. "The Calendar of Sabbath Years During the Second Temple Era: A Response," Hebrew Union College Annual 54 (1983), *p.* 123-133.

Internet Resources

Jewish Calendar Conversions in One Step, automatic calendar generator (available online from Stephen P. Morse, San Francisco, California, at http://www.stevemorse.org).

Jewish Virtual Library, a free-content encyclopedia of Jewish history (published online by AICE, the American-Israeli Cooperative Enterprise, at http://www.jewishvirtuallibrary.org).

Journal of Biblical Literature, published by the Society of Biblical Literature (searchable archive available online at http://www.sbl-site.org).

JSTOR, an archive of hundreds of academic journals dating back to 1665 (searchable database available online at http://www.jstor.org).

Livius.org, articles on ancient history (published online from Amsterdam, The Netherlands, by historian Jona Lindering at http://www.livius.org).

Wikipedia ®, the free-content encyclopedia (available online at http://www.wikipedia.org).

Bible-study Software

PC Study Bible ®, a searchable Bible-study program with numerous Bible translations, commentaries, original-language texts, Hebrew and Greek word studies, and an extensive library of classical and modern books and articles related to history and religion, and more (available on CD in PC format only from BibleSoft, Inc., at http://www.biblesoft.com).

SCRIPTURE INDEX

Bible references with page numbers where mentioned in this book; the letter "f" following page number denotes item found in a footnote.

Scripture Index

Bible references with page numbers where mentioned in this book; the letter "f" following page number denotes item found in a footnote.

General Index

A listing of names, places, and topics most frequently mentioned in this book; the letter "f" following page number denotes item found in a footnote.